Security Perception and China-India Relations

Li Li

KNOWLEDGE WORLD

KW Publishers Pvt Ltd
New Delhi

KNOWLEDGE WORLD

A KW Publishers Book
www.kwpublishers.com

ISBN 10: 81-87966-98-X
ISBN 13: 978-81-87966-98-2

Published in India by

Kalpana Shukla
KW Publishers Pvt Ltd
4676/21,First Floor, Ansari Road, Daryaganj, New Delhi 110002
email: knowledgeworld@vsnl.net

Typeset by Black Innovation, New Delhi and Printed at Rajkamal Electric Press, New Delhi

Contents

	List of Tables	v
	Acknowledgements	vii
	Introduction	ix
1	**Security Perception and Constructivism: A New Approach to Analyze China-India Relations**	1
1.1	Security Perception and Wendt's Constructivism: The Effects of Ideas on International Relations	1
1.2	Components of Security Perception	9
	1.2 (1) Security and Security Perception	9
	1.2 (2) Contents of Security Perception	11
	1.2 (3) Evolution of an International Strategic Culture	21
1.3	Parameters of Security Perception	23
	1.3 (1) Assessment of the Security Environment	24
	1.3 (2) National Security Strategy	25
	1.3 (3) Mutual Perception	26
2	**The Cold War Mindset and China-India 'Cold' Relations during the Cold War (1950-1990)**	33
2.1	China's Security Perception	33
	2.1 (1) Mao's Era	34
	2.1 (2) Deng's Era	38
2.2	India's Security Perception	42
	2.2 (1) Nehru's Era	43
	2.2 (2) Mrs. Gandhi's Era	49
	2.2 (3) Rajiv Gandhi's Era	54
2.3	The Cold War Mindset and its Implications for China-India Relations during the Cold War	56
3	**China's Security Perception After the Cold War**	69
3.1	China's Assessment of its Security Environment	69
	3.1 (1) A Better Security Environment than ever Before (1991-2002)	70
	3.1 (2) A Complex Picture (2002 till the Present)	74

3.2 China's National Security Strategy 76
3.2 (1) Objectives of China's National Security Strategy 76
3.2 (2) China's National Security Interests 78
3.2 (3) China's National Security Policy 81
3.3 China's India Perspective 85
3.4 Nature of the Change in China's Security Perception 92

4 India's Security Perception After the Cold War 101

4.1 India's Assessment of its Security Environment 101
4.2 India's National Security Strategy 107
4.2 (1) Objectives of India's National Security Strategy 107
4.2 (2) India's National Security Interests 109
4.2 (3) India's National Security Policy 111
4.3 India's China Perspective 116
4.4 India's Security Perception in Transformation 123

5 Perception Change and the Transformation of China-India Relations since 1991 135

5.1 Perceptible Improvements in China-India Relations Preceding Pokhran II (1991-April 1998) 136
5.1 (1) China's India Policy 136
5.1 (2) India's China Policy 138
5.1 (3) Perceptible Improvements in China-India Relations 141
5.2 Post-Pokhran II Hiatus and Fence-Mending Efforts (May 1998-June 1999) 146
5.3 New Stage of China-India Relations (July 1999-till Date) 150
5.3 (1) China's India Policy 150
5.3 (2) India's China Policy 154
5.3 (3) New Stage of China-India Relations 158

6 Conclusion 171

Index 179

List of Tables

Table 1.1 Three Cultures of Anarchy 5

Table 1.2 Evolution of International Strategic Culture 23

Table 5.1 Sino-Indian High-Level Exchange Visits, 1991-1997 142

Table 5.2 China-India Bilateral Trade 1991-1999 146

Table 5.3 Sino-Indian High-Level Exchange Visits, 2000-2008 158

Table 6 China-India Bilateral Trade 1991-2007 160

Acknowledgements

This book was born out of my research experiences in India between 2004 and 2008, mainly as a PhD candidate at the School of International Studies of Jawaharlal Nehru University. I owe a profound debt of gratitude to many people who have helped in making this book possible.

My deepest gratitude goes first and foremost to Dr. Alka Acharya, my PhD supervisor, for her constant encouragement and guidance. By sharing her immense knowledge and insightful comments, she has walked me through all the stages of the writing of this book. Without her generosity and invaluable instruction, this book could not have reached its present form. She also put me in touch with my publisher. This book is dedicated to her.

Second, I am greatly indebted to Professor Sreemati Chakrabarti and Professor Manoranjan Mohanty, who showed a lot of patience in reading through the manuscript and gave me many enlightening suggestions.

I am especially grateful to Ms. Kalpana Shukla, my publisher, for her quick responses to my book proposal and the first draft of the manuscript. My gratitude also to Mr. Jose Mathew for guiding me through the publishing process.

I would also like to thank all the academic and support staff at the Centre for East Asian Studies and the School of International Studies, who extended to me various kinds of support during my study and research in the Jawaharlal Nehru University. Much respect goes to Professor Lalima Varma and Professor H.S. Prabhakar, who offered me varied help over the years. Thanks also to Dr. Srikanth Kondapalli and Dr. Varaprasad Sekhar for their valuable advice and warm encouragement.

Furthermore, I would like to express my gratitude to Dr. C. Raja Mohan, who allowed me to attend his classes on India's foreign policy and South Asian security between August 2004 and May 2005, when he was a professor with the Centre for South Asian Studies, SIS, JNU. I especially appreciate the valuable insights he offered during those discussions, both within and outside the classroom.

A special word of thanks also goes to Professor Yan Xuetong, Director of the Institute of International Studies at the Tsinghua University. Despite his many preoccupations, he found time to share his insights into Wendt's constructivism and China's new security concept, through direct discussions or by emails.

I also appreciate the respective discussions over the years with Professor He Xiquan, Professor Hu Shisheng, and Professor Ma Jiali. Their advice and encouragement are of great help. I especially owe a debt of gratitude to Tang Zhichao, who offered me a lot of help in finding the Chinese source materials.

Above all, I want to thank my family for their love, support and encouragement. Being a New Delhi-based journalist covering India and South Asia since 2002, my dear husband, Yaodong, gave me invaluable suggestions for the manuscript. His belief in me has been an important source of confidence and strength. My primary school-aged son, Yunchong, has supported me in his specific way. His straight-A marks in school and his talent in piano have been the greatest rewards for me.

Li Li
New Delhi

Introduction

As neighbours sharing a long and varied border, China and India both take their relationship with each other to be one of the most significant in their foreign policy dealings. Adding the fact that they are the world's two most populous countries and two Asian giants, this relationship has important implications for both regional and global affairs. The past few years have especially witnessed an increasing interest in this relationship by the international community, mainly because of the rapid economic growth of both countries and the conspicuous transformation of the relationship itself. There is a fundamental question involved here: What characterizes the China-India relationship? Rivalry, alliance, or selective cooperation? It is this question that constitutes the foundation of this research.

A good and healthy China-India relationship will contribute not only to the development and prosperity of the two countries themselves, but also to the peace and stability of the region and the world. Nevertheless, the record of the past indicates that this relationship has been rather unsatisfactory. Except for the short period of the 'honeymoon' around 1954-551,[1] China-India relations have seen dramatic fluctuations and stalemates of many kinds in the period since the late 1950s, including a direct military conflict in 1962. Notwithstanding a restoration of ambassadorial ties in 1976, tensions remained throughout the 1970s.

From the 1980s, some relation-mending efforts by both sides led to a certain alleviation of the hostility. The 1988 visit to China by Indian Prime Minister Rajiv Gandhi represented a new starting point of the process of normalization between the two countries. Since then, China-India relations had been gradually normalized through their steady re-engagement after a gap of nearly three decades. However, they suffered a serious setback in 1998 when India used the 'China Threat' as the justification for its series of nuclear tests. This led to many speculations and suspicions about the future of this relationship.

Even as worries about the probable fallout from the new tensions persisted, the China-India relationship took a new, and to some extent, an unexpected turn at the beginning of the 21st century. Instead of deteriorating, it has picked up a strong momentum towards maturity. On the political front, the two countries kept frequent exchanges of high-level visits. During Indian Prime Minister Vajpayee's visit to Beijing in 2003, both sides agreed for 'comprehensive cooperation' and promotion of 'a long-term constructive and cooperative partnership'.[2] In 2005, when the Chinese Premier Wen Jiabao visited New Delhi, they announced the establishment of 'an India-China strategic and cooperative partnership for peace and prosperity'.[3] With the bilateral trade volume touching US$ 38.7 billion in 2007, the economic ties have displayed the growing interdependence between them. On the military front, besides the re-instatement of the regular military to military exchanges, the two navies held the first ever joint exercises in November 2003. In 2006, the two sides signed an MoU for military cooperation, and the Annual Defence Dialogue was also initiated at the end of 2007.

On the evolution of China-India relations, different people have different interpretations. With regard to the relationship before 1988, however, there was a consensus that since the late 1950s, hostility and confrontation had featured in the China-India relations. Assessments varied greatly on the development since 1988. They fell into three categories. The first group argued that the relationship had not changed much, and the two countries remained rivals. The improvement of China-India relations had been over-hyped.[4] There was no substantive progress in any aspect in bilateral ties except trade, and 'strong economic relations are no insurance against political, military and strategic confrontations' of China and India.[5]

The second stream of analysis acknowledged the visible improvement in bilateral ties since 1988, but it pointed out the 'paradox or contradiction' that could not be ignored.[6] On the one hand, the bilateral trade had increased remarkably and there had been noticeable multi-level engagement and cooperation between the two countries. On the other, due to the unresolved border dispute, the so-called 'Tibetan issue' and the 'Pakistan issue' among others, the level of mutual trust and confidence remained low.[7] The future of their relationship would, to a large extent, depend on how artfully they could overcome this contradiction.

Those in the third group were rather optimistic. They believed that the relations between China and India had entered an era of comprehensive cooperation since 2000. There was substantive progress in bilateral trade, cultural exchanges, military ties as well as border talks.[8] The China-India ties were currently characterized by friendship rather than rivalry or brotherhood.[9]

No matter how divergent the conclusions, the study of China-India relations has been dominated by traditional approaches, especially the Realist perspective. Scholars from both sides attributed the ups and downs of this relationship either to the changes of the power structure or to the effects of the common/contradicting interests between the two countries. Many Indian scholars emphasized the implications of changes of the international system, i.e. the power structure of international community, for the evolution of China-India relations. For example, some believed that the emerging Sino-Soviet rapprochement since 1986 made it possible for China and India to rethink their policies toward each other and finally drove Rajiv Gandhi to visit China in 1988.[10] Some argued that the Sino-Soviet rapprochement and the end of the Cold War left India with strategic vulnerabilities, forcing her to reduce the decades-long two-front pressure by 'buying' peace with China.[11]

Many Chinese scholars highlighted the role of common interests, however. They believed that 'the convergence of their strategic objectives and interests has served as a catalyst for bringing the two Asian nations closer' since the end of the Cold War.[12] As the two largest developing nations, both China and India need a peaceful international environment that is favourable for their own economic development. Moreover, their stance on promoting a multi-polar world in the new century has also given them further cause for cooperation.[13]

Those scholars, who argued that there was no substantive improvement in the relations between China and India in the past two decades, also emphasized the effects of interests. In contrast to the above Chinese scholars, they believed that the interests of China and India conflicted in many aspects, including trade.[14] According to J. Mohan Malik, a US-based scholar, "there is a fundamental clash of interests between China and India,"[15] and their "overlapping spheres of influence forestall the chances for genuine Sino-Indian rapprochement".[16]

By scanning these arguments, however, one can find that there are many questions that they cannot answer. First, if the improvement of China-India relations can be attributed to changes of the international system, it is difficult to explain why tension arose between them in the late 1950s when there was no major structural shift in the bipolar world. Second, for those who overstate the role of common interests, it seems that China and India shared no significant common interests during the decades of 'cold' relations. This is clearly not the case. On the contrary, the two countries could always find commonality, even in the worst period of bilateral relations. In the beginning of the 1950s, China and India, two newly independent and populous developing countries, both faced the task of maintaining independence and striving for a bigger say in regional and international affairs. Although their relations took a downturn after that 'honeymoon', and they even went to war in 1962, it did not mean that the common interests disappeared. What actually changed were their perceptions about each other, i.e. from 'friend' to 'threat'. Moreover, it is ironic that, from the same perspective, some scholars have drawn a totally different conclusion. They saw a still hostile relationship with a lot of clashing interests between the two countries.

The blurring in these analyses of China-India relations indicates the shortcomings and deficiencies of the traditional approaches. Therefore, this book attempts to examine the China-India relations from a fresh perspective. It introduces Constructivism into the framework of analysis. Constructivism is an IR theory that emerged at the end of the 1980s and has become as popular in international studies as Realism and Liberalism. As Constructivism emphasizes that ideas play a significant role in international politics, this book attempts to explore the implications of security perceptions for the evolution of China-India relations. It hypothesizes that the respective security perceptions of China and India have experienced a great change since the end of the Cold War. These perception changes have led to the respective adjustments of their policies toward each other. As a result, China-India ties have been transformed from hostility to partnership.

By introducing the arguments of Constructivism, Chapter One explains why security perception is selected by this book as the variable to analyze China-India relations. It illustrates how this theory will be applied to the following analysis and what kind of limitations it has. It also sets up a theoretical framework of analysis by elaborating upon both the contents and the parameters of security perception.

Chapter Two examines the features of China-India respective security perceptions during the Cold War, how they were affected by the then strategic culture of international politics, i.e. the Cold War mindset, with the confrontation between the US and the Soviet Union as its backdrop, and how these security perceptions contributed to the evolution of this relationship during that period.

Chapter Three and Chapter Four respectively deal with the security perceptions of China and India since the end of the Cold War. By examining their respective assessments of the security environment and their respective security strategies, the two chapters probe their respective shift from the Cold War mindset to the new security perspective. They also explore how their mutual perceptions have changed accordingly.

Chapter Five explores how the perception changes have influenced their respective policies toward each other, and how their respective policy adjustments have led to an impressive transformation in their bilateral relations. The last decade of the 20th century witnessed the two countries emerging from their three-decade cold relationship and replacing it with a normal one. In spite of the brief hiatus after Pokhran II, China-India relations not only resumed a year later but also started a new phase of comprehensive cooperation and marched ahead along the track of "strategic and cooperative partnership".

Chapter Six draws a conclusion of this research and makes a prediction of the future of China-India relations accordingly.

Notes

1. Zhou Weiping, *Bainian Zhongyin guanxi* (A Century of China-India Relations) (Beijing: Shijie zhishi chubanshe, 2006), 187.
2. *Declaration on Principles for Relations and Comprehensive Cooperation between the Republic of India and the People's Republic of China,* June 23, 2003, Beijing, available at http://www.fmprc.gov.cn/eng/wjdt/2649/t22852.htm.
3. *Joint Statement of the Republic of India and the People's Republic of China,* April 11, 2005, New Delhi, available at http://www.meaindia.nic.in.
4. Brahma Chellaney, 'The Three Ts of India-China Relations', The *Asian Age,* January 15, 2008.
5. Rajeev Sharma, 'Pitfalls of Hindi-Chini Bhai Bhai', *The Tribune,* April 11, 2005.
6. Alka Acharya, 'Climbing Down', *The Economic Times,* November 17, 2006.
7. Ibid. Also see Harsh V. Pant, 'China and India: Cooperation or Conflict', *The Statesman,* April 11, 2005.
8. Zhou Weiping, *Bainian Zhongyin guanxi,* 424.
9. S. Nihal Singh, 'Friends, Not Brothers', *The Asian Age,* April 21, 2005.
10. C.V. Ranganathan and Vinod C. Khanna, *India and China: The Way Ahead, second* edition (New Delhi: Har-Anand Publications, 2004), pp. 59-62.
11. Brahma Chellaney, 'The Regional Strategic Triangle', in Securing India's *Future in the New Millennium,* ed. Brahma Chellaney (New Delhi: Orient Longman, 1999), p. 330.
12. 'Sino-Indian Ties Enter New Stage: New Analysis', *People's Daily Online,* June 23, 2003, available at http://english.people.com.cn/200306/23/eng20030623_118739.shtml.
13. Xia Liping, 'China-India Security Relationship: Retrospects and Prospects', in *A Presentation Collection for Conference on India in 21st Century: External Relations,* SIIS (Shanghai Institute for International Studies) (Shanghai: SIIS Publication, 2002), p. 111.

14. Brahma Chellaney, 'The Drag of a Dragon', *The Asian Age*, April 21, 2007.
15. J. Mohan Malik, 'India-China Relations in the 21st Century: The Continuing Rivalry', in *Securing India's Future in the New Millennium*, ed. Brahma Chellaney, 337.
16. J. Mohan Malik, 'China's Strategy of Containing India', February 6, 2006, available at http://www.pinr.com/report.php?ac=view_report&report_id=434.

1

Security Perception and Constructivism: A New Approach to Analyze China-India Relations

By introducing the arguments of Constructivism, this chapter will set up a theoretical foundation for the entire research. It will illustrate the relationship between security perception and constructivism, how this theory will be applied to the following analysis, and what kind of limitations it has. On this basis, it will further construct a concrete framework of analysis by elaborating upon both the contents and the parameters of security perception.

1.1 Security Perception and Wendt's Constructivism: the Effects of Ideas on International Relations

To answer the question as to why security perception is preferred as a variable to analyze China-India relations, it is necessary to first turn to the international relations (IR) theory. In the semantic sense, perception is the process of acquiring, interpreting, selecting, and organizing sensory information,[1] while idea is defined as something "that potentially or actually exists in the mind as a product of mental activity".[2] Therefore, perception and idea are treated as synonyms by many disciplines including international studies. Security perception is hereby a state actor's ideas about security, i.e. its recognition and interpretation of security. Since security perception is an idea or a strategic culture[3] of nations, it is necessary to find out what kind of role ideas play in international politics.

Realism and Liberalism have long occupied pre-eminent positions in IR theory. Realists, from Morgenthau's classical Realism to Waltz's Neorealism, have explained the world in terms of power and interest, "with power understood ultimately as military capability and interest as an egoistic desire for power, security, or wealth."[4] Liberalism covers a more broad perspective, ranging from Wilsonian Idealism through to contemporary neo-liberal theories and the democratic peace thesis. Liberal thought postulates that states are but one actor in world politics, while other actors such as Transnational Corporations, the IMF and the United Nations also play a role. Since the 1980s, the main academic debates of IR theory have been dominated by the debate between Waltz's Neorealism and Keohane's Neoliberal Institutionalism or Neoliberalism. In his book, *Theory of International Politics*, Kenneth Waltz combines a micro-economic approach to the international system with Realists' traditional emphasis on power and interest, suggesting that international structure has effects on state's behaviour.[5] While conceding the importance of power and interest, Keohane argues that international institutions also play a significant role in international politics, since they could dampen, if not entirely displace, the effects of power and interest.[6] Therefore, the basic difference between Neorealists and Neoliberalists lies in the relative weight of power and interest, and at times, their debate "seems to come down to no more than a discussion about the frequency with which states pursue relative rather than absolute gains".[7]

According to the above mainstream of IR theory, power, interest and institutions have together become 'the three factors' that explain most of the variance in international outcomes.[8] The isomorphic tendency between Neorealism and Neoliberalism has blocked the development of the IR theory. To break their long-term dominance or even 'hegemony', in the mid-1980s, a fourth factor, 'idea', was introduced and emphasized by some IR scholars. Scholars like Nicholas Onuf,[9] Friedrich Kratochwil[10] and Alexander Wendt[11] explored constructivism, fundamentally a social theory, in the context of international relations. The end of the Cold War has especially provided more room for the enhancement of this school, since mainstream IR theory fell short of providing satisfactory explanations for the drastic changes in world politics. For example, both Neorealists and Neoliberalists have difficulties in explaining why various partnerships were established among major powers after the Cold War. According to their respective hypotheses, the international system is by nature a self-help anarchy, in which cooperation among intrinsically self-interested state actors is impossible. As Wendt said in his most significant work, *Social Theory of International Relations* (1999), "the revival of constructivist thinking about international politics was accelerated by the end of the Cold War, which caught scholars on all sides off guard but left orthodoxies looking particularly exposed. Mainstream IR theory simply had difficulty explaining the end of the Cold War, or systemic change more generally".[12] Thanks to this book, which provides a comprehensive framework of constructivist IR theory, not only has Wendt strengthened his position as the leading theorist of this school but also contributed to enshrining constructivism as one of the three predominant schools of thought in international relations, along with realism and liberalism.

Wendt's constructivism challenges the fundamental assumption held by both Neorealism and Neoliberalism that national interest and anarchy should be taken as given in international politics. It emphasizes the role of shared ideas in international interaction, the implications of cultures in the international system, and the importance of the structure in constituting the identities and interests of the state.[13] The following are the four basic arguments by Wendt:

First, national interests are constituted mostly by ideas. In IR scholarship, national interests are normally defined as needs or the reproduction requirements of states, which consist of life, liberty and property, i.e. physical survival, autonomy and economic well-being. Hypothesizing that these interests are "rooted in some combination of human nature, anarchy, and/or brute material capabilities", Realists assume that states are inherently self-interested or egoistic. States are power-, security-, and/or wealth-seekers by nature accordingly, while the international system is by definition a self-help system. Realists believe that states do what they do because it is in their national interest. Therefore, interest and power are the only proper variables or factors to explain international politics. Neoliberalists also assume that self-interest is the core of the national interest, while admitting that ideas and institutions, independent of power and interest, can explain a substantial proportion of state action.[14]

Wendt rejects the fully material-oriented interpretation of national interest. He argues that interest involves not only an actor's intrinsic desire but also its belief based on cognition and deliberation. Interest is not 'mind independent' but constituted by the 'perception of value' that is learned through 'socialization to culture'. Interest refers to what actors want, and "we want what we want because of how we think about it". Like mankind, therefore, states are not inherently selfish or power-seeking. Human nature does not tell us whether people are good or bad, aggressive or pacific, power-seeking or power-conferring, even selfish or altruistic. These are all socially contingent, not materially essential. Human beings are animals whose material needs are a key constituting element of their interests, but in the end their interests are mostly a function of their ideas, not their genes. This is no less true of states. States, no matter they are status quo, revisionist or collectivist, define their interests by virtue of their perceptions of the international order and their place within it, rather than any egoistic or altruistic intrinsic desire.[15]

Second, the structure of the international system is a 'distribution of ideas' rather than a 'distribution of capabilities'. For Waltz the nature of international politics is shaped by power relations. He assumes that the distribution of capabilities is the only variable dimension of international structure. When IR scholars today use the word 'structure', they almost always imply Waltz's definition. Wendt rejects this proposition by emphasizing that the meaning of the distribution of power in international politics is first constituted in important part by the distribution of interests. The nature of the international structure does not depend on the number and size of major powers but the interests of members in the system. In other words, what states want matters more than how powerful they are. The nature of structure (or the logic of anarchy) can vary when states have different interests. The logic of anarchy among revisionist states takes the form of a fight to the death; among status quo states, arms racing and some brawls; among collectivist states, perhaps heated but ultimately non-violent arguments about burden sharing. Since Wendt assumes interests are ideas, he further argues that the structure of international system is a distribution of ideas.[16] He believes that "ideas usually are far more important... if we want to say a small number of big and important things about world politics we would do better to focus first on states' ideas and the interests they constitute, and only then worry about who has how many guns." For the US, for instance, five hundred British nuclear weapons are less threatening than five North Korean ones, because the US believes that North Korea has the will to use them against it whereas Britain does not.[17]

Third, the structure of international politics is not by nature a self-help system but it can have multiple logics. The Neorealists believe that, in a world composed of egoistic states, anarchy is the only structure characterized by self-help that tends to produce military competition, balances of power, and war. Against this, Wendt argues that the definition of anarchy is no more than the absence of centralized authority in the international system. There is no inevitable relationship between anarchy and conflict. Anarchy is actually an empty vessel and has no intrinsic logic. The logic of anarchy depends on "what we put inside" it. Here comes the well-known assumption by Wendt: anarchy is what states make of it. The interaction among state actors generates shared ideas (or culture); then these shared ideas constitute the structure of anarchy. The material polarity of the international system matters, for example, but how it matters depends on whether the poles are friends or enemies, which is a function of shared ideas.[18]

Anarchy can have at least three kinds of structure, based on what kind of roles[19]—enemy, rival, and friend—dominate the system. Wendt dubs these structures as Hobbesian, Lockean, and Kantian. In the Hobbesian culture, states see each other as enemies, who will observe no limits in their violence toward each other. As a result, the logic of this anarchy is the 'war of all against all' in which actors operate on the principle of kill or be killed. The Hobbesian structure is truly a self-help system. In the Lockean culture, states treat each other as rivals who will use violence sometimes to advance their interests or settle disputes but refrain from killing each other. The logic of this anarchy is 'live and let live'. There is a shared expectation that states will recognize each other's right to life and liberty, i.e. sovereignty. In contrast to

Table 1.1 Three Cultures of Anarchy

	Hobbesian	Lockean	Kantian
Role	Enemy (unlimited aggressive intentions, not recognizing the Self's right to life and liberty at all, 'deep' revisionism, unlimited violence)	Rival (limited aggressive intentions, recognizing the Self's right to life and liberty, 'shallow' revisionism, self-restraint violence)	Friend (non-violence, team play)
Logic of Anarchy	Kill or be killed (war of all against all)	Live and let live	Perpetual peace (all for one, one for all)
System	Self-help	Self-restraint (in part Self-help, in part Other-help)	Mutual aid
Tendencies (generated by the structure)	(1) Endemic and unlimited warfare; (2) The elimination of 'unfit' actors; (3) States powerful enough to avoid elimination will balance each other's power; (4) The system will tend to suck all of its members into the fray, making non-alignment or neutrality very difficult.	(1) Limited warfare, since warfare is simultaneously accepted and constrained; (2) The system can have a relatively stable membership or low death rate over time; (3) States will balance power, and balancing is more of an effect of the mutual recognition of sovereignty; (4) Neutrality or non-alignment becomes a recognized status.	(1) Pluralistic security[21]; (2) Collective security[22].

the Hobbesian anarchy, the Lockean structure is self-restraint rather than self-help. In the Kantian culture, states perceive each other as friends who will not use violence to settle their disputes and work as a team against security threats. The logic of this anarchy is perpetual peace or 'all for one, one for all'. Mutual aid is the feature of this structure.[20]

Flowing from the above discussion, the three cultures of anarchy can be placed in a tabular form for facilitating comparison: (See Table 1.1)

Since the establishment of the Westphalian system in the seventeenth century, international politics has experienced a qualitative structural change, from Hobbesian to Lockean. "In the late twentieth century," he believes, "the international system is undergoing another structural change, to a Kantian culture of collective security."[23] "Even if there is no guarantee" of such an end, he further points out, at least the international time is unlikely to move backward.[24]

Fourth, the structure of international politics also has constitutive effects on states. Wendt claims that there is an interaction between actors and social structure. The interactions between state actors constitute the anarchic structure; the international system in turn constitutes states. Since Neorealists and Neoliberalists treat interests as given, they assume that only the behaviour of states is affected by system structure. In contrast, Wendt proposes that anarchic structures do affect state identities and interests as well as their behaviour. As elements of structure, states will be under pressure to internalize the corresponding role — enemy, rival, or friend — in their identities and interests. In short, culture (or shared ideas) has become part of the background knowledge in terms of which states define their national interests. For example, in a Lockean culture, states normally define their interests according to the internalized sovereignty norms, i.e. recognizing the Other's right to life and liberty. That just explains why small states have not only survived but thrived in the modern history of international politics. Thanks to the interaction between structure and its elements, culture (or shared ideas) become "a self-fulfilling prophecy". Once the cultural formation known as the 'Cold War' was in place, the US and Soviets had a shared belief that they were enemies. This shared ideas or culture helped constitute their identities and interests in any given situation, which they in turn acted upon in ways that confirmed to the Other that they were a threat, reproducing the Cold War.[25]

By challenging the given factors (such as interests and anarchy) determined by mainstream IR theory Constructivism is trying to redefine the agenda of IR studies. This is precisely the most significant contribution it has made to the IR theory. Most schools of mainstream IR theory have taken the rational choice theory as the starting point of their studies. Like classical economics, they have treated states as 'economists', who will always try their best to maximize their gains.[26] In doing so they have assumed that the international system is a single anarchy composed of state actors who are born egoists. They have thereby neglected the social feature of the international system and its elements. Wendt's constructivism, in contrast, attributes human qualities to state actors and pays significant attention to the ways in which these actors are socially constructed. In recent years, constructivism is gaining weight among quantities of critique. Although a consensus has not been reached on whether constructivism is better than Neorealism or Neoliberalism in terms of explaining international politics, constructivism is at least broadly 'permitted' to join the mainstream group, and some scholars have even started talking about the possible transformation of IR studies: from rationalism to constructivism.[27] To comment on the position of constructivism in contemporary IR theory is not the objective of this research, but this author agrees with Wendt that his theory "makes a difference for thinking about international politics".[28] This is the reason why this author has chosen constructivism as the basic theoretical foundation for the ensuing analysis of China-India relations.

Although this author accepts Wendt's assumption that ideas play a more significant role in international politics than normally imagined, two points should be clarified. One, to accept the importance of ideas does not mean the rejection of the significance of power and interest. As Wendt points out, his claim does not mean that a substantial proportion of state action can be explained by ideas rather than power and interest.[29] From his point of view, power and interest are just as important and determining as before, but "their meaning and effects depend on actors' ideas".[30] The relationship between ideas and power or interest is actually a philosophical issue of ontology. It is obviously beyond the scope of this work. In this book, therefore, what this author would like to emphasize is that more attention should be paid to the role of ideas in international politics, and nothing goes beyond that. When looking into the studies of China-India relations that have been dominated by the traditional analytical framework, this author finds it imperative to deal with the role of security perception, which is an idea or a strategic culture, in this relationship.

Two, in practice, no IR theory can claim to provide a full-fledged explanation of international politics. Some schools, such as Neorealism and Neoliberalism can only claim to have done better than the others. This is no less true of constructivism. To choose constructivism as a starting point of this research only means that this author believes that constructivism provides a better alternative explanation of international politics. It does not mean that constructivism is the only possible one. As mentioned above, idea is the 'fourth' factor of international studies, apart from power, interest and institutions. It is impossible to put everything within one study. This author neither denies the contributions made by traditionalists to the studies of China-India relations, nor thinks that this analysis is the only solution. This book only intends to suggest a new approach or perspective, namely, security perception, which has seldom been discussed in the past.

While being cautious about Wendt's assumption on ontology, this author does not fully adopt his methodology either. Although Wendt proposes that state actors and the international system are mutually constituted, he seems to emphasize the international system's constitutive effects on states, rather than the other way around. He claims that a key feature of constructivism is holism, which means that "social structures have effects that cannot be reduced to agents and their interactions".[31] Since "the ideas held by individual states are given content or meaning by the ideas which they share with other states—that state cognition depends on states systemic culture," he argues, "in analyzing what states think it makes sense to start with the culture of the international system and work top-down, rather than start with unit-level perceptions and work bottom-up."[32]

The nature of Wendt's constructivism underlies his preference for this top-down methodology. As mentioned above, a significant contribution of Wendt to IR theory is that he problematizes one of the latter's basic assumptions that anarchy is a given logic of international system. In his book, Wendt suggests that the international anarchy can have at least three kinds of logic: Hobbesian, Lockean, and Kantian. In a world with a single given anarchy, there is no need to pay too much attention to its effects on its elements. These effects are always clear and relatively static. When there is more than one logic, however, the situation will become complicated, and there is a lot of work to do in this regard. IR scholars who have not paid sufficient attention to the structure's effects on states, therefore, should do more of the 'top-down' work.

This author will follow the suggestion of Wendt and deal with the effects of international strategic culture on the respective security perceptions of China and India. As a mainstream IR theory now, however, constructivism should provide more theoretical perspectives and be more widely applied. This author hereby suggests that, although Wendt says his three kinds of structure are at the macro level, it can also explain how mutual perceptions are constituted between two nations. In sum, in this book, the analysis is not about working 'top-down' or 'bottom-up', but applying an international structural theory to the explanation of bilateral relations.

1.2 Components of Security Perception

While constructivism provides an answer to the question of how perception or idea is relevant in explaining international relations, it does not go further in elaborating upon what *security perception* is exactly about. However, the literature of international politics has no dearth of discussions on 'security', a core concept of international studies. As Wendt points out, traditional mainstream political science has made valuable explorations into perception. They, however, depart on the issue of the role perception plays in international relations.[33] Therefore, in the following, this research tries to develop a concrete analytical framework on the basis of the hitherto relevant studies on security perception.

1.2 (1) Security and Security Perception

Generally speaking, security perception is a state actor's ideas about security. Before going further, one must address a basic question: what is *security*? In a world where every state regards security as its fundamental concern, the term 'security' seems to be usually left as an axiom, which means that everyone knows what it is about. When looking into literature of international relations, however, one may find that the definition of security is so complex and ambiguous that there is not a fixed definition at all. Most dictionaries and encyclopaedias basically define *security* in the following ways: (i) as a psychological feature or a feeling, security is freedom from anxiety or fear; (ii) as a condition or a status, security is the state of being free from danger or injury; (iii) as a measure or an act, security is protection or defence against threats.[34] In IR scholarship, security is generally defined in similar ways. Numerous definitions have been provided and "each one emphasizes different aspects".[35] The following are some well-known definitions of security that have respectively enjoyed a certain support.

- Ian Bellany: "Security itself is a relative freedom from war coupled with a relatively high expectation that defeat will not be a consequence of any war that should occur."[36]
- John E. Marz: "Security is relative freedom from harmful threats."[37]
- Arnold Wolfers: Security is a value "of which a nation can have more or less and which it can aspire to have in greater or lesser measures. It has

much in common, in this respect, with power or wealth, two other values of great importance in international affairs. But while wealth measures the amount of a nation's material possessions, and power its ability to control the actions of others, security, in an objective sense, measures the absence of threats to acquired values, in a subjective sense, the absence of fear that such values will be attacked."[38]

- Bernard Brodie: Security is a "derivative value, being meaningful only in so far as it promotes and maintains other values which have been or are being realized and are thought worth securing, though in proportion to the magnitude of the threat it may displace all others in primacy."[39]
- Jules Comban: "Security means more indeed than the maintenance of a people's homeland, or even of their territories beyond these seas. It means the maintenance of the world's respect for them, the maintenance of their economic interest, every thing in a word, which goes to make up the grandeur, the life itself of the nation."[40]

Among the above definitions, with John E. Marz defining security as condition, Ian Bellany and Arnold Wolfers emphasize both state and feeling, while Bernard Brodie and Jules Comban talk about ability, i.e. guarantee of security. Barry Buzan cites several reasons for the "conceptual underdevelopment of security". The first is simply that the idea has proved too complex to be explained. The second lies in the scope for overlap between it and the concept of power. The third is due to the vague boundary between security studies and strategic studies. The fourth is the consequence of the efforts by the practitioners of state policy to maintain its symbolic ambiguity.[41] After the end of the Cold War, the vagueness of the term 'security' actually increased as new paradigms emerged to approach the new security challenges. Although the debate on the meaning of security gets more heated, scholars have at least reached one consensus: that it is imperative for the security studies to have a clear agenda. A large amount of literature in recent years on the redefinition of the agenda or the framework of security studies has reflected this consensus.

The ambiguity of the concept of security is also manifested in the context of its connection with *national security*. In IR literature, *security and national security* are sometimes, and in most cases, used interchangeably as if they are synonymous.[42] Some IR scholars even take it for granted that the term 'security' in security studies refers to *national security*. According to the evolution of security studies, the relationship between these two concepts actually depends on the extent to which national security is defined.

The traditional approach, which characterizes the period before and during the Cold War, refers to national security as the security of the state and narrowly concentrates on military threats. According to Walter Lippmann, national security is closely associated with the ability of a nation to deter an attack or to defend itself successfully if attacked. As he put it, security meant that "a nation is secure to the extent to which it is not in danger of having to sacrifice core values, if it wishes to avoid war, and is able, if challenged, to maintain them by victory in such a war".[43] This overwhelmingly military character of security is based on the assumption that principal threats to security come from beyond the border of a nation.[44] In this classical view, therefore, national security is a 'derivative' of security or a branch of security.[45]

The modern approach, which characterizes the period after the end of the Cold War, has extended the concept of national security beyond the above scope and defines it in a holistic sense. Apart from military concerns and national perspective, it covers almost all the non-military aspects and non-state factors of security, from economic security to environmental security, and from societal security to human security. In this case there is no difference between national security and overall security. Security is only an abbreviation of national security. In the view of this author, there is another significant reason for regarding these two terms as one concept. The end of the Cold War has not changed the fact that states are the dominant actors in contemporary world politics, and the state-centrism still characterizes the mainstream IR theories as a result. This state-centrism in security studies, therefore, has justified the homogeneity between *security* and *national security*.

The lack of a common understanding of the concept of security underscores the difficulty for this research to develop its arguments and discussions on the one hand; above all it compels this author to develop a specific agenda of analysis on the other. As security is basically defined in terms of status, scope and ability, security perception may accordingly involve the following three aspects: threat perception, types of security, and approaches to security.

1.2 (2) Contents of Security Perception

Threat Perception

Threat perception is a "process of appraisal" and judgment of the status or condition of security.[46] It is "above all a cognitive construct which creates an image of reality as a hypothesis".[47] According to Raymond Cohen, the perception of threat should be understood as anticipation on the part of an observer—the decision maker—of impending harm (usually of a military, strategic, or economic kind) to the state.[48]

While Raymond Cohen considers threat as impending harm to the state, in IR literature, *threat*, like security, is also an ambiguous concept. Taking all the above definitions of security into account, one may find that security is always defined in terms of threat, no matter how distinct these definitions are. Richard Ullman simply offers a definition of security by describing the relations between threat and national security. He assumes that "a threat to national security is an action or sequence of events that (1) threaten drastically and over a relatively brief span of time to degrade the quality of life for the inhabitants of a state, or (2) threaten significantly to narrow the range of policy choices available to the government of a state or to private non-governmental entities (persons, groups, corporations) within a state."[49] Klaus Knorr says that threats either may be "actual", that is inferred from more or less definite signal or intent, or "potential", that is inferred from some state or the environment or the mere capability of an opponent.[50] For Haftendorn, Robert Keohane, and Celeste Wallander, threats are posed when a state (or a group of states) has both the intention and capability to circumscribe the security of another state.[51] For Wendt, however, intention matters more than capability, just as discussed earlier. Although the introduction of the term 'threat' into the definition of security has not made any change of the uncertain nature of security, it offers an indicator or a parameter of security. For instance, analysis of a particular threat or group of threats allows us to examine the area of security that is threatened,[52] helping us have a better understanding of security as a result. Therefore, threat perception is a part and an indicator of security perception. This author postulates that how China or India assesses the threat facing it will, to a great extent, reflect its security perception, and any change of its threat perception will, to a large degree, mirror the change of its security perception.

Threat identification of a nation depends on its scope determination of security, i.e. types of security. For example, if a nation views security only in a military sense, it usually identifies the threat facing it within the same area. This happened in the past, especially during the Cold War, when security and threat referred mainly to political and military aspects. According to David Singer, threat arises out of a situation of armed hostility, in which each body of policymakers assumes that the other entertains aggressive designs; each side further assumes that such a design will be pursued by physical and direct means if estimated gains seem to outweigh estimated losses.[53] Since the end of the Cold War, as scope of security extends to economic and other non-traditional aspects, threat identification has been broadened in many ways.

Types of Security

If threat identification of a nation depends on its scope determination of security, conversely, how a state actor identifies the threat facing it reflects its determination on types of security. Types of security are the sectors or dimensions of security classified by the character of threats. As mentioned above, before and during the Cold War, the traditional approach narrowly concentrated on the military threats and the sovereignty of the state. In fact, security experts at that time did not pay much attention to the types of security, because they had taken the military and political characters of security for granted. Some scholars, like Walter Lippmann, as mentioned above, even tried to define security primarily in these terms. After the end of the Cold War, however, sectors of security broadened dramatically as a result of the emergence of many new threats, like environmental threats and terrorism. To be accurate, to call these threats *new* does not mean that they did not exist before and during the Cold War but refers to the new characters "that previously had not been perceived, or were given little attention".[54] According to recent security literature, military security and political security are generally classified as *traditional security*, and the others as *non-traditional security*. Security is thus now being examined in the following typology:

(1) **Military security.** Military security is freedom from military threats. This type of security constitutes the core of traditional security perception, as "military threats occupy the traditional heart of national security concerns".[55] Military threats are predicated on the fear that another state or group of states could use military force to subjugate the incumbent government, and armed forces are believed to be the only means to counter military action.[56] Military threats are of many types. At the extreme end are threats of invasion and occupation aimed at obliterating the state. Military threats may also be of punitive nature whose objective, usually, is to force a change in government policy rather than to seize territory or to overturn institutions. Military threats may also be indirect, in the sense that they are not applied directly to the state itself but aim at its external interests, like threats to allies, shipping lanes, or strategically placed territories.[57]

(2) **Political security.** Political security is freedom from political threats. The core of this sector is about non-military threats to state sovereignty. Normally, the target of political threats is supposed to be the idea of the state, particularly its organizing ideology, and the institutions which express it.[58] In other words, the objectives of political threats are, first, against the internal legitimacy of the political unit, which relates to ideologies and other issues defining the state, and second, against the external position of the state and its external legitimacy.[59] Political threats traditionally stem from ideological competition, cultural penetration and secessionism fomentation. Cultivating an anti-ideology, as the Americans have done with anti-communism and the Soviets with anti-imperialism during the Cold War, may constitute a political threat to the state that represents this ideology. Both intended and unintended cultural exports may produce political threats to local cultural tradition, especially to those that are weak or small. Secessionism fomentation involves such political activities as propaganda support for secessionist groups[60] of the rival state, and from there into the funding and creation of such groups, all the way up to the military training and arms aid to rebels.[61] Political threats "are not less significant than military threats as ignorance of political threats may drastically hamper the security of a nation".[62]

(3) **Economic security**. Economic security is the top sector of security perceptions after the end of the Cold War. Attentions drawn by the 'comprehensive power' and development of the economic globalization have dramatically upgraded the significance of economic security. As meaningful participation in the global economy has become the ultimate objective of every state, increased economic competition could increasingly expose the country to various threats and vulnerabilities, like the Asian financial crisis of the late 1990s, while increased commercial interactions between states do generate growth and wealth.[63] According to Barry Buzan, economic security refers to "access to the resources, finance and markets necessary to sustain acceptable levels of welfare and state power".[64] Economic threats include all those activities that could hamper the state's economic growth and erode citizens' standard of living.[65] The objective of a state's economic security is to ensure access to global markets, continuity of supply of essential resources and to buffer vulnerability to turbulent global market changes.[66] Energy security therefore is a part of economic security.

(4) **Societal security.** Societal security is about identity problem that may threaten the organizational stability of social order: state, system of government, and ideology that gives the state and the government legitimacy. Societal security is so closely related to political security that it used to be regarded as an aspect of political security. After the end of the Cold War, as civil wars and regional conflicts caused by identity crises like ethnic competition and religious quarrel increased dramatically, the salience of societal security has emerged to such an extent that it is being dealt with as an independent sector of security. According to Waever, there is a significant distinction between the terms 'social' and 'societal', as each of them refers to different aspects of identity. *Social security,* therefore, refers to individuals and the economic aspects of their life, whereas *societal security* refers to collectives and their identity.[67] The most common issues concerned with societal security are migration, horizontal competition, and vertical competition. Migration may bring about a shift in the composition of the population, which may threaten the identity of the indigenous people. Horizontal competition designates that people change their ways of thinking because of overriding cultural and linguistic influence from a neighbouring culture (e.g. Canadian fears of Americanization). Vertical competition prescribes that people will stop seeing themselves as one group because of the process of integration (e.g. the EU), or because of a secessionist 'regionalist' process (e.g. Quebec, Catalonia, and Kurdistan).[68]

(5) **Environmental Security.** Environmental security "concerns the maintenance of the local and the planetary biosphere as the essential support system on which all other human enterprises depend".[69] The threat posed by environmental factors to human survival was not largely recognized until 1972, when the United Nations Conference on the Human Environment was held. Environmental threats are very broad and complex, ranging from scarcity of clean air and water, fuel and arable land, degradations of lands, forests and fisheries, to impacts of climate change and population growth.[70] Most of the threats stem from human activities. Industrialization in significant part plays a role in such phenomena as global warming, ozone depletion and acid rain. Nuclear accidents (for instance, the meltdown of the Chernobyl reactor) or proliferation of weapons of mass destruction may lead to man-made environmental disasters. Environmental security can be a cause of political instability and conflict. For example, the scarcity of water in the Middle East is cited as one reason for worsening of the Arab-Israeli

conflict and a future war.[71] Though there are still heated debates on the security relevance of environmental variables,[72] it may be generally accepted that the higher the potential severity and durability of the impact of man-made biospheric imbalance, the higher the chances that such an imbalance would be regarded as a security threat.[73]

(6) **Terrorism.** Terrorism is a sector of security directly named after the threat, though there is no international consensus on the definition of terrorism so far. According to Walter Laqueur, terrorism is "the substate application of violence or threatened violence intended to sow panic in a society, to weaken or even overthrow the incumbents, and to bring about political change."[74] There are two features of terrorism that distinguish it from other acts of violence: political goals usually lie behind terrorist acts, on the one hand; innocent people are the direct target of the violence, on the other.[75] Terrorism is not a new phenomenon and is traditionally perceived as a political threat. It has been known since the mid-1970s, when the world started to get used to it as an unconventional and violent method of gaining 'political' goals used by such groups as the Irish Republican Army (IRA), the Euskadi ta Askatasuna (ETA), and many other groups.[76] After the end of the Cold War, terrorism has reached a new high because it is considered by the 'weaker' as an effective method to coerce the 'stronger' into concessions. Terrorism has become a great security challenge for most countries in the world. Terrorism has therefore started to be treated as a separate area in security studies. The bombing of the World Trade Center in New York on September 11, 2001, has further enhanced terrorism's place in many countries' security perceptions, since it revealed the potential and scale of destruction of this asymmetric threat. The United States has announced that terrorism is currently the biggest security challenge to it. As technology advances, terrorism may carry new characters. For example, cyber terrorism could severely threaten a state's national security. Cyber-terrorist threats could inflict considerable damage to both defence and civilian sectors by employing software commands or malicious programmes. Such attacks could disable a state's key military computer systems or paralyze its critical infrastructure such as communications, transportation, power systems, and industrial enterprises.

Taking the current situation of security studies into account, it is not possible to discuss all the emerging ramifications of the types of security. There are many criteria by which security can be categorized. Apart from the above types, security can also be categorized into global, regional, state and individual securities in terms of the levels of the threat's source, symmetric and asymmetric securities in terms of the power gap between the target and the attacker, etc. There are also some emerging conceptions, like 'human security', which is still being debated. For the purpose of this research, the above broad typology is sufficient. By examining how China and India respectively categorize their own security and how they prioritize these types of security, one may get a better understanding of their respective security perceptions. By exploring the changes in these categorizations and priorities, one may discover the changes in their security perceptions, which, as stated at the outset, is the fundamental impetus of the transformation of China-India relations in recent years.

Approaches to Security

Approaches to security are the methods or ways taken by a state in dealing with its security issues to accomplish or preserve its national security. According to Wendt's ideal model of international structure, there are primarily three approaches to security: unilateral security based on the Hobbesian logic of "all against all"; alliance security on the Lockian "live and let live"; and collective security on the Kantian "all against one". These approaches have on the whole represented the ways for security pursued by most countries in the world before the end of the Cold War. After the end of the Cold War, and consequent on the great changes concerning threats' structure (as mentioned above) and the lessons that state actors drew from their experiences in the past, especially those in the period of the Cold War, many countries have started seeking, experimenting and promoting new security approaches. Among these numerous and controversial means to security, common security, cooperative security and comprehensive security are the three which have drawn most attention and worth discussing here therefore.

(1) **Self-help security.** This approach originates from the logic of the Hobbesian anarchy, the "war of all against all", in which state actors operate on the principle of kill or be killed. In such a true 'self-help' system, actors cannot trust anyone or count on each other. States can only rely on themselves, and survival depends solely on military power. As a result, the state actor sees security as a deeply competitive, zero-sum affair and attempts to establish absolute military superiority by unrestricted expansion of unilateral military power. The big problem of this approach is in terms of a vicious cycle of mistrust, since increases in the security of A necessarily reduce that of B, who can never be sure that A's capabilities are defensive. Therefore, B is compelled to "prepare for the

worst" by taking counter-measures to enhance its own power. A security dilemma arises herefrom.[77] Self-help security was broadly implemented during the Cold War, and the all-out arms race between the United States and the Soviet Union was typically characteristic of the security dilemma.

(2) **Alliance security.** According to Wendt, alliance security is made possible by the logic of the Lockean anarchy. Although in the Lockean world there is still no Leviathan that states can count on for security, the system is not self-help all the way down. State actors see each other as rivals that may use violence to settle disputes but do so within 'live and let live' limits due to the institution of sovereignty. Although actors still to a great extent believe that they cannot count on each other and they themselves bear the ultimate responsibilities for their own security, the self-restraint nature of the system enables them to ally themselves with those who also have an interest in this alliance. Alliance security is preferred especially when one's own power is insufficient. An alliance is in fact a temporary, mutually expedient arrangement. Each state in the alliance feels individually threatened by the same threat. Their collaboration is self-interested and will end when the common threat is gone. Military power is still important, because allies expect to eventually revert to a condition in which war between them is an option. Therefore, alliance security is usually adopted by state actors along with self-help security. This has been characterized by the confrontation between the two blocs during the Cold War, in which both the United States and the Soviet Union attempted to anticipate each other by building up their own power on one hand, and by recruiting allies on the other. Like self-help security, alliance security can also lead to a security dilemma.[78]

(3) **Collective security**. The introduction of collective security represents a shift away from a competitive, self-help approach to security, to one that is premised on collaboration.[79] The theoretical genesis of collective security can be traced back to the idea of mutual aid, or "all for one, one for all", advocated by Immanuel Kant's "perpetual peace".[80] IR history has witnessed the implementation of collective security by several concretized institutional frameworks, from the Concert of Europe in the nineteenth century, through the League of Nations in the 1920s-1940s, to the current United Nations. Externally, collective security means that, when the security of any one member of the system is threatened by aggression, all members are supposed to come to its defence even if their own individual security is not at stake. Internally, collective security implies that disputes within the system will be handled by negotiation or

arbitration rather than war or the threat of war.[81] According to Wendt, the basic difference between alliances and collective security lies in how the system's members define each other. Parties to the former treat each other as rivals, whose capabilities pose a latent threat to each other, and they collaborate only because that threat is temporarily suppressed by the greater threat of external aggression. Parties to the latter regard each other as friends whose capabilities are believed to be used only on behalf of the collective.[82] In spite of being traditionally defined as a universal system, collective security has been, to a certain extent, practised at the regional and sub-regional level, such as NATO after the end of the Cold War, and the Economic Community of West African States (ECOWAS).[83] Without a universal consensus on its definition, however, the failure of this approach to prevent World War II, the Cold War and countless regional wars, and the weakness and inefficacy of the current UN, have made it a rather confusing idea and led to heated debates.[84]

(4) **Common security.** The idea was initially introduced in Europe during the Cold War by the Independent Commission on Disarmament and Security Issues that was commonly known as the Palme Commission—named after the Swedish Prime Minister, Olof Palme, who chaired the commission. In 1982, the Palme Commission published a report, claiming that common security refers to "achieving security with others, not against them", and that security would be best assured through cooperation rather than competitive power politics.[85] In essence, the Palme Commission attempted to verify that "the unilateral self-help security system" was obsolete due to the existence of nuclear weapons, and sought to rid the world of the arms race and nuclear weapons by introducing far-reaching arms control and disarmament.[86] This idea underlay the activation of the Conference for Security and Cooperation in Europe (CSCE)[87] in 1980s. After the end of the Cold War, this Euro-centric notion found an echo in Asia-Pacific, when the Canadians and Australians advocated applying it to this region.[88] In practice, common security has carried some new characters, with its nucleus shifting from arms control and disarmament to cooperation and dialogue. It is believed that "in the interdependent world, it is impossible for one country to achieve lasting security at the expense of the security of others".[89] As countries share greater common security interests and are more interdependent on one another for security, they should "respect each other's interests and concerns and create conditions for others' security while ensuring their own security".[90]

(5) **Cooperative security.** Cooperative security expands the understanding of security to include non-military issues and emphasizes the significance of cooperation rather than competition. The concept can be traced back to the late 1980s, and was first raised by American scholars with a focus on the competitive relations with the former Soviet Union. Later, it was reconceptualized by the Canadians. This approach promotes "consultation rather than confrontation, reassurance rather than deterrence, transparency rather than secrecy, prevention rather than correction, and interdependence rather than unilateralism".[91] For these to materialize, various confidence- and security-building measures (CSBMs) are introduced. These CSBMs include joint training exercises, demilitarization of common borders, exchange of military personnel and weapon acquisition programmes.[92] As security goes beyond the military issue, security cooperation should be sufficiently broad to involve political, economic, and other aspects as well. The essence of cooperative security is to shift the emphases of approach to security from contingency reaction to systemic prevention.[93] Cooperative security has been broadly implemented both at the bilateral level and regional level. The current bilateral relationship of the major powers, compared with that during the Cold War, is characterized more by cooperation than confrontation. The ASEAN Regional Forum (ARF) represents a good example of regional cooperative security.

(6) **Comprehensive security.** The proponents of comprehensive security argue that security is a comprehensive matter far beyond the military dimension. It intentionally downplays the role of military means with regard to security, and stresses the importance of non-military aspects, such as national development, internal stability and social harmony. Therefore, to safeguard one's national security requires a comprehensive approach: active diplomacy, multilateral cooperation, as well as military preparedness.[94] Originating from the Ohira Administration in Japan in the 1970s, the concept was taken up and strongly advocated by ASEAN countries in the 1980s. Since the end of the Cold War, this approach has played an important role in promoting security cooperation in the Asia-Pacific. Both the ARF and CSCAP (Council for Security Cooperation in the Asia Pacific), the major Track I and Track II regional dialogue mechanisms, have discussed and implemented major principles of comprehensive security.[95]

Since definition has always been a problem for security studies, there are no clear dividing lines among the above six approaches. Sometimes they share a concrete step, for example, CBMs can be implemented in any of the approaches except the first one. Sometimes they share a behavioural principle, for example, the latter two approaches all emphasize the non-military means. Furthermore, in reality, none of them is exclusive for a state actor. In other words, usually a state may simultaneously take more than one approach to cope with its security issues. Which approach to security a state will take depends on how it categorizes and prioritizes its security, and the approach or approaches to security it takes will, thereafter, determine its national security strategy and policy.

1.2 (3) Evolution of an International Strategic Culture

The foregoing examination of the hitherto relevant studies on security perception not only helps this research set up an analytical framework but also reveals the evolution of security perception on the macro-level, i.e. from the *Cold War mindset* to *the post-Cold War new security perspective,* or in Wendt's words, the tendency of structural change or change of international strategic culture.

The first aspect of change comes to the source of threat. Although the Cold War mindset and the new security perspective concur on the point that threat is constituted by both capability and intention, they disagree on the role each of the two factors plays. According to the Cold War mindset, capability plays a major role in the construction of threat, while the intention of a state to obtain benefits through force can be taken for granted. When a state or a group of states has acquired military superiority, it is bound to use force to enlarge its benefits. Therefore, the major threat to a nation's security is derived from the military superiority of its opponent. As for the new security perspective, intention is far more important than capability. Whether a state poses a threat to the other depends more on its intention than its capability. Weak actors can cause insecurity within strong ones. Although the US has an absolute military superiority over North Korea, the former still worries about the latter's military capability. Similarly, after the Cold War, many countries consider terrorism as a prominent threat to their national security, even though the military capability of terrorists is far inferior to that of a nation.[96] Moreover, states are not born aggressive. It is not inevitable that a state with outstanding military capability will entertain aggressive designs. Only with the intention will its military capability carry the nature of threat. Manifestations of this can be seen in the peace among the major powers since the end of the Cold War.

The second aspect of change lies in the categorization and priorities of security. The Cold War mindset takes the military and political characters of security for granted. It believes that military threats always occupy the heart of national security concerns. As a nation faces a threat due to the military superiority of its opponent, the threat will be greater if the opponent enjoys a divergent ideology. In other words, an opponent with ideological differences may pose a greater threat to a nation than those who share a similar political system. The new security perspective extends the dimension of security from military and political to economic and other non-traditional aspects. In the post-Cold War era, external military threats are not imminent for many countries, especially for the major powers, and ideological difference does not cause confrontation thanks to the disappearance of bipolar confrontation. As economic globalization develops rapidly, and the world becomes more interdependent, non-traditional threats become more and more salient. In the light of the lessons of the disintegration of Soviet Union, economic security should get much more attention. The military capability of a nation should be underpinned by its economic strength. Therefore, many countries regard economic security as important as military security, while some, like China in the 1990s, give priority to economic security.

The third change is with regard to the approaches to security. The Cold War mindset believes that a nation's security depends on its overwhelming military strength against its opponent. Approaches to preserve a nation's security, therefore, are military build-up (self-help security) and military alignment (alliance security). The new security perspective conceives that the foundation of security is mutual trust and common interests. The new security perspective considers that the Cold War mindset leads nowhere but to a security dilemma, since one side's military superiority will make the other side feel insecure, which will force the latter to search for a stronger military strength, and hence initiate a vicious cycle between the two opponents. To get out of this security dilemma, it would be better for countries to replace the zero-sum confrontation with cooperation when dealing with security. Cooperation promotes mutual trust. When one side thinks it can trust the other, it means that the former believes that the latter has no intention of using force against it, no matter how powerful the latter is. If mutual trust develops between the two sides, neither of them will find the urgency to strengthen its capability. Then this will lead their security relations to a healthy spiral. Cooperation grows common interests. If common interests between two countries outweigh each side's estimated gains from a war, it will rid both sides of any intention of using force. Common security, cooperative security and comprehensive security, the prevalent approaches to security in the post-Cold War era, all lay stress on cooperation.

Table 1.2 Evolution of International Strategic Culture

	Cold War Mindset	Post-Cold War New Security Perspective
Source of Threat	States are born aggressive. Capability plays a major role in the construction of threat. The major threat to a nation's security is derived from the military superiority of its opponent.	States are not born aggressive. Intention is far more important than capability in the construction of threat.
Categorization of Security	(1) Military security (2) Political security	(1) Military security (2) Political security (3) Economic security (4) Other non-traditional security
Priorities of Security	Military threats always occupy the heart of national security concerns.	Non-traditional threats, especially economic security, attract more attention.
Approaches to Security	(1) Self-help security (2) Alliance security	(1) Common security (2) Cooperative security (3) Comprehensive security (4) Collective security

As change of the international strategic culture is still in the process, it is the transition period when both the Cold War mindset and the new security perspective exist simultaneously. As a result, each country's security policy is, to a different extent, influenced by both these security perceptions. Some countries incline to the new security perspective, some tilt to the Cold War mindset, while others stay in between. The dual impacts of the two security perceptions lead many countries to a complex, sometimes contradictory, security policy that includes both competition and cooperation. For example, the US has taken a contradictory security policy toward China since the end of the Cold War. On the one hand, it is trying to build a constructive and cooperative partnership with China, which represents a new security perspective. On the other, it is seeking to strengthen the US-Japan military alliance, a legacy of the Cold War, to cope with the 'potential threat' of China.[97]

1.3 Parameters of Security Perception

The foregoing discussion about the contents of security perception provides a theoretical direction for the following and concrete analysis of the respective security perceptions of China and India. Before starting this analysis, however, there is still another important question to answer: how to identify and define a state's security perception. In the real world, no state actor makes a formal or informal announcement in this regard. Therefore, some measures or parameters are needed to solve this problem. Parameters of security perception here refer to the factors that reflect the security perception. In the light of the above direction of analysis, this author will take recourse to such parameters as assessment of the security environment, security strategy and policy, and mutual perception. Assessment of the security environment will, to a great extent, reflect a state's perception of threat, while security strategy and policy will unravel how a state categorizes and prioritizes its security and through which ways it deals with its security problems. Mutual perception is especially pertinent to the analysis of bilateral relations, including China-India relations.

1.3 (1) Assessment of the Security Environment

Security environment is another concept taken for granted by IR scholarship. According to *The American Heritage Dictionary of the English Language* (2000), environment refers to surroundings, which is further explained as "the external circumstances, conditions, and objects that affect existence and development". Based on this explanation, security environment therefore can be defined as the circumstances and conditions that affect the existence, maintenance and development of a state. When examining IR literature, one will find that there are not many discussions on the definition. This kind of theoretical negligence has not mitigated any relevance of security environment to IR studies, however. On the contrary, everybody, from the IR scholars to the decision-makers of states, refers to security environment. Although there is neither a unanimous definition nor a rigorous analytical framework, it is widely accepted that assessment of the security environment is the first step for a state to shape its security strategy.[98]

Traditionally, assessment of the security environment is undertaken as a process of threat-identification.[99] In other words, to assess a state's security environment is to identify the real and the potential threats or challenges it faces. Both Barry Buzan and Stephen Walt have tried to provide an ideal framework for understanding the security environment, but neither of them can make "a fundamental departure from the threat-identifying approach".[100] In Buzan's 'security complex', factors such as geography, distribution of power, and patterns of amity and enmity are introduced to illustrate the regional security, but understanding threats is finally emphasized as the basis for understanding security.[101] According to Walt's 'balance of threat' theory, the assessment of a state's security environment involves factors such as power, geographical proximity, offensive capability, and perception of intention, and the objective of this assessment is to identify threats, on which states choose to balance threat rather than balance power to ensure its security.[102]

In the real world, this threat-identifying approach is usually combined with 'level analysis'.[103] According to the sources of threats, the assessment of a state's security environment can be divided into global (or international), regional (or neighbouring), and domestic ones. For instance, when a state is talking about its regional security environment, it is in fact trying to enumerate the threats it faces in the region.

To sum up, the assessment of security environment is to identify threats from each level. How a state defines its security environment will reflect its threat perception. Since the assessment of security environment underlies the formation of a state's security strategy, and the implementation of the security strategy will eventually have certain implications for its external relations, to examine how China and India respectively assess their own security environment will not only provide a significant parameter for understanding their security perceptions but also help in understanding their security strategies and the interaction between them.

1.3 (2) National Security Strategy

National security strategy is "the art and science of developing, applying, and coordinating the instruments of national power (diplomatic, economic, military, and informational) to achieve objectives that contribute to national security".[104] The formulation of a national security strategy varies from country to country. Some states have a specific report on it and also make regular announcements, while others implicitly include it in various official documents.

The US is the country that currently enjoys the most sophisticated system of both the formulation and the implementation of national security strategy. According to the *US National Security Act of 1947,* "the President [shall] transmits to Congress each year a comprehensive report on the national security strategy of the United States," and each report "[shall] sets forth the national security strategy of the United States and [shall] includes a comprehensive description and discussion of the following: (1) the worldwide interests, goals, and objectives of the United States that are vital to the national security of the United States; (2) the foreign policy, worldwide commitments, and national defense capabilities of the United States necessary to deter aggression and to implement the national security strategy of the United States; (3) the proposed short-term and long-term uses of the political, economic, military, and other elements of national power of the United States to protect or promote the interests and achieve the goals and objectives referred to in paragraph (1); (4) the adequacy of the capabilities of the United States to carry out the national security strategy of the United States, including an evaluation of the balance among the capabilities of all elements of national power of the United States to support the implementation of the national security strategy; (5) such other measures as may be helpful to inform Congress on matters relating to the national security strategy of the United States."[105] In short, a state's national security strategy normally should outline its major national security concerns and its plans to deal with them.

National security strategy is a comprehensive parameter for a state's security perception. How a state defines its security interests and concerns will reflect its categorization of security, the objectives of its national security strategy will illustrate the priority of its security, and how a state is supposed to use its national power to achieve these objectives will manifest its approaches to security. Although neither China nor India has the same arrangement of a specific report as the US does, there are other sources that can provide a contour of their respective national security strategies. This book will examine at least three major sources: the government documents, especially those on foreign policy and national development, the speeches by the top leaders, and the strategic analysts from each side who have various connections with the government and play a role in policy-making.

1.3 (3) Mutual Perception

Mutual perception can be categorized into the assessment of security environment and be analyzed at the regional level mentioned above. Regional security environment consists of multilateral and bilateral sublevels. When a state assesses its regional security environment, it not only deals with the region as a whole, but also takes major bilateral relations into account. Therefore, mutual perception is about two specific nations' threat-identification vis-à-vis each other. Since this book is about a bilateral relationship, and its theoretical basis, viz. Wendt's constructivism, provides a sophisticated explanation of mutual perception's effects on bilateral relations,[106] this author will treat mutual perception as an independent parameter of security perception.

According to Wendt, mutual perception refers to role-identification between two nations. As mentioned above, he basically sorts them into three roles: enemy, rival and friend. How the *Self* (one side) defines the role of the *Other* (the other side) will first affect its own policy towards the *Other*. Representing the *Other* as an enemy tends to have at least four implications for a state's foreign policy posture and behaviour. First, it will act like a deep revisionist and try to destroy or conquer its enemy. Second, its decision-making will tend to heavily discount the future and be oriented toward the worst case. Third, it will see relative military capabilities as crucial. Fourth, it will observe no limits on its own violence if there is an actual war.[107] Representing the *Other* as a rival also has at least four implications for the *Self's* foreign policy. The most important is that it will behave in a status quo fashion, no matter what conflict it may have with the *Other*. Second, its anxiety about security will be less intense due to the institution of sovereignty. Third, relative military power is still important but no longer dominates all decision-making, and allies can be more easily trusted when its own power is insufficient. Finally, it will limit its own violence during war.[108] When the *Self* represents the *Other* as friend, the implications for its foreign policy are two-fold. On the one hand, it will settle its disputes with the *Other* without war or the threat of war; on the other, it will cooperate with the *Other* if either of their security is threatened by a third party.[109]

In Wendt's mind, the roles here are more of a structural phenomenon than is often assumed at the unit level. In other words, "roles are structural positions, not actor beliefs".[110] How the *Self* defines the role of the *Other* will not only affect its own policy toward the *Other*, but also have constitutive effects on the *Other's* perception of it, which will in turn influence the *Other's* policy toward the *Self*. Therefore, mutual perception implies a process of interaction, which may finally create a structure of logic. For example, when the *Self* represents the *Other* as enemy, it is forced to mirror back to become the *Other's* enemy. When the *Self* acts like an enemy toward the *Other*, this enmity will confirm whatever hostile intentions the *Other* has attributed to the *Self*, forcing the *Other* to actually enact its role as an enemy, which will in turn reinforce the *Self's* perception of the *Other*. Once this logic of enmity gets started, whether or not states really are existential threats to each other is not relevant. In short, real or imagined, if actors think enemies are real, then they are real in their consequences.[111]

Based on the aforementioned model of Wendt's, this research will examine how China and India have perceived each other, how their mutual perception has interacted, how the mutual perception has affected their respective decisions-making, and what implications they have had for their ties.

Notes

1. *The Free Online Dictionary,* available at http://www.thefreedictionary.com/perception.
2. *The American Heritage Dictionary of the English Language,* Fourth Edition, 2000, available at http://www.bartleby.com/61.
3. The term 'strategic culture' is loosely defined in IR theory. This book treats strategic culture as a synonym of security perception. On the development of strategic culture study, refer to Alastair Iain Johnston, 'Thinking About Strategic Culture', *International Security,* Vol.19, No.4 (Spring, 1995), pp. 32-64.
4. Alexander Wendt, *Social Theory of International Politics* (Cambridge: Cambridge University Press, 1999), p. 92.
5. See Kenneth N. Waltz, *Theory of International Politics* (MA: Addison Wesley, 1979).
6. See Robert Keohane, *After Hegemony: Cooperation and Discord in the World Political Economy* (Princeton: Princeton University Press, 1984).
7. Wendt, Social Theory of International Politics, p. 3.
8. Ibid, p. 92.
9. See Nicholas Onuf, *World of Our Making* (Columbia: University of South Carolina Press, 1989).
10. See Friedrich Kratochwil, *Rules, Norms, and Decisions* (Cambridge: Cambridge University Press, 1989).
11. Alexander Wendt, 'The Agent-Structure Problem in International Relations Theory', *International Organization,* New York, Vol. 41, No.3 (1987): 335-370.
12. Wendt, *Social Theory of International Politics,* p. 4.
13. Qin Yaqing (2001), *'Guoji zhengzhi de shehui jiangou—Wente ji qi jiangou zhuyi guoji zhengzhi lilun'* (Social Construction of International Politics: Alexander Wendt and the Constructivist Approach to International Relations), *Mei Ou jikan (Americas & Europe Quarterly),* Taipei, Vol. 15, No. 2 (Summer, 2001): 264.
14. Wendt, *Social Theory of International Politics,* pp.113, 114, 130, 135, 234, 235, 239.
15. Ibid, pp. 115-130, 133, 231.
16. Ibid, pp. 93-113.
17. Ibid, p. 256.
18. Ibid, pp. 24, 249.
19. Each involves a distinct posture or orientation of the Self toward the Other with respect to the use of violence. Roles, therefore, here are structural positions and exist only in relation to the Others. See Wendt, *Social Theory of International Politics,* pp. 227-229, 257-259.

20. Wendt, *Social Theory of International Politics,* pp. 246-312.
21. Members of a community will not fight each other physically, but will settle their disputes by negotiation, arbitration, or the courts. See Wendt, *Social Theory of International Politics,* pp. 299-300.
22. When the security of any one member of the system is threatened by aggression, all members are supposed to come to its defence even if their own individual security is not at stake. See Wendt, *Social Theory of International Politics,* p. 300.
23. Wendt, *Social Theory of International Politics,* p. 314.
24. Ibid, pp. 250-251.
25. Ibid, pp. 184-189, 247-250.
26. Qin Yaqing, *'Guoji zhengzhi de shehui jiangou',* p. 258.
27. Jeffrey T. Checkel, 'The Constructivist Turn in International Relations Theory', *World Politics,* Vol. 50 (Summer, 1998): 324-348.
28. Wendt, *Social Theory of International Politics,* p. 2.
29. Ibid, p.135.
30. Ibid, p. 25.
31. Ibid, p.138.
32. Ibid, p. 372.
33. Ibid, p. 93-96.
34. *The Free Online Dictionary.* Also see Mieczyslaw Malec, *Security Perception: Within and Beyond the Traditional Approach,* MA Thesis (California: Naval Postgraduate School, 2003), 6, available at http://handle.dtic.mil/100.2/ADA417522.
35. Moses Bongani Khanyile, *South Africa's Security Relations with the Mercosur Countries,* Doctoral Thesis (Pretoria: University of Pretoria, 2003) at http://explore.up.ac.za/search?/akhanyile%2C+moses+bongani/akhanyile+moses+bongani/1%2C1%2C2%2CZ/l856&FF= akhanyile+moses+bongani&2%2C%2C2%2C1%2C0.
36. Ian Bellany, 'Towards a Theory of International Security', *Political Studies,* Vol. 29, No. 1 (1981): 102.
37. John E. Marz, *Beyond Security: Private Perceptions Among Arabs and Israelis* (New York: International Peace Academy, 1980), p.105.
38. Arnold Wolfers, *Discord and Collaboration* (Baltimore: John Hopkins University Press, 1962), p.150.
39. Brodie Bernard, 'Strategy as a Science', *World Politics,* Vol.1, No.4 (1949): 477.
40. Norman J. Padelford, and George A. Lincoln, *International Politics: Foundations of International Relations* (New York: Macmillan Company, 1954), p. 291.

41. Barry Buzan, *People, States, and Fear: The National Security Problem in International Relations* (New Delhi: Transasia Publishers, 1987), pp. 6-9.
42. Khanyile, *South Africa's Security Relations with the Mercosur Countries,* p.19.
43. Walter Lippmann, *US Foreign Policy: Shield of the Republic* (Boston: Little, Brown and Company, 1943), 51, cited in Iqbalur Rehman, *National Security and the Problems of Unconventional Warfare* (Delhi: Kanishka Publishing House, 1992), p. 4.
44. Rehman, *National Security and the Problems of Unconventional Warfare,* p. 4.
45. Khanyile, *South Africa's Security Relations with the Mercosur Countries,* p.19.
46. Raymond Cohen, *Threat Perception in International Crisis* (Madison: University of Wisconsin, 1979), pp. 79-80.
47. Malec, *Security Perception,* p.15.
48. Cohen, *Threat Perception in International Crisis,* 5.
49. Richard Ullman, 'Redefining Security', *International Security,* Vol.8, No.1 (1983): 135.
50. Klaus Knorr, 'Threat Perception', in *Historical Dimensions of National Security Problems,* ed. Klaus Knorr (Lawrence: University of Kansas Press, 1976), p.78.
51. Helga Haftendorn, Robert O. Keohane, and Celeste A. Wallander, *Imperfect Unions, Security Institutions over Time and Space* (Oxford: Oxford University Press: 1999), p. 2.
52. Malec, *Security Perception,* p.13.
53. David Singer, 'Threat Perception and the Armament Tension Dilemma', *Journal of Conflict Resolution,* No.1 (1958): 93-94.
54. Malec, *Security Perception,* p.1.
55. Buzan, *People, States, and Fear* (1987), p.75.
56. Khanyile, *South Africa's Security Relations with the Mercosur Countries,* p. 29.
57. Buzan, *People, States, and Fear* (1987), pp. 75-76.
58. Ibid, p. 76.
59. Barry Buzan, Ole Waever, and Jaap de Wilde, *Security: A New Framework for Analysis* (London: Lynne Rienner Publishers, 1998), p.144.
60. Sometimes dissident groups are included.
61. Buzan, *People, States, and Fear* (1987), pp. 76-77.
62. Rehman, *National Security and the Problems of Unconventional Warfare,* p.10.
63. Khanyile, *South Africa's Security Relations with the Mercosur Countries,* pp. 31-32.
64. Barry Buzan, *People, States, and Fear: An Agenda for International Security in the Post-Cold War Era,* Second Edition (London: Harvester Wheatsheaf, 1991), p.19.
65. Khanyile, *South Africa's Security Relations with the Mercosur Countries,* p.32.
66. Barry Buzan, *People, States, and Fear* (1991), pp. 237-242.

67. For details, see Ole Waever, Barry Buzan, Morten Kalstrup, and Pierre Lemaitre, *Identity, Migration and the New Security Agenda in Europe* (London: Pinter, 1993).
68. Malec, *Security Perception,* pp. 40-41.
69. Barry Buzan, *People, States, and Fear* (1991), pp.19-20.
70. Malec, *Security Perception,* pp. 41-42.
71. P.K. Gautam, 'India's Security in the 21st Century: The Environmental Aspect', in *India's Security in 21st Century: Challenges & Responses,* ed. Rajendra Prasad (New Delhi: Dominant Publishers and Distributors, 2002), pp.115-116.
72. Malec, *Security Perception,* p. 42.
73. Khanyile, *South Africa's Security Relations with the Mercosur Countries,* p. 31.
74. Walter Laqueur, "Postmodern Terrorism: New Rules for an Old Game," *Foreign Affairs,* Vol.75, No.5 (September/October 1996): 24.
75. Li Shaojun, *"Kongbu zhuyi gainian de jieding"* (Determining the Definition of Terrorism), in Kongbu zhuyi suyuan (Tracing Terrorism), ed. Wang Yizhou (Beijing: Social Sciences Academic Press, 2002), pp.1-42.
76. Malec, *Security Perception,* p. 51.
77. Wendt, *Social Theory of International Politics,* p. 265; John H. Herz, *International Politics in the Atomic Age* (New York: Columbia University Press, 1959), pp. 231-235.
78. Wendt, *Social Theory of International Politics,* pp. 229, 301.
79. Khanyile, *South Africa's Security Relations with the Mercosur Countries,* p. 38.
80. Wendt, *Social Theory of International Politics,* p. 300.
81. Ibid, pp. 299-300.
82. Ibid, p. 301.
83. Khanyile, *South Africa's Security Relations with the Mercosur Countries,* p. 40.
84. Ding Kuisong, 'East Asia: Evolving Security Concepts', in *Security Cooperation in East Asia,* ed. Yan Xuetong, and Zhou Fangyin (Beijing: Peking University Press, 2004), p.146.
85. Ibid.
86. Khanyile, *South Africa's Security Relations with the Mercosur Countries,* p. 48.
87. Now the Organization for Security and Cooperation in Europe (OSCE).
88. Ding, 'East Asia: Evolving Security Concepts', p.146.
89. Rajpal Budania, *India's National Security Dilemma: The Pakistan Factor and India's Policy Response* (New Delhi: Indus Publishing Company, 2001), pp. 34-35.
90. Wang Yizhou, *SARS yu fei chuantong anquan* (SARS and Non-Traditional Security), 2003, available at http://www.iwep.org.cn/zhengzhi/SARSyufeichuantonganquan_

wangyizhou.htm.

91. C.A. Snyder, 'Regional Security Structures', in *Contemporary Security and Strategy,* ed. C.A. Snyder (London: Macmillan Press, 1999), p.114.
92. Khanyile, *South Africa's Security Relations with the Mercosur Countries,* p. 49.
93. Zhang Yunling, *Zonghe anquan guan ji duiwo guojia anquan de sikao* (Comprehensive Security Concept and China's National Security), *Dangdai Ya Tai yanjiu (Contemporary Asia-Pacific Studies),* Beijing, No.1 (2000), available at http://iaps.cass.cn/Bak/ddyt/0001-1.htm.
94. Ibid.
95. Ding, 'East Asia: Evolving Security Concepts', p.147.
96. Yan Xuetong, *Guoji zhengzhi yu Zhongguo* (International Politics and China) (Beijing: Peking University Press, 2005), p.162.
97. Ibid, p.164.
98. Tang Shiping, 'A Systemic Theory of the Security Environment', *The Journal of Strategic Studies,* Vol. 27, No.1 (March 2004): 1-34.
99. Ibid.
100. Ibid, p. 3.
101. Ibid, p. 2.
102. See Stephen M. Walt, *The Origin of Alliances* (Ithaca: Cornell University Press, 1987).
103. Malec, *Security Perception,* pp. 52-66.
104. *Online Encyclopedia,* available at http://encyclopedia.thefreedictionary.com.
105. *National Security Act of 1947,* United States of America, available at http://www.iwar.org.uk/sight/resources/national-security-act/1947-act.htm.
106. As mentioned in the previous introduction of Wendt's constructivism.
107. Wendt, *Social Theory of International Politics,* p. 262.
108. Ibid, pp. 282-283.
109. Ibid, p. 299.
110. Ibid, p. 258.
111. Ibid, pp. 262-263.

2

The Cold War Mindset and China-India 'Cold' Relations During the Cold War (1950-1990)

This chapter examines the respective security perceptions of China and India during the Cold War as well as their implications for the bilateral relationship between the two countries. When India achieved independence in 1947 and the People's Republic of China (PRC) was founded in 1949, the Cold War had already commenced and the world was being divided into two opposing and confrontational camps: the Western camp led by the United States and the Eastern camp led by the Soviet Union. In spite of their desires and efforts to keep aloof from the two-bloc confrontation, in the following decades, China and India got involved into the Cold War to different extents. What is more important is that neither of them was capable of staying immune to the then prevalent international strategic culture. For most of the time from 1950 when the two countries established diplomatic relations till the end of the Cold War in 1991,[1] China and India saw and dealt with each other through the prism of the Cold War mindset; and hence underwent a three-decade-long 'cold' relationship.

2.1 China's Security Perception

Since the foundation of the PRC in 1949 till 1991, the Chinese had experienced two generations of leadership, i.e. Mao Zedong and Deng Xiaoping. Mao was at the helm for nearly three decades, and he viewed security issues through the prism of "war and revolution".[2] After Deng came into power in 1978, China started to depart from Mao's era in terms of both domestic focus and external strategy, although it was not an overnight transformation. The launch of the Chinese economic reforms at the end of the 1970s was followed by a big change in its security perception and foreign policy in the mid-1980s.

2.1 (1) Mao's Era[3]

China's security perception under Mao was characterized by 'war and revolution'. On the one hand, 'war and revolution' represented Mao's general assessment of the then international security environment. His two well-known judgments in this regard were: "The danger of a new world war still exists"; "the main trend of the current world is revolution."[4] On the other, it is not difficult to find the deep mark of 'war and revolution' in the way by which China safeguarded its national security interests in this period.

Mao's Assessment of China's Security Environment

In Mao's perspective, Imperialism and Hegemonism were the biggest threat to China's national security. In the first decade of New China, Mao conceived the 'imperialist' United States as the major threat to China's territorial unity and independence. Even on the eve of the founding of the PRC, Mao had already started to worry about a future military intervention in the Communist China by the United States, which had firmly supported Chiang Kai-Shek during the 1946-1949 Civil War of China.[5] After New China came into being, a series of actions taken by the United States in Asia seemed to justify Mao's suspicion of America's intentions. The US' refusal to recognize the PRC and its continuous support to the Chiang Kai-Shek nationalist government in Taiwan were viewed by Mao Zedong as a big challenge to the safety of China's territory and the stability of the new communist regime. Mao saw the Korean War as a prelude or a trial balloon of the US' ultimate aggression vis-à-vis China.[6] Along with the US military actions and deployments in the Korean Peninsula and Taiwan, the creation of the Central Treaty Organization (CENTO) and the later Southeast Asian Treaty Organization (SEATO) military alliance by John Foster Dulles in the 1950s was seen by Mao Zedong as an accelerated implementation of the US intrigue of containing China and the Soviet Union.[7]

After the Sino-Soviet split in the early 1960s, the 'revisionist'[8] USSR became another major threat to China. While the ideological debates between China and the Soviet Union had major effects on China's image and status in the international socialist community as well as in the entire world, the military strength of the Soviet Union had turned into a major security concern for China. Meanwhile, the American government, especially the Kennedy administration, continued its hostility to China due to its then assessment that "China was more belligerent than the Soviet Union".[9] Therefore, Mao saw a very dangerous picture: a massive and surprise aggression by either of the two superpowers or even jointly by them, in which the very existence of the PRC would be seriously threatened.[10]

Entering into the 1970s, the 'hegemonist' Soviet Union singly was viewed by Mao Zedong as China's major enemy. The rapidly deteriorating Sino-Soviet relations, especially the outbreak of the Sino-Soviet border conflict in 1969, made Mao draw the conclusion that the major threat to China came from its neighbour in the north and that the Soviet Union was more malevolent to China than the United States.[11]

Apart from the above direct war threat to China posed by the 'imperialist' and the 'hegemonist', Mao's China had been haunted for three decades by the fear of an imminent Third World War, which would very possibly be nuclear. In the first decade of New China, Mao looked at the post-war world through the prism of his own 'two camps' theory. He named the socialist camp led by the Soviet Union as "the world front of peace and democracy" and the Western camp led by the United States as the 'imperial camp'. Although the socialist camp appreciated peace very much, Mao argued, the risk of a new world war was very high due to the aggressive nature of the imperialists.[12] In the 1960s, when Beijing was trapped in open antagonism with both superpowers, Mao's security forecasts were locked by "a nightmare of an immediate, large-scale and nuclear strike".[13] He thus talked more about a 'nuclear war' than about a new world war during this period.[14] In the 1970s, Mao conceived that the new world war might be triggered by the 'expansionist' Soviet Union that was active in worldwide military 'adventures' rather than the United States that was in "a state of strategic withdrawal".[15]

National Security Strategy of China under Mao

Worrying about the above-mentioned severe war threats throughout the first three decades of New China, the maintenance of the very existence of the PRC led by the Communist Party of China (CPC) was the top objective of the national security strategy of China under Mao, while safeguarding China's territorial unity came second. Specifically, these strategic objectives were reflected in the following security interests of China. First, the PRC being able to survive the coming war, no matter whether it was an aggression by either of the superpowers or a new world war, and irrespective of whether it was a conventional war or a nuclear war, was the most significant.[16] Second, the PRC led by the CPC should be capable of preventing the Chiang Kai-Shek nationalists in Taiwan, who were enjoying strong support from the United States, from overthrowing the new China.[17] Third, the PRC should replace Chiang Kai-Shek nationalist government to represent China in the United Nations.[18] Fourth, the PRC should prevent the secessionist tendencies in its border regions, like Tibet and Xinjiang.[19]

In this period, the approaches that China used to realize its strategic objectives and safeguard its national security interests were characterized by alignment, self-reliance, Third-Worldism, and 'World Revolution'. As early as in June 1949, Mao asserted that the upcoming new China should side with the Soviet Union to confront the United States and its allies.[20] The weakness of China and its ideological similarity with the Soviet Union were the two decisive factors contributing to this policy that was called "leaning to one side". In the first decade of New China, the alliance with Moscow and the unity of the communist bloc were deemed as major security guarantees for the PRC, and neutralism was firmly rejected by Mao Zedong.[21] In the 1970s, learning lessons from its confrontation with both superpowers throughout the 1960s, Mao decided to side with the United States to confront the Soviet Union, which was then viewed as the No.1 enemy of China.

Self-reliance carries two meanings. On the one hand, it refers specifically to the strategy Mao used in the 1960s in dealing with its strains with both the United States and the Soviet Union. In this context, self-reliance is a concept contrary to alignment. On the other hand, the word 'self-reliance' has reflected Mao's emphasis on the significance of military power in safeguarding China's national security. Mao attributed the ill intentions of the superpowers toward China to the big gap of military strength between the powerful former and the weak latter, especially the nuclear superiority that the former enjoyed over the latter. Therefore, Mao never shunned talking about China's desire and efforts to build a strong army and to "make some nuclear weapons".[22]

As a weak country, China had been exploring a moral alignment with the underdeveloped nations in Asia and Africa, which shared a common feeling toward colonialism, imperialism and hegemonism, although sometimes they disagreed on which countries should be put into this category. China actively participated in the Bandung Conference in 1955, which aimed at Afro-Asian solidarity. In the 1960s, despite its own poverty and economic difficulties, China provided economic aid for African countries, like Tanzania and Zambia.[23] In the 1970s, China joined hands with other Third World countries to call for a new international economic order in their favour.[24]

To promote global revolutionary movements was considered by Mao as another significant approach to China's security. As early as in November 1949, the Chinese government openly declared its obligation to aid revolutions in other countries.[25] Mao argued that imperialism and capitalism were the source of war; to put an end to war, it was imperative to put an end to imperialism and capitalism through revolution.[26] In the 1950s, this kind of aid was represented by China's own participation in the socialist camp and its moral support for the movements for national liberation in Asia, Africa, and Latin America.[27] In the 1960s, due to its domestic excesses of ideological fervour, particularly the Cultural Revolution (1966-1976), China went as far to put forward the strategy of 'world revolution'. The goal of world revolution was to found a new world free from imperialism, capitalism, and system of exploitation; and the way was to "take on the form of surrounding cities (i.e. North America and West Europe) from the countryside (i.e. Asia, Africa and Latin America)", which featured the Chinese revolution.[28] In this period, China made a vocal propaganda for world revolution. "Spreading Mao Zedong thoughts worldwide" was the central mission of Chinese envoys all over the world.[29] Activists of the Cultural Revolution launched protests against and even attack on foreign diplomatic missions in China.[30] To get rid of the diplomatic isolation caused by this kind of chaos, Mao started to depart from this strategy of world revolution since 1969.

Mao's India Perspective

Like Nehru's perspective of China, Mao's perspective of India also experienced a shift, from viewing it as a friend in the 1950s to considering it as a threat to China from the early 1960s onwards; and Mao's India perspective had a strong ideological element.

In the first decade of the PRC, Mao firmly treated India as a friend in spite of their divergence on ideology and even some friction on the Tibet issue. In his talks with Nehru in 1954, Mao made it clear that China and India were friends. He said, "China and India do not need to be on alert against each other," and the Chinese "have no apprehension that India would harm us".[31] Mao gave the following reasons for this stance. First, facing a strong opponent like the United States, China was in great need of friends. Second, the fact that India was not an ally of the US made it possible for it to be considered as China's friend.[32] Third, having commonalities in terms of their Asian identities, their weakness, and their revulsion against colonialism, imperialism and war, China expected that a moral solidarity with India might become a supplement to its security strategy based on the then Sino-Soviet alliance.[33] Fourth, China could not deal with two-front threats. Even in mid-1959, when the strain between China and India rapidly increased due to the Tibet rebellion, Mao reiterated to the Indian government that China "cannot, nor is it necessary to, focus its attention to the southwest" while its major threat came from the east.[34]

Notwithstanding his insistence on China-India friendship, Mao's India perspective turned negative after the Tibet rebellion. Mao used the dichotomy to explain the contradictory nature of the Indian 'bourgeoisie' represented by Nehru. On the one hand, as the leading class in its independent movement, the Indian bourgeoisie had a tendency of anti-colonialism and anti-imperialism. On the other hand, it could not get rid of "its lust for expansion", an intrinsic nature of its class. Nehru's support and instigation of the Tibet rebellion had exposed the negative part of the Indian bourgeoisie's nature.[35] The China-India border clashes at Longju and Kongka in the same year accentuated Mao's negative feeling about Nehru and the Indian government. As the rift between China and the Soviet Union grew, the proximity developed between India and the Soviet Union confirmed Mao's perception of India's threat to China. This was explained in detail by Deng Xiaoping in an interview with an Indian statesman in 1981, which will be discussed later in this section.

2.1 (2) Deng's Era[36]

As Deng Xiaoping took power in 1978, the PRC entered into a new era characterized by significant transformations in terms of its domestic politics and external policies. In contrast to Mao's war/threat-featured security perception, Deng introduced fresh air into the cognition of the Chinese decision-makers. This culminated in his affirmation in 1985 that "peace and development are the two outstanding issues in the world today".[37]

Deng's Assessment of China's Security Environment

Deng's repeated assumptions in the 1980s that the new world war was avoidable indicated a fundamental transformation of China's assessment of the international security environment. As early as in 1983, when the second Cold War was at its peak, Deng assumed that "[world] war is not going to break out...I don't think there will be war for at least the next ten years."[38] He attributed such possibility to the unreadiness of both superpowers and the increasing voice from the international anti-war forces.[39] As a détente between the two superpowers emerged in the mid-1980s after Mikhail Gorbachev's assumption of power in the Soviet Union in 1985, Deng was more convinced that a "relatively long-lasting peace is possible and that war can be avoided".[40]

Although China was still facing the military threat from the Soviet Union, mainly caused by the "three hurdles",[41] Deng perceived that it was not serious enough for an immediate military intervention in China. This assessment was accentuated by the messages Moscow passed to Beijing for reconciliation, especially by the 1986 Vladivostok speech of Gorbachev.[42] Deng therefore believed that China was enjoying the best security environment since the PRC was founded.

While the external military threat to China's existence was rapidly decreasing, China started to come under increasing political and ideological pressures, mainly from the Western countries. In the mid-1980s, China launched a movement against the so-called 'bourgeois liberalization', which was challenging domestic stability and the communist rule in China. While Deng insisted that China could not 'copy' Western democracy, he did not relate it, until 1989, with the intention of the Western countries to promote 'peaceful evolution' in the socialist countries.[43] Witnessing the 'democratization' of many socialist countries in Eastern Europe and the disintegration of the Soviet Union as well as the Tiananmen Incident at home, Deng warned against the risk of "a third world war without gunsmoke" waged by the Western countries to overthrow the socialist regimes in the world.[44] The Western sanctions and their increasing criticism of China's human rights records alerted Deng to a new type of intervention in China's internal affairs and impingement on China's sovereignty.[45]

National Security Strategy of China under Deng

Viewing peace and development rather than war and revolution as the main trends of the world at that time, Deng made the creation of a peaceful environment for China's economic development a major objective of its national security strategy, though he insisted that "first priority should always be given to national sovereignty and [territorial] security".[46] In his address to the 12th National Congress of the CPC held in September 1982, he listed the three main tasks for the Chinese people in the 1980s as follows: "to accelerate socialist modernization, to strive for China's reunification and particularly for the return of Taiwan to the motherland, and to oppose hegemonism and work to safeguard world peace".[47] Among them the economic development was the core issue, which formed "the basis for the solution of our external and internal problems".[48] In other words, Deng conceived economic strength as a more important means than military capability for China to safeguard its national interests.

A peaceful security environment of China should start from its peripheral regions, which demanded that China improve its relationship with the Soviet Union. According to Deng Xiaoping, China's coordination since 1972 with the United States in opposing the Soviet Union did increase China's sense of security, on the one hand; it also aggravated the Soviet hostility to China and therefore further deteriorated China's security environment, on the other.[49] Second, it was in China's interests to be flexible and innovative on issues of the return of Hong Kong and Macao to China and the peaceful solution of the Taiwan question.[50] Third, defence build-up should be subordinate to economic development. In the context of China's new focus on economic growth and the assessment of no imminent war threat, Deng insisted that the major destination of China's limited resources should be shifted from the military sections to the economic fields. To quote him:

> What is essential now is that the Party, government, army and people throughout the land work wholeheartedly for national development, taking it into account in everything they do. The army has its role to play here. It must do nothing harmful to the general interest, and all its work must conform to it and be governed by it. Since the development of all our armed services is tied to national development, they should devise ways to assist and actively participate in it. The air force, the navy and the Commission in Charge of Science, Technology and Industry for National Defense should divert some of their resources to foster the development of the economy.[51]

Moreover, keeping a low profile on defence would show China's goodwill and help China set up a peace-loving image on the world stage.[52]

Independence, economic cooperation, "one country, two systems", and disarmament can be summed up as the keywords of Deng's approaches to safeguarding China's strategic security interests in this period characterized by significant transformation both domestically and internationally. While independence had been perceived as a fundamental principle of China's external strategy since the PRC was founded in 1949, it was not till 1982 that it carried the specific meaning of non-alignment.[53] China's independent foreign policy, in Deng's words, meant "truly non-aligned".[54] China decided to keep aloof from the Cold War for the first time by discarding its earlier strategy of siding with one superpower against the other. As Deng further explained, in dealing with the world affairs, "We will not play the 'United States card' or the 'Soviet Union card'. Nor will we allow others to play the 'China card'".[55] Apart from pursuing a normalization of its bilateral ties with the Soviet Union, China also explored the improvement of its relations with other neighbours, like India and Indonesia.

Second, Deng was convinced that economic cooperation could precede political normalization.[56] This was not only meant to expand foreign trade and attract investments but also bound to contribute to the political relationship due to the emergence and the increase of the common economic interests.

In China's talks with the British about the return of Hong Kong and with the Portuguese about that of Macao, Deng put forward his idea of "one country, two systems".[57] He also expressed China's willingness to realize Taiwan's reunification with China by applying the same principle.[58] By thinking out of the box, Deng was trying to convince the world that China was a peace-lover and it would try its best to solve its territorial problems peacefully.

Another significant step to win over the international confidence in China was its efforts with respect to disarmament. At home, the People's Liberation Army (PLA) volunteered to demobilize one million servicemen.[59] Internationally, China took part in negotiations on multiparty security regimes under UN, including treaties on chemical weapons, comprehensive disarmament, and outer space.[60]

Deng's India Perspective

In the early years of his era, Deng basically inherited Mao's perspective of India. In a meeting with Dr. Subramanian Swamy, the Janata Party MP, [61] in 1981, Deng made it very clear that China had a strong will to befriend India but viewed India as a threat only because the latter had been siding with the Soviet Union, China's major enemy since the 1960s.[62] India could not be a threat by itself, he said, even taking into account the fact that "you have many more troops on your side of the border than we have on ours". The real danger was the Soviet hegemonism. The USSR was threatening China's security from all directions, he further explained. In the north, there were a million Soviet troops deployed along the Sino-Soviet border and the Sino-Mongolian border. In the south, the USSR was instigating Vietnam to be a threat to China. In the southwest, it attempted to "get to the Indian Ocean" by way of its aggressive action in Afghanistan. Therefore, what was of greater concern to China was that the Soviet Union "may take a hand" in the subcontinent, especially in view of the fact that "the Russians always tried to use others even the war between China and India".[63] According to these remarks, Deng obviously attributed the major barrier in the China-India relations to the quasi-military alliance[64] between India and the Soviet Union.

One and a half years later, Deng made another important remark on improving China-India relations during his meeting with an Indian delegation. This time he did not mention the Soviet threat to China or

China's suspicion of India's quasi-military alliance with the USSR. On the contrary, he said:

> The problem between China and India is not a serious one. Neither country poses a threat to the other. The problem we have is simply about the border. Both countries should make an effort to restore the friendship that existed between them in the 1950s. As long as we go about it in a reasonable way, I think it will be easy for us to settle our border question.[65]

This represents a prominent shift in China's perspective of India. China no longer viewed India through the prism of the two-bloc confrontation. On the basis of Deng's reassessment, just as discussed earlier in this chapter, of the international security environment and China's national security interests, China viewed India as a natural and near neighbour, with which it had boundary dispute, rather than an ally of its major enemy.

On the solution of the Sino-Indian boundary dispute and the improvement of their bilateral relations, Deng made two important points in the same remark as follows. First, the approach to border issue required mutual concessions. Second, bilateral exchanges in areas such as trade, economy and culture could precede the solution of the border problem. In other words, the normalization of the bilateral relations between China and India should not be predicated on the solution of the boundary problem. This was in accord with Deng's belief that economic cooperation could promote political proximity. To quote him:

> When I met your former foreign minister in 1979, I put forward a "package solution" to the problem. If both countries make some concessions, it will be settled...We have settled border questions with many other countries simply by having both parties make concessions. I believe that we shall eventually find a good solution. Even if the border question cannot be resolved for the time being, we can leave it as it is for a while. We still have many things to do in the fields of trade, the economy and culture and can still increase our exchanges so as to promote understanding and friendship between us. The two countries have broad prospects for cooperation. We hope that we shall develop and that you will too.[66]

2.2 India's Security Perception

In the four decades from its independence in 1947 to 1990, the Indian strategic perspective had been dominated by Jawaharlal Nehru's view of India and the world, which is generally known as 'Nehruvianism'. The lengthy dominance in Indian politics by the Congress Party and the Nehru-Gandhi family contributed quite significantly to this domination of strategic thought. As the first prime minister of the Republic of India (RoI), Nehru served his country in the same position till the last second of his life. He was succeeded by Lal Bahadur Shastri, his disciple from 1964 to 1966. Nehru's daughter, Indira Gandhi, served as prime minister in 1966-77 and 1980-84. Nehru's grandson, Rajiv Gandhi, succeeded his mother in power from 1984 to 1989. This power chain of the Congress party was only shortly broken by governments like the Janata government under the leadership of Morarji Desai from 1977 to 1979 and the Janata Dal government led by V.P. Singh from the end of 1989 to the end of 1990. Therefore, this section will only examine the security perceptions of the three longest lasting governments during this period, i.e. the Jawaharlal Nehru, the Indira Gandhi and the Rajiv Gandhi governments.

2.2 (1) Nehru's Era

As the first prime minister of independent India, Nehru took charge at a time when the world order was experiencing a significant change. On the one hand, the ideological conflict and the competition for strategic influence between the United States and the USSR had finally evolved into the Cold War, in which the world was divided into two camps of confrontation: the Western camp, led by the former and the Socialist camp, led by the latter. On the other hand, the old colonial system was wavering due to the widespread freedom movements by the African and Asian colonial countries who wanted to follow India's example. Unlike his Chinese counterpart, Nehru held a relatively optimistic view of India's security environment. Apart from the specific threat from its immediate neighbour Pakistan, Nehru saw 'remote' chances of external attack on or invasion of India.[67] While the Cold War posed a general challenge to India's security, it also provided room for India to play a meaningful role in world politics. As the leader of a weak state, Nehru conceived that an effective foreign policy could make up for military preparedness in safeguarding national security.[68]

Nehru's Assessment of India's Security Environment

Internationally, Nehru saw no imminent war threat by outside powers to the newly independent India, although the politics of Cold War did challenge its independence to a certain extent. He argued that the danger from powers like Russia was caused solely by the rivalry between them and Britain. After independence, as British domination was removed, India was free from this kind of rivalry. Therefore, India should not "be unduly worried about external threats to its security".[69] In other words, in early years of the Cold War, Nehru had ruled out the possibility of any invasion of India by either the United States or the Soviet Union.

In his view, the real challenge of the Cold War to India's security was its threat to India's national independence. From the first day of its independence, India was expected to take sides by each camp. The United States expected it to join them in the ideological confrontation against the Soviet Union. This expectation was mainly based on "India's historical connections with Britain'.[70] The Soviet Union recognized the geopolitical significance of India for its influence on Central and West Asia as well as South Asia itself. Especially after the anti-Soviet strategic arrangements like the CENTO and SEATO were created, the Soviet Union believed that it was imperative to have India on its side.[71] The choice before India was either to accept a policy of alignment or keep independent and stay away from bloc politics. The former would put India in a subordinate position and let "foreign relations get out of hand into the charge of somebody else".[72] The latter would be a difficult path to pursue, since "both America and Russia are extra-ordinarily suspicious of each other as well as of others...and we may be suspected of leaning towards the other."[73]

Moreover, as the forerunner of freedom movements after the World War II, Nehru considered that Colonialism and Imperialism were still threatening India's independence. He was really worried about the remnants of the influence of colonial powers. He believed that India's independence and sovereignty "could not be sustained in a vacuum, when other countries and societies remained under colonial rule".[74]

Regionally speaking, Pakistan was accorded a prime place in Nehru's threat perception. In his view, the Pakistani threat had a "multidimensional nature", i.e. territorial, ideological and politico-strategic.[75] Pakistan's defiance of the accession of Jammu and Kashmir to India was considered a direct threat to the sovereignty and territorial consolidation of the newly independent India. Pakistan's promotion of the argument that Kashmir should belong to Pakistan in view of its Muslim majority "also posed an ideological threat to India's secular edifice".[76] India even suspected that Pakistan was seeking to exploit its relationship with the Islamic States of West Asia to 'embarrass' India in the region.[77] Pakistan's decision of joining the CENTO and SEATO pacts added a politico-strategic dimension to the threat it posed to India, especially when Pakistan claimed that the commitments by the West to support it politically and militarily in its disputes with India were the quid pro quo for its membership of the anti-communist alliances.[78] Apart from Pakistan, Nehru considered China, India's largest neighbour, another major security concern for India. Although Nehru was convinced that a friendly working relationship with China was essential for Asian resurgence, he was "conscious of China's influence, and also of its great power orientations towards Asia, and the Sino-centric assertive mindset of the Chinese leadership'.[79] Nehru's China perspective will be discussed later in detail in this section.

Domestically, India's primary security concern was regarding the possibility of some large and important Princely States rejecting accession to India, which would fragment the geopolitical cohesion and territorial integrity of the Indian Republic, especially in the context of British 'connivance' and Pakistan's 'encouragement' towards the independent tendencies of these Princely States. After these Princely States were successfully integrated with India, due to the multinational and multi-religious nature of India, ethnic centrifugal tendencies emerged quite soon as manifested in the demand for linguistic states.[80]

National Security Strategy of India under Nehru

Based on the aforementioned assessments of India's security environment, Nehru set two-fold objectives for India's national security strategy. Preserving India's independence and maintaining its national unity and territorial integrity was the one fundamental task, while playing a leading role in Asian and world affairs was the other, which was more ambitious. The latter objective derived from Nehru's belief in India's greatness. India's geographical size and the demographic and natural resources entitled it a unique position in the international system. Its civilizational legacy constituted a source of tremendous influence over other Asian countries.[81] Furthermore, in spite of its poverty and backwardness, the ancient and yet young India was "industrially more developed than many less fortunate countries'.[82] Therefore, India merited a leading role at the regional level on contemporary politico-cultural grounds and at the global level due to the moral stance it adopted on world issues.[83]

In Nehru's perspective, India's security interests comprised a number of inter-related dimensions. First, Nehru was convinced that India's stability and influence depended on genuine independence. He insisted that India should avoid involvement in Cold War power politics. India should not take sides with one bloc or the other in the East-West confrontation but "keep aloof from that and at the same time develop closest relations with all the countries'.[84] Second, the freedom of all the colonies and the creation of an equitable world order would consolidate India's independence and stability. India should promote the unity of the newly independent nations in Asia and Africa and lead them to become a significant force in international relations.[85] Third, Nehru considered that a friendly and peaceful equation with China was in the interest of India. On the one hand, Chinese support was imperative for Nehru's vision of Asian resurgence and Third World solidarity. On the other, in view of its military weakness, India "was not in a position to protect and preserve its security if it had to face two enemies on its borders—Pakistan and China'.[86] Fourth, as far as Pakistan was concerned, the 'idealist' Nehru turned into a complete realist, insisting that strong defence capacities and friends were needed to meet the Pakistani threat to India.[87]

Bearing in mind the above aspirations and the understanding of India's security interests, Nehru considered non-alignment, Third-Worldism, moralism and defence preparedness as the core approaches to India's national security. Nehru responded to the Cold War with non-alignment, which became a fundamental term of reference for India's foreign policy. Guided by this principle, Nehru sought equally good relations with both the United States and the Soviet Union while refusing to take anyone's side, especially in the first decade of India's independence.

Third-Worldism found manifestation in Nehru's endeavour to consolidate Afro-Asian unity on the basis of common interest in anti-colonialism and anti-imperialism. Bilaterally, India extended substantive support to Indonesia, to other countries of South-East Asia and later to the African countries in their freedom struggle.[88] Multilaterally, this endeavour had commenced with the convening of the Asian Relations Conference in March 1947, followed by the Afro-Asian Conference at Bandung in 1955, culminating in the creation of the Non-Aligned Movement (NAM) in 1961.

Convinced by the unique experience of India's freedom struggle, Nehru emphasized the role of moral force in safeguarding the national security for a weak and vulnerable state like India. He saw India "as a torch-bearer of freedom, of conscience, mediation and as a peace-maker in the world'.[89] He believed that India could transform the world by promoting "the universal causes of disarmament, racial equality, international cooperation for economic development, and peaceful resolution of disputes'.[90] Guided by this principle, Nehru clearly ruled out the possibility of India's going nuclear. India under him took the lead in the global campaign for nuclear disarmament, although he kept the option open for the future generations of Indian leaders to make nuclear weapons.

Defence preparedness was illustrated by Nehru's effort to constitute a sub-continental security order based on India's special relationship with its smaller neighbours and the way in which he responded to the Pakistani challenge. The Indo-Sikkimese Treaty of 1950 made the defense of Sikkim a responsibility of the Indian Government; the Indo-Bhutanese Friendship Treaty of 1949 asked Bhutan to be "guided by the advice of Government of India in regard to its external relations"; the Indo-Nepalese Treaty of Peace and Friendship of 1950 provided for mutual consultations and devising of effective counter-measures to deal with threats to their security.[91] A secret codicil of the Indo-Nepalese treaty not made public until 1959 went even further, providing that any aggression against Nepal would be considered as aggression against India and would be dealt with accordingly.[92] On the one hand, Nehru saw these special relationships as a guarantee of keeping the subcontinent an exclusive sphere of influence for India and preventing the great powers from intervening in the region.[93] On the other, these diplomatic/security arrangements were specifically regarded as a supplement to India's engagement with China, in order to cope with the Chinese challenge for India's security in the Himalayan perimeter.[94]

As for Pakistan, Nehru assumed a decisive politico-military posture. Within a few months after partition, India, without hesitation, took 'necessary' military steps against Pakistan to "protect India's vital interests in the Kashmir" and hasten the process of Kashmir's accession to India.[95] An objective of Nehru's search of friendship with China and the post-Stalin Soviet Union was to counterbalance Pakistan buttressed by Western military aid.[96] After the border war of 1962 with China, Nehru started to lay more stress on military preparedness in safeguarding India's national security. In 1963, he wrote: "We will have to clearly give considerably more attention to strengthening our armed forces and to the production within the extent possible, of all weapons and equipment needed by them".[97]

Nehru's China Perspective

Nehru's perspective on China experienced a categorical change during his 17-year-long tenure as the prime minister of India, from regarding China as a friend in the first decade to a rival and even an enemy in the rest years of his life.

Nehru made significant and substantial efforts to build a national consensus on defining communist China as a friend rather than an enemy of India during the early years after the People's Republic of China was founded in 1949, when some of his cabinet members like the then Home Minister

Sardar Vallabhbhai Patel were very suspicious of China's intentions. In his letter of 18 November 1950 to Patel, whose apprehension was accentuated especially by China's liberation of Tibet, Nehru clearly illustrated his perspective on China.

First, he assumed that China was not an enemy to India. Being hostile to India was not in the interests of New China, which was preparing for a fight on the main front in South and East against a real threat to its very existence. Any major attack on India by China would be "a wild adventure" which would "greatly weaken China's capacity to meet its real enemies".[98] Nehru thus considered an Indo-China war "exceedingly unlikely".[99] He also rejected the idea that communism inevitably means expansion and war. He thought it important to distinguish military invasion from infiltration of ideas. Chinese communism might have a tendency of exporting ideology, but it did not mean inevitably a military expansion vis-à-vis India.

Second, he was convinced that a friendly China would serve India's interests. Taking into account the limitations of India's strength, it was not wise to have two enemies on either side of India. When Pakistan was India's "major possible enemy", unreasoning fears of and preparations for a war with China would only play into the hands of Pakistan.[100] On the other hand, as mentioned earlier, Nehru considered a friendly working relationship with China essential for his vision of Asian resurgence. As he wrote in the same letter, "India and China, at peace with each other, would make a vast difference to the whole set-up and balance of the world".[101]

Third, any dispute with China could only be solved on the diplomatic level. As India shared a tremendously long common frontier with China and the "present" communist government in China was quite unlikely to "collapse giving place to another", any decision of India to have a really hostile China on its doorstep would mean continuous tension and apprehension.[102] Unlike other powers, like the UK and the US, who were just interested in embarrassing China, India had vital interests in Tibet. Helping Tibet to retain a large measure of autonomy would better serve that interest than trying to prevent China from taking possession of it, which would be an impossible mission.[103] He even believed that the PLA's march into Tibet might help ensure the security of its northern borders as long as good relations with China could be maintained.[104]

While advocating a friendly relationship with China, at the very beginning, Nehru had "no romantic or idealistic views about Sino-Indian relations".[105] He was conscious of China's influence and kept a close watch on China's act in Tibet and its attitude toward their border problem as well. To quote him:

> Ever since the Chinese Revolution we naturally had to think of what the new China was likely to be. We realised that this revolution was going to be a very big factor in Asia, in the world and in regard to us...Taken also with the fact of China's somewhat inherent tendency to be expansive when she is strong, we realised the danger to India...If any person imagines that we have followed our policy without realising the consequences, he is mistaken.[106]

Two developments in early 1959 deepened his suspicions about China. One was Zhou Enlai's letter of January 1959 to Nehru, in which China affirmed that border disputes did exist between India and China, rejecting Nehru's claim that the Indo-China boundary was a settled matter. The other was China's quelling of the rebellion in Tibet and its accusation of India's involvement in this incident. Insisting that there were private promises by Zhou Enlai on China's willingness to accept the McMahon Line and preservation of Tibetan autonomy, Nehru viewed these two events as signs of China's betrayal and hostility to India.[107] Moreover, China's diplomatic activities in the subcontinent during the same period also raised serious apprehensions in Nehru's mind. Neither China nor Burma preinformed India about the settlement of their border dispute on the basis of the 1941 line drawn by the then British authority. Without consultation with India, China and Nepal concluded the Kathmandu-Tibet highway agreement in 1961. Nehru interpreted the intensification of China's relations with both Burma and Nepal as "an incipient act of strategic encirclement of India".[108] As tensions between China and India heightened in the early 1960s, Nehru warned about the emergence of an impossible alliance between China and Pakistan on the basis of their common dislike of India.[109] After the 1962 war with China, Nehru was obsessed with the danger of renewed conflict between the two countries.[110]

2.2 (2) Mrs. Gandhi's Era

India's military defeat in the Sino-Indian armed conflict of 1962 had a significant impact on the world view and strategic thinking of Mrs. Indira Gandhi, Nehru's daughter, who was India's prime minister from 1966 to 1977 and from 1980 to 1984. While sharing Nehru's assumptions about the greatness of India and remaining committed to non-alignment, Indira Gandhi rejected her father's "softness" and sought "tangible" power to cope with the threats facing India.[111] In other words, she downplayed the role of moral force in India's national security strategy and believed that safeguarding security interests of India "primarily depended on India becoming self-reliant and strong".[112]

Mrs. Gandhi's Assessment of India's Security Environment

Nehru looked at the world in the Cold War through a "positive" prism.[113] As mentioned before, although he was aware of the strategic threat to India by the confrontation between the two camps, he was convinced that there was an opportunity for India to play a leading role outside the bipolar system in the world affairs. Taking office in the post-1962 era, Indira Gandhi found it difficult to inherit Nehru's "rather benign" threat perception.[114] In her view, new developments in international and regional environments put India in a more unfavourable and insecure position.

Internationally, as the transformation of strategic and power equations between important members of the international community led the Cold War into the subcontinent, Mrs. Gandhi's distrust of Washington was greatly accentuated by the fact that the United States opposed India's support for the Bangladesh movement in 1971 and allied with China in the 1970s and 1980s.[115] Earlier, it had adopted the policy of arming Pakistan in the 1950s and 1960s. The Afghan crisis, which commenced in 1979 contributed to the consolidation of relations among Pakistan, the US and China, especially the revival of the erstwhile US-Pakistan military alliance. Indira Gandhi was convinced that "the general international environment, dominated by the US and the Soviet Union, was hostile to the development of India as an independent power centre challenging their respective assumptions of security management and world order."[116]

Regionally, India first faced the threat posed by Pakistan, against which it fought two wars respectively in 1965 and in 1971. Second, a more powerful China after the 1962 Sino-Indian military conflict, which became a nuclear weapon power endowed with missile capacity and politically a permanent member of the UN Security Council, was a major security concern for India.[117] Third, Sino-Pak collaboration established soon after 1962 and greatly accelerated thereafter, compounded India's regional security environment that was characterized by a two-front threat.[118] Fourth, as "the entire Indian Ocean region was increasingly militarised by the direct presence of outside powers and the flow of arms to the littoral states of the Persian Gulf," and the smaller regional states like Bangladesh, Nepal and Sri Lanka "turn[ed] to China and the US at various times", India's "natural" regional dominance was under a great challenge.[119]

Domestically, the political uncertainties that accompanied Indira Gandhi for most years of her tenures, from the break-up of the Congress in 1969 to the declaration of a state of emergency in India in 1975, had weakened India's position in defending its national security and damaged India's prestige in the international community.[120] Meanwhile, rebels "in the culturally distinct and strategically vulnerable northeastern part of India" were a very difficult security problem for Indira Gandhi.[121]

National Security Strategy of India under Mrs. Gandhi

Like her father, Indira Gandhi also conceived preserving India's independence and maintaining its territorial integrity as the predominant objective of India's national security strategy. Where she disagreed with Nehru was only over the magnitude of the toughness of this task. Facing a considerably deteriorated security environment, Indira Gandhi laid much more stress on Nehru's first objective while toning down the second. Although she shared her father's assumption about the greatness of India, "she consistently scorned the idea of India becoming a 'great power' in the conventional sense".[122] Thus, she focused on achieving an "Indo-centric" role for India, which means autonomy and stability of its own on the one hand, and India's dominance in the subcontinent rather than a pivotal role in the world on the other.[123]

From the perspective of Indira Gandhi, the following security demands assumed greater urgency than before. First, India should be capable of "preventing any further military adventurism" by either of its two major enemies, i.e. Pakistan and China.[124] Second, the support of the Soviet Union was imperative for India to protect its economic and defence interests, even though she clung to her father's view that India had to remain outside of the major international alliances.[125] Third, India should prevent external powers from changing the status quo in the subcontinent and make "a discernible effort to have its own superior position in the region recognised by all other states concerned".[126] Fourth, India should develop its own nuclear weapons capacity to respond to China's explosion in 1964, to counterbalance the increasing deployment of tactical nuclear weapons in the Indian Ocean region by the US, and to neutralize the possible threat posed by Pakistan's nuclear weapons acquisition programme.[127]

While inheriting her father's vision and principles in dealing with the challenges to India, Indira Gandhi made some significant changes in India's national security policy. She emphasized the role of tangible power in international politics, deviating from Nehru's moralism.

First of all, "she brought an increased preoccupation with the need for military power, and she demonstrated a willingness to use this power boldly in her response to the Bangladesh crisis".[128] The Indian military reforms, which commenced after 1962 due to India's defeat at the hands of the Chinese, were accelerated by Mrs. Gandhi's government. These reforms consisted of the review of India's military doctrines, the upgrading of the weapons system, the military logistical infrastructure, the arms production, the defence supplies acquisition, etc.[129] In Mrs. Gandhi's era, India became a military power whose might in southern Asia could not be ignored either by regional or by outside powers.[130] While pursuing a conventional military superiority of India over Pakistan and China, Indira Gandhi adopted a nuclear option strategy that "implied clearly India's right to make the bomb".[131] Indira Gandhi and her cabinet decided not to sign the Nuclear Non-Proliferation Treaty (NPT) of 1968. Defying the intense international pressure at that time, Indira Gandhi "authorised India's Department of Atomic Energy and the Department of Space to commence research for making India self-reliant in the spheres of nuclear weapons and missile capacity," which culminated in India's first underground nuclear test in 1974.[132]

Second, barring the upgrading of India's military capabilities, Indira Gandhi regarded balance of power or alliance security as an effective approach to cope with the strategic threat to India. At the beginning of her first tenure, "she looked both to the US and to the USSR for strategic deterrence against China and subtle pressure on Pakistan."[133] Thanks to the cold shoulder from the United States but the warm response from the Soviet Union, in 1971 she decided to sign a de facto alliance treaty with the latter.[134] This decision seems to have been justified by the subsequent transformation of the strategic chessboard in India's neighbourhood, characterized by the proximity between China and the United States.

Third, as far as the smaller neighbours of India are concerned, Indira Gandhi buttressed Nehru's approach[135] through the principle of bilateralism. She insisted on bilateralism in solving problems in the region, eschewing any role for external powers.[136] Furthermore, Indira Gandhi was tough in "demanding that the smaller countries of the subcontinent desist from activities which could be construed as anti-Indian".[137] Her forceful actions in the protectorate of Sikkim and hard line in dealing with what she called "anti-Indian nonsense" in Nepal and Bangladesh, contributed to the image of her seeking hegemony.[138]

Mrs. Gandhi's China Perspective

Indira Gandhi's perception of China was rather negative. When she first came to power in 1966, rivalry with China appeared to be an inescapable fact.[139] Throughout her two tenures, Indira Gandhi viewed China with alertness and suspicion. She was convinced that the rivalry between China and India went beyond the border dispute. She asserted that China had a more complex policy that was aimed at defeating India in an Asian power rivalry game. China was seeking a dominant position in Asia by eclipsing India's international standing and prestige and reducing it to a position of subordination.[140] To quote her:

> It would be an over-simplification to regard this merely as the result of a border dispute. Simultaneous or subsequent developments—such as China's systematic support of Pakistan against India, her provocative criticism of India for alleged subservience to the United States and later the Soviet Union, and her persistent, though futile efforts to promote internal subversion—leave us no option but to infer that border dispute was the outcome of a more complex policy which was aimed at undermining India's stability and at obstructing her rapid and orderly progress.[141]

In Indira Gandhi's perspective, China then posed a great threat to India in both military-strategic and political categories. In the military-strategic dimension, Indira Gandhi first kept a close eye on the implication of China's acquisition of nuclear capability for India's security. Not having fully recovered from the trauma of the humiliating military defeat by the Chinese in 1962, Indira Gandhi considered that the nuclear bomb gave China further superiority over India in terms of defence capability. Mrs. Gandhi's government even feared that "China might use nuclear weapons or resort to nuclear blackmail in the event of a future conflict".[142] Second, the proximity that rapidly grew between China and Pakistan after 1962 was a grave security concern to India. The Sino-Pak border agreement signed in March 1963 and their later formal arrangements for defence and strategic cooperation were interpreted in India as the outcome of an anti-India alliance. The risk of a joint Sino-Pak military attack on India appeared very real to Indira Gandhi during the 1971 Eastern Pakistan Crisis, though China took a relatively low-key approach to this crisis in contrast to the United States, which embarked on naval diplomacy[143] on Pakistan's behalf.[144] China's support for Pakistan and the use of veto on Bangladesh's application of membership to the United Nations "fuelled hostile opinion in India".[145] Third, when the US-China rapprochement emerged in the early 1970s, China's threat to India was put into a much broader picture that was dubbed as the "China-Pakistan-US axis".[146]

In the political dimension, India accused China of endangering India's national security through "fomenting dissent and subversion within India and in the neighbourhood".[147] Indira Gandhi's government was convinced that

China's intention of giving moral and material support to the Naxalbari Movement that started in 1967 and Naga rebellious elements was to undermine India's stability by exploiting the "two basic weaknesses in the governance of India".[148] Meanwhile, Indira Gandhi was very alert to China's efforts to strengthen its relations with the smaller countries in the subcontinent, which might dilute India's influence and position in the region.

2.2 (3) Rajiv Gandhi's Era

Compared with Nehru and Indira Gandhi, Rajiv Gandhi's five-year tenure from 1984 to 1989 as India's prime minister was quite short. However, the tasks he assumed were not easier, especially taking into account the then dramatic transformation of world politics, which ultimately led to the end of the Cold War.

Rajiv Gandhi's Assessment of India's Security Environment

When Rajiv Gandhi took charge as prime minister, he was conscious of the changing international power equations. Keeping a close watch on the emerging USSR-USA détente and the Vladivostok speech of Gorbachev, Rajiv Gandhi perceived that the great challenge for India's national security at that stage was how to respond appropriately to those dramatic changes. In his view, the good news for India was that the strategic pressure on India for decades due to the superpowers' confrontation in the world and in the subcontinent as well might decrease.[149]

On the regional level, Rajiv Gandhi saw a less 'aggressive' China, whereas there were many 'troublesome' neighbours within the subcontinent.[150] Taking note of the fact that China was focusing on its internal consolidation and economic development and that the antagonistic Sino-Soviet relations were thawing, Rajiv Gandhi expected that Beijing would adopt "a more tactful approach towards India".[151] As far as Pakistan was concerned, it remained a major threat to India. First of all, Rajiv Gandhi was extremely worried about Pakistan's nuclear programme and its acquisition of ultra-sophisticated armaments, which might lead to a transformation of the South Asian military balance.[152] Second, the likelihood of Soviet withdrawal from Afghanistan would increase the regional influence of Pakistan, whose involvement in Afghanistan, backed by the US, was then at its peak.[153] Moreover, Pakistan's support for "the separatist Sikhs in the Punjab" was challenging Rajiv Gandhi's capability in dealing with the thorniest issue facing him internally.[154] As a fallout of Mrs. Gandhi's tough stance on regional issues, a negative perception about India came into being in the subcontinent. India's other neighbours, such as Nepal, Bangladesh and Sri Lanka were forging political and defence relationships with the US, China and Israel due to their suspicion of India's hegemonic ambitions.[155]

India's National Security Strategy under Rajiv Gandhi

Upholding most of Indira Gandhi's views about India's national security strategy, Rajiv Gandhi made some detailed adjustments on India's national security policy in accordance with the changing security environment. In the context of the détente emerging between the two superpowers, Rajiv Gandhi perceived that it was in India's interests to readjust its relations with both the United States and the Soviet Union and seek a balance between them. Taking into account his still deep suspicions of the United States, his doubts about China's intentions toward India, and India's heavy dependence on the Soviet Union in terms of defence supplies, high technology and trade, Rajiv Gandhi insisted on giving "the central place in his foreign policy to Moscow".[156] Meanwhile, he "worked assiduously to expand and strengthen relations with America", despite their differences over the questions of nuclear disarmament and Pakistan.[157]

Second, Rajiv Gandhi believed that the profound changes occurring in China under the leadership of Deng Xiaoping offered India an opportunity to improve its prolonged bitter security environment. He paid a historic visit to Beijing in December 1988. It had been 34 years since the last visit to China by an Indian prime minister.

Moreover, Rajiv Gandhi, like his mother, also believed in tangible power. During his time, there was a considerable strengthening of India's armed forces.[158] Despite his world-level anti-nuclear campaign, an important theme of his foreign policy, he continued to keep India's nuclear option open. Although he tried to improve India's relations with all countries in the subcontinent and endorsed South Asian regional cooperation, Rajiv Gandhi maintained a strong attitude toward issues that had effects on the vital interests of India.[159] During his tenure, India imposed a trade embargo against Nepal, intervened in Sri Lanka's internal turmoil, and offered help in quelling the coup in the Maldives.[160]

Rajiv Gandhi's China Perspective

Rajiv Gandhi's perception of China was ambivalent due to the complex international situation of his time. Taking note of the fact that China was placing greater emphasis on internal consolidation and economic development and trying to keep aloof from the Cold War, Rajiv Gandhi felt a decreasing military threat from China. With "an economically resurgent and politically assertive China" on the northeastern flank of India, however, Rajiv Gandhi thought that India's position in the world as a whole and its dominance in the subcontinent in particular, were under a new type of pressure.[161]

In spite of his doubts about China's intentions, the rapidly transforming international situation, especially the Soviet decision to improve its relations with China, convinced Rajiv Gandhi that a tense relationship with China would not serve India's security interests. In his 1986 visit to India, Gorbachev conveyed a very clear message to Rajiv Gandhi that a normal China-India relationship was in Soviet interests and that India should not expect as before the Soviet Union to extend its unqualified and categorical support in any possible conflict between India and China.[162] This message made a significant contribution to Rajiv Gandhi's decision to send P.N. Haksar as Special Envoy to China to assure the Chinese leaders that India desired good relations with China and that "India was prepared to adopt a forward looking policy without being mired in the past".[163] This indicated that India would get ready to accept Deng Xiaoping's proposal on improving China-India relations, which he had put forward several years' back.

2.3 The Cold War Mindset and its Implications for China-India Relations during the Cold War

Despite their respective resistance, to a certain extent, against getting involved into the Cold War of bipolar confrontation, it is not difficult to find the imprint of Cold War mindset on the above-discussed security perceptions of China and India. This has in turn verified one of Wendt's assumptions that the structure of international politics has constitutive effects on states, as discussed in Chapter One.

On China's part, Mao's security perception was deeply influenced by the Cold War mindset. It was not till the early 1980s that Deng Xiaoping brought about a sea change in the cognition of Chinese decision-makers, leading China to a gradual departure from the mindset that was still prevalent around the world. During Mao's era, China considered that the imbalance of military power among nations was the major source of threat. Mao took for granted the intention of a state with outstanding military capability to obtain benefits through force. Therefore, as a newly liberated and weak country in the post-war era, China under Mao had been staying under the shadow of an imminent Third World War as well as a military invasion by the superpowers, i.e. the United States in the 1950s, both the United States and the Soviet Union in the 1960s, and the Soviet Union in the 1970s. In the early 1980s, Deng Xiaoping started to downplay the role of the imbalance of military power in threat construction. Though China's military capability was still prominently inferior to either of the two superpowers, he predicted the possibility that China could enjoy a relatively peaceful security environment for a comparatively long time.

Second, China's security perception during the Cold War was imbued with the colour of ideology. As discussed earlier, ideology had been a principal prism through which Mao looked at the security issues. While the ideological consideration to a great extent contributed to China's decision to side with the Soviet Union in the 1950s, it also led to the Sino-Soviet split. To pursue and safeguard pure socialism, China took an extremely difficult journey to fight both US capitalism and Soviet revisionism throughout the 1960s. China's strategic alliance with the United States in the 1970s and 1980s did not mean that it had given up its ideological pursuit in its national security strategy. On the contrary, it was only an expedient move for China, which was by then convinced that the Soviet revisionism or social hegemonism posed a much greater threat to China than the US capitalism did.

Mao's India perspective manifested his emphasis on the ideological factor. Although Nehru held sympathy for the socialist cause of the Soviet Union and adopted a socialist-oriented policy in managing the national economy, Mao had never viewed Nehru as a socialist but a representative of the big bourgeoisie of India. In the early days when the PRC was just founded, Mao expressed his profound suspicion of the Indian bourgeois government under Nehru. In a message to B.T. Ranadive, Secretary General of the Communist Party of India, he wrote, "I firmly believe that India, relying on the brave Communist Party of India and the unity and struggle of all Indian patriots, will certainly not remain long under the yoke of imperialism and its collaborators."[164] As mentioned earlier, Mao attributed Nehru's "instigation" of the 1959 Tibet rebellion and the follow-up border crisis between China and India to the aggressive and expansive nature of the big bourgeoisie of India. China's later support to the Naxalbari movement was also justified by this ideological backdrop. An article in the *People's Daily* entitled 'A Single Spark can Light a Prairie Fire' extolled the movement as an authentic peasant armed rebellion against the big bourgeoisie, proving its earlier prophecy that India was ripe for a revolution.[165]

Even Deng Xiaoping, who had tried to downplay the role of ideological factor in China's domestic policy and external relations since 1978, had to keep an eye on the political and ideological pressures on China by the

Western countries at that time. Since the mid-1980s, he had warned against the conspiracy of the Western countries to promote "peaceful evolution" in the socialist countries. He called it a third world war without gunsmoke. However, there was no trace of ideology in Deng's India perspective.

Third, during Mao's era, China was convinced that military strength played a vital role in safeguarding national security. On the one hand, in order to build a strong army, Mao gave the army the priority of access to the limited resources China had at that time. He also resolutely allowed China to go nuclear in 1964. On the other hand, China regarded alignment as an effective way to enhance its military capability along with military build-up. In the early days of the PRC, Mao firmly chose to ally with the Soviet Union to neutralize the threat by the United States. In the 1970s, facing the intensifying threat from the Soviet Union, China forged a de facto strategic alliance with the United States. Meanwhile, China also explored a moral alignment with the Third World countries. In short, self-help security plus alliance security were Mao's approaches to security. It was since 1982 that China started to drop alliance security and try to safeguard its national security through economic cooperation and international security dialogue.

Although Nehru tried to give India and the world an alternative way to address security issues, since the mid-1950s, the more India got involved into the bipolar confrontation, the more its security perception was influenced by the Cold War mindset. First of all, India, like China, attributed its sense of insecurity to its inferiority in national power, especially in military strength. Despite Nehru's not seeing any prospect of direct military invasion by the superpowers, he was worried about the military threat from Pakistan backed by the United States and the remnant influence of the colonialism as well.

As mentioned earlier, in the days of his advocating a friendly relationship with China, Nehru was realistic enough to believe that China had an "inherent tendency to be expansive when she is strong". In other words, he took China's intention of expansion for granted and attributed the fact that China did not constitute a threat to India to China's lack of capability. As China showed its political influence in Bandung and military strength in its 1959 action in Tibet, Nehru's China perspective underwent a negative change. From 1962 onwards, China, the winner of the China-India border conflict and a nuclear weapon power since 1964, was viewed, along with Pakistan, as a major military threat to India. During Mrs. Gandhi's era, India's feeling of its military inferiority was enhanced by the Sino-Pak, the Sino-US and the Sino-US-Pak collaborations, which emerged in sequence since the mid-1960s. Therefore, Mrs. Gandhi was very pessimistic about India's security environment at her time and concerned about military threats all around.

Apart from military threat, India during the Cold War laid stress on the political dimension of national security. Unlike China, which focused on the survival of the Chinese communist regime, India attached great importance to its external position, i.e. its political influence in the region and in the world. Due to Nehru's political aspiration of a leading role of India in Asian and world affairs, India was very sensitive to the emergence of China. Through the 1960s and 1970s, India was upset by the fact that, "to many in the Third World, including some Indians, the revolutionary and self-reliant path tried by Mao Zedong's China appeared more appealing and more honourable than India's middle way of nonalignment and mixed economy".[166] On the subcontinent, as India considered this region naturally an exclusive sphere of influence of India, it had been on the alert for the relationship between its smaller neighbours and outside powers, including China. As history indicated, from time to time, this led India into tensions not only with outside powers but also with its smaller neighbours.

Finally, during the Cold War, India also viewed self-help security and alliance security as the major approaches to national security. The successive top leaders of India during the Cold War attached great importance to its own military build-up. In the light of its three wars with Pakistan and one war with China during this period, military superiority over Pakistan and China was viewed as a guarantee to India's security, and wars were sometimes thought to be the best way to get out of insecurity. During Mrs. Gandhi's first tenure, India even exploded a nuclear device in 1974. Meanwhile, in the 1970s and 1980s, India considered its quasi-military alliance with the Soviet Union as a major provider of security. Before that, Nehru tried to form a moral alliance with the Third World through the Non-Aligned Movement to preserve India's security interests.

Based on the foregoing analysis, it is not difficult to draw the conclusion that the security perceptions of China and India, both of which were characterized by the Cold War mindset, have played a significant role in the ups and downs of the bilateral relationship during the Cold War era, despite the fact that there have already been so many explanations. Obviously, it was the determination of Mao and Nehru to befriend each other that has contributed to the China-India 'honeymoon' till the mid-1950s. However, the mutual distrust inherent in their respective security perceptions gained momentum with the passage of time. As discussed earlier, since both Nehru's India and Mao's China took each other's expansive nature for granted, they were very sensitive to any change of their power relations. China's gain in Bandung and military action in Tibet appeared to be alarms for Nehru; Nehru's sympathy for the Tibet rebellion, claim to the British legacy of the Sino-Indian border and intimacy with Khrushev sounded a series of warning for Mao. The mutual distrust led to a lot of mutual misperception, culminating in a military confrontation. As many scholars have argued, the 1962 armed conflict between China and India might have been avoided if there were not so many mutual misperceptions.[167] This author concurs with the view that there were opportunities for Nehru and Mao to have lowered down their temper and shunned the extremity, but also argues that it appeared to be very difficult for them to overcome these mutual misunderstandings given the nature of their respective security perceptions at that time.

From 1962 onwards, with both sides getting further involved in the Cold War, especially when the hostility between China and India was formally fixed in the structure of Cold War confrontation since the 1970s, with the US-China-Pak strategic collaboration on one side and the Soviet-Indian alliance on the other, it was impossible for them to find an exit for their mutual distrust. As a result, the rest of the Cold War era witnessed lengthy 'cold' relations between China and India, although the bilateral diplomatic relations were restored at the ambassadorial level in July 1976.

It was Deng Xiaoping who brought some light to the China-India relations in the dark. In his meeting of February 1979 with the visiting Indian Foreign Minister Vajpayee, Deng Xiaoping put forward the proposal for the first time that China and India could normalize their relations without predicating the process on the resolution of their boundary dispute. As mentioned earlier, in 1982, when he was determined to keep aloof from the Cold War and put China's focus on its economic development, Deng Xiaoping repeated this view to India. Due to the slow pace of perspective adjustment on the Indian side, Rajiv Gandhi caught up with Deng only by late 1988.

Rajiv Gandhi's visit to Beijing of December 1988 is a major landmark in China-India relations. It broke the impasse of the process of normalization between the two countries. Based on the consensus the two sides reached during this visit that the improvement and development of bilateral relations should not be predicated on the solution to the boundary dispute, some concrete agreements were made to promote all-round cooperation between them.[168] A joint working group at the level of vice ministers for negotiations on the boundary question was established, whereas another joint working group at the level of ministers was set up to promote trade and investment. Three agreements were also signed on cooperation in the field of science and technology, on civil aviation and on cultural exchanges.

To sum up, if the China-India 'cold' relations during the Cold War can be attributed to their respective Cold War mentalities, Rajiv Gandhi's visit, which led China-India relations into a new page of increasingly positive interaction, can be attributed to their perspective adjustment in accordance with the rapidly changing world situation. Against this backdrop, the following chapters will focus on the transformation of their security perceptions in the post-Cold War era, and its implications for the development of this relationship, which is one of the most important bilateral relations in the 21st century.

Notes

1. Although Mikhail Gorbachev and George H.W. Bush declared the Cold War officially over at a summit meeting in Malta in December 1989, the drastic changes of the political scenario in Eastern Europe during 1989-1990 and the dissolution of the Warsaw Pact in July 1991 were also seen as symbols of the end of the Cold War.
2. Qi Chengzhang, *'Zhongguo duiwai zhanlue de queli yu tiaozheng'* (The Establishment and Adjustment of China's External Strategy, in *Zhongguo waijiao xinlun (New Dimensions of China's Diplomacy)*, eds. Liu Shan, and Hsueh Chun-tu (Beijing: Shijie zhishi chubanshe, 1997), p. 44.
3. From 1949 to 1976. Mao passed away on September 9, 1976.
4. *Mao Zedong on Diplomacy* (Beijing: Foreign Languages Press, 1998), p. 444.
5. Ibid, pp. 75-80.
6. Ibid, pp. 106-111.
7. Ibid, pp. 126-136.
8. In the 1960s, Mao called the USSR 'revisionist,' a word characterized by ideological elements. From the early 1970s, China replaced 'revisionist' with 'hegemonist', a word Mao used to specify the 'expansionist ambition' of the Soviet Union.
9. Zhang Xiaoming, *'Lengzhan shiqi xin Zhongguo de si ci duiwai zhanlue jueze'* (Four Choices of New China's External Strategy in the Cold War Era), in *Zhongguo waijiao xinlun*, eds. Liu Shan et al. pp. 7-8.
10. Xie Yixian, *Dangdai Zhongguo waijiao sixiang shi* (Contemporary History of China's Diplomatic Thoughts) (Kaifeng: Henan University Press, 2004), pp. 242-243.
11. Zhang Xiaoming, *'Lengzhan shiqi xin Zhongguo de si ci duiwai zhanlue jueze'*, pp. 10-11.
12. *Mao Zedong on Diplomacy*, pp. 104, 264-269.
13. Wu Baiyi, *'The Chinese Security Concept and Its Historical Evolution'*, paper

from a conference sponsored by the Stanley Foundation in 2000, available at http://www.stanleyfoundation.org/papers/wub.pdf.

14. *Mao Zedong on Diplomacy,* pp. 413-414, 416-428.
15. Xie, *Dangdai Zhongguo waijiao sixiang shi,* pp. 285-286.
16. *Mao Zedong on Diplomacy,* pp. 221, 416-428.
17. Ibid, pp. 293-297.
18. Ibid, pp. 204-212.
19. Zhang Zhirong, *Zhongguo bianjiang yu minzu wenti* (China's Border Regions and Ethnic Nationalisms) (Beijing: Peking University Press, 2005), pp. 232-234, 268-269.
20. Zhang Xiaoming, *'Lengzhan shiqi xin Zhongguo de si ci duiwai zhanlue jueze',* p. 2.
21. *Mao Zedong on Diplomacy,* pp. 215-216.
22. Ibid, pp. 87-89, 364-365.
23. Yang Gongsu, *Dangdai Zhongguo waijiao lilun yu shijian:1949-2001* (Theory and Practice of Contemporary Diplomacy of China: 1949-2001) (Hong Kong: Lizhi Publishing House, 2002), pp. 96-99.
24. Xie, *Dangdai Zhongguo waijiao sixiang shi,* pp. 300-304.
25. Niu Jun, 'The Formation of Diplomatic Policy in New China and its Main Characteristics', *Social Sciences in China,* Beijing, No.1 (2001): 3, also available at http://niujun.coldwarchina.com/ywlz/lw/000297.htm.
26. Ibid, p. 1.
27. China's decisions to aid Korea against the US and Vietnam against France were made more on the basis of pragmatic security requirement than out of ideological consideration.
28. Xie, *Dangdai Zhongguo waijiao sixiang shi,* pp. 239-241.
29. Niu Jun, 'The Historical Background of the Shift in Chinese Policy Toward the United States in the Late 1960s', paper from the Conference 'New Evidence on China, Southeast Asia and the Indochina Wars', Hong Kong, January 11-12, 2000, available at http://niujun.coldwarchina.com/ywlz/index.htm.
30. Yang, *Dangdai Zhongguo waijiao lilun yu shijian,* pp. 152-153.
31. *Mao Zedong on Diplomacy,* p. 134.
32. Ibid, pp. 126-135.
33. Yang, *Dangdai Zhongguo waijiao lilun yu shijian,* p. 75.
34. *Mao Zedong on Diplomacy,* pp. 291-292.
35. "Xizang de geming he Nihelu de zhexue" (The Revolution in Tibet and Nehru's Philosophy), Renmin ribao (People's Daily), Beijing, May 6, 1959, available at http://myy.cass.cn/file/2006010618276.html.
36. The convocation of the Third Plenary Session of the CPC's Eleventh Central Committee indicated the beginning of Deng's era. From then on till the early 1990s, Deng had been the de facto leader of China, though his official posts (such as chairman of the State and Communist Party Central Military Commissions) were not the highest, and though the third generation of collective leadership with Jiang Zemin at the core was formed in 1989. After 1993, Deng gradually retired from the political scene of China. He passed away

on February 19, 1997.

37. *Deng Xiaoping wenxuan* (Selected Works of Deng Xiaoping), Vol. III (Beijing: Renmin chubanshe, 1993), p. 104.
38. Ibid, p. 25.
39. Ibid, pp. 82, 127.
40. Ibid, p. 233.
41. This refers to the Soviet heavy military deployment in the Sino-Soviet and Sino-Mongolian border areas, its occupation of Afghanistan, and its support for Vietnam's invasion of Cambodia.
42. On July 28, 1986, President Mikhail Gorbachev made a speech in Vladivostok dealing with the Soviet Union's Asia policy, including relations with China. With regard to China, he made the following points: the Soviet Union was ready to hold serious discussions with China at any time and at any level to create a good-neighbourly atmosphere and hoped that the border between the two countries would soon become an area of peace and friendship; the Soviet Union was willing to take the main course of the Heilongjiang (Amur) River as the official boundary line between the two countries; the Soviet and Mongolian leaders were studying the withdrawal of a considerable portion of the Soviet troops from Mongolia; the Soviet Union would withdraw six regiments from Afghanistan before the end of 1989; and the Soviet Union understood and respected China's goal of modernization.
43. *Deng Xiaoping wenxuan*, pp. 123-125, 194-197, 207-209.
44. Ibid, p. 344.
45. Ibid, pp. 344-349.
46. Ibid, 348; Qi, *'Zhongguo duiwai zhanlue de queli yu tiaozheng'*, p. 47.
47. *Deng Xiaoping wenxuan*, p. 3.
48. Ibid.
49. Zhang Xiaoming, *'Lengzhan shiqi xin Zhongguo de si ci duiwai zhanlue jueze'*, p. 15.
50. Yang, *Dangdai Zhongguo waijiao lilun yu shijian*, pp. 260-262.
51. *Deng Xiaoping wenxuan*, p. 99.
52. Ibid, pp. 126-129.
53. Zhang Xiaoming, *'Lengzhan shiqi xin Zhongguo de si ci duiwai zhanlue jueze'*, p. 14.
54. *Deng Xiaoping wenxuan*, p. 57.
55. Ibid.
56. Ibid, p. 99.
57. Ibid, pp. 12-15, 58-61.
58. Ibid, pp. 30-31, 58-61.
59. Ibid, p. 126.
60. Xie, *Dangdai Zhongguo waijiao sixiang shi*, p. 353.
61. Member of Parliament.
62. Subramanian Swamy, *India's China Perspective* (Delhi: Konark Publishers, 2001), Appendix III: pp. 175-181.

63. Ibid. All the quotations of Deng in this paragraph are extracted from Dr. Subramanian Swamy's historic 100-minute interview with Chinese top leader Deng Xiaoping in Beijing in 1981.
64. See the later discussion of India's national security strategy under Mrs. Gandhi.
65. *Deng Xiaoping wenxuan*, p. 19.
66. Ibid, pp. 19-20.
67. P.S. Jayaramu, *India's National Security and Foreign Policy* (New Delhi: ABC Publishing House, 1987), p. 13.
68. Ibid, p. 14.
69. Ibid, pp. 12-13.
70. J.N. Dixit, *India's Foreign Policy 1947-2003,* updated edition (New Delhi: Picus Books, 2003), p. 22.
71. Ibid, pp. 23, 53.
72. Jayaramu, India's National Security and Foreign Policy, p. 16.
73. K.P.S. Menon, *Many Worlds: An Autobiography* (London: Oxford University Press, 1965), p. 229.
74. Dixit, *India's Foreign Policy 1947-2003,* p. 31.
75. Jayaramu, *India's National Security and Foreign Policy,* p. 19.
76. Ibid.
77. Ibid.
78. Dixit, *India's Foreign Policy 1947-2003,* pp. 51-52.
79. Ibid, p. 48.
80. Ibid, pp. 29, 52.
81. *Jawaharlal Nehru's Speeches,* Vol. I, September 1946 to May 1949 (New Delhi: Publications Division, Government of India, 1958), p. 253.
82. *Jawaharlal Nehru's Speeches,* Vol. II, 1949 to 1953 (New Delhi: Publications Division, Ministry of Information and Broadcasting, Government of India, 1963), p. 199.
83. Dixit, *India's Foreign Policy 1947-2003,* p. 21.
84. *Jawaharlal Nehru's Speeches,* Vol. I, p. 247.
85. Dixit, *India's Foreign Policy 1947-2003,* pp. 18, 35.
86. Jayaramu, *India's National Security and Foreign Policy,* p. 25.
87. Stephen P. Cohen, *India: Emerging Power* (New Delhi: Oxford University Press, 2002), 39-40; Dixit, *India's Foreign Policy 1947-2003,* p. 37.
88. Dixit, *India's Foreign Policy 1947-2003,* p. 18.
89. Surjit Mansingh, *India's Search for Power: Indira Gandhi's Foreign Policy 1966-1982* (New Delhi: Sage Publications, 1984), p.15.
90. Ibid.
91. Jayaramu, *India's National Security and Foreign Policy,* pp. 25-26.
92. John W. Garver, *Protracted Contest: Sino-Indian Rivalry in the Twentieth Century* (New Delhi: Oxford University Press, 2001), p.141.
93. C. Raja Mohan, *Crossing the Rubicon: The Shaping of India's New Foreign Policy* (New Delhi: Penguin-Viking, 2003), pp. 238-239.

94. Jayaramu, *India's National Security and Foreign Policy,* pp. 25-26.
95. Ibid, p. 20.
96. Ibid, pp. 22-23.
97. Jawaharlal Nehru, 'Changing India', *Foreign Affairs,* Vol. 41, No. 3 (April 1963): p. 459.
98. 'Prime Minister Jawaharlal Nehru's Note on China and India', in *India's China Perspective,* Swamy, Appendix II: pp. 171-172.
99. Ibid, p. 171.
100. Ibid, p. 172.
101. Ibid, p. 173.
102. Ibid, p. 171.
103. Ibid, pp. 173-174.
104. C.V. Ranganathan and Vinod C. Khanna, *India and China: The Way Ahead,* second edition (New Delhi: Har-Anand Publications, 2004), p. 28.
105. Dixit, *India's Foreign Policy 1947-2003,* p. 18.
106. Jawaharlal Nehru, *India's Foreign Policy: Selected Speeches, September 1946 to April 1961* (New Delhi: Publications Division, Ministry of Information and Broadcasting, Government of India, 1961), p. 369.
107. Ibid, pp. 185-192.
108. Dixit, *India's Foreign Policy 1947-2003,* p. 62.
109. *Jawaharlal Nehru's Speeches,* Vol. IV, September 1957 to April 1963 (New Delhi: Publications Division, Ministry of Information and Broadcasting, Government of India, 1964), p. 225.
110. Ibid, pp. 267-268.
111. Mansingh, *India's Search for Power,* pp. 32-41.
112. Dixit, *India's Foreign Policy 1947-2003,* pp. 88-89.
113. Jawaharlal Nehru, 'Speech to Bandung Conference Political Committee', 1955, available at http://www.fordham.edu/halsall/mod/1955nehru-bandung2.html
114. Jayaramu, *India's National Security and Foreign Policy,* p. 13.
115. *Selected Speeches and Writings of Indira Gandhi 1972-1977,* Vol. III (New Delhi: Publications Division, Ministry of Information and Broadcasting, 1984), pp. 634-636; Mansingh, *India's Search for Power,* pp. 4-5.
116. Mansingh, *India's Search for Power,* p. 55.
117. Dixit, *India's Foreign Policy 1947-2003,* pp. 89-90, 119.
118. Jayaramu, *India's National Security and Foreign Policy,* p. 29.
119. Mansingh, *India's Search for Power,* pp. 38, 55, 302.
120. Dixit, *India's Foreign Policy 1947-2003,* pp. 89, 91, 119.
121. Mansingh, *India's Search for Power,* pp. 55-56.
122. Ibid, p. 2.
123. Dixit, *India's Foreign Policy 1947-2003,* p. 96; Mansingh, *India's Search for Power,* p. 41.
124. Dixit, *India's Foreign Policy 1947-2003,* p. 90.
125. *Selected Speeches and Writings of Indira Gandhi 1972-1977,* Vol. III, p. 634.

126. Mansingh, *India's Search for Power,* pp. 41, 264.
127. Dixit, *India's Foreign Policy 1947-2003,* pp. 95-96, 116.
128. Mansingh, *India's Search for Power, Foreword,* p. xi.
129. Dixit, *India's Foreign Policy 1947-2003,* pp. 57-60, 97.
130. Mansingh, *India's Search for Power,* p. 52.
131. Jayaramu, *India's National Security and Foreign Policy,* p. 28.
132. Dixit, *India's Foreign Policy 1947-2003,* p. 95.
133. Mansingh, *India's Search for Power,* p. 142.
134. Dixit, *India's Foreign Policy 1947-2003,* pp. 91-92; Mohan, *Crossing the Rubicon,* p. 11.
135. It has been dubbed as 'India's Monroe Doctrine'. See Mohan, *Crossing the Rubicon,* pp. 238-239.
136. Mansingh, *India's Search for Power,* p. 293.
137. Ibid, p. 27.
138. Ibid, pp. 39, 263.
139. Ibid, p. 196.
140. Ranganathan et al., *India and China: The Way Ahead,* p. 54.
141. *Selected Speeches and Writings of Indira Gandhi 1972-1977,* Vol. III, p. 633.
142. Jayaramu, *India's National Security and Foreign Policy,* p. 28.
143. The Nixon Administration sent its naval aircraft carrier Enterprise into the Bay of Bengal in December 1971.
144. Garver, *Protracted Contest,* p. 22.
145. Mansingh, *India's Search for Power,* p. 205.
146. Ibid, p. 247.
147. Ranganathan et al., *India and China: The Way Ahead,* p. 54.
148. Mansingh, *India's Search for Power,* p. 202.
149. Dixit, *India's Foreign Policy 1947-2003,* p. 170.
150. Ibid, p. 171.
151. Ibid.
152. *Prime Minister Rajiv Gandhi: Statements on Foreign Policy, May-August 1985* (New Delhi: External Publicity Division, Ministry of External Affairs, 1985), pp. 15, 59.
153. Dixit, *India's Foreign Policy 1947-2003,* pp. 170-171.
154. *Prime Minister Rajiv Gandhi: Statements on Foreign Policy,* p. 50.
155. Dixit, *India's Foreign Policy 1947-2003,* pp. 171-172.
156. Maharajakrishna Rasgotra, 'Overview', in *Rajiv Gandhi's India: A Golden Jubilee Retrospective, Volume 3, Foreign Policy: Ending the Quest for Dominance,* eds. Mani Shankar Aiyar and Maharajakrishna Rasgotra (New Delhi: UBS Publisher's Distributors Ltd, 1998), p. 14.
157. Ibid, pp. 14-15.
158. Ibid, p. 17.
159 Ibid, p. 18; *Prime Minister Rajiv Gandhi: Statements on Foreign Policy,* p. 20.
160. Urmila Phadnis, 'India and its Neighbours with Special Reference to Sri Lanka:

Prospects for the Future', in *India's Foreign Policy in the 1990s,* eds. M. Rasgotra, V.D. Chopra, and K.P. Misra (New Delhi: Patriot Publishers, 1990), p. 262.

161. Dixit, *India's Foreign Policy 1947-2003,* p. 135.
162. Ranganathan et al., *India and China: The Way Ahead,* pp. 59-60.
163. Ibid, p. 60.
164. Ibid, p. 25.
165. Ibid, p. 55.
166. Mansingh, *India's Search for Power,* p. 196.
167. Ranganathan et al., *India and China: The Way Ahead,* pp. 25-55.
168. See *Sino-Indian Joint Press Communiqué,* 23 December 1988, Beijing, available at http://www.fmprc.gov.cn/eng/topics/wzlcflyeng/lsbjyd/dindia/t15913.htm.

3

China's Security Perception After the Cold War

China's security perception has undergone a major change since the end of the Cold War, compared to the previous one that was shaped by the Cold War mindset. With its concentration on economic construction, China has attached great importance to economic security while seeking comprehensive national security in the political, military, social as well as economic areas. In spite of its insistence on the basic role of 'active defence' in safeguarding China's territorial security, China has been practising and promoting common security to address the security issues. As the international situation continues to undergo profound and complex changes in the new century, China continues to make adjustments in its security perception in accordance with these changes.

3.1 China's Assessment of its Security Environment

Since the end of the Cold War, the international situation has experienced dramatic changes. As the bipolar confrontation disappeared due to the collapse of the Soviet Union, and the political multipolarity and economic globalization started to gradually develop, the international configuration has shifted into a form of "one superpower and several major powers", which is characterized by both cooperation and competition.[1] At the same time, this post-Cold War period has also witnessed a rapid growth of the Chinese economy, with an annual average rate of 10.3%. China's ranking in terms of economic total in the world rose from 11th in 1990 to 4th in 2005.[2] Under these circumstances, China has held a relatively optimistic assessment of its post-Cold War security environment, in contrast to the pessimistic one that prevailed during the Cold War. Furthermore, since the beginning of the 21st century, China has continued to adjust its assessment of the security environment in light of the sustained changes internationally and regionally. According to China's government documents on security, the year 2002 seems to be a minor watershed in its assessment of the post-Cold War security environment. From 1991 to 2002, by emphasizing the positive side of its security situation after the Cold War, the PRC was of the view that it was enjoying the best security environment it had ever had. However, since 2002, China has started to pay more attention to the negative elements of its security.

3.1 (1) A Better Security Environment than Ever Before (1991-2002)

China's national security "can be said to be in a better condition than at any time during the Cold War".[3] First and foremost, China has been completely immune from direct military threats for the first time since the founding of the PRC in 1949. As mentioned earlier, China suffered military threats from the two superpowers at different periods and had military conflicts with them at different places. Although such external military threats started to decrease in the mid-1980s when the weakened Soviet Union adjusted its foreign policy and expressed its desire of reconciliation with China, they "did not disappear until the end of the Cold War".[4] In 1992, Russia withdrew all of its troops from Mongolia and agreed with China to minimize their respective military deployments in their border area.[5] As a result, the confrontation between China and the former Soviet Union turned into cooperation between China and Russia. Since then, for the first time in the PRC's history, China has been able to simultaneously keep normal relations with all major powers, including the US, Russia, and the European countries.

Furthermore, the Chinese government also perceives that the international security situation has improved considerably due to the end of the Cold War. Although regional conflicts are still frequent and sometimes even show a trend of escalation, the Chinese government under the third generation leadership led by Jiang Zemin has constantly reaffirmed what Deng Xiaoping had earlier assessed, that is, "peace and development are the major themes of the present era...and the new world war is avoidable".[6] China has mainly put forward three arguments, as follows:

First, the disappearance of the military confrontation between the two blocs has dramatically changed the logic of the outbreak of the world war. As mentioned in Chapter 2, for three decades of Mao's era, China had been preparing against an imminent third world war. In light of the tense arms race between the US and the Soviet Union and their worldwide fierce contention for influence of power, China believed that both military adventurism by either of them and some local wars might trigger a new world war. After the Cold War, as the direct military confrontation between the two blocs, i.e. the major source of the new world war, passed into history, "the influence of armed conflicts and local wars on the overall international situation has been remarkably weakened".[7] The present regional conflicts "are relatively limited in terms of scale, intensity and region, and are under control to varying degrees".[8]

Second, in the post-Cold War era, the competition among nations is characterised by the integrated national power rather than the military strength.[9] Although military factors still occupy an important position in national security, "economic development, scientific and technological innovation, and the growth of aggregate national strength remain the priorities for many countries".[10] Therefore, "the forces for peace are prevailing over the forces for war".[11]

Third, coordination and cooperation among major powers are gaining momentum. Since the end of the Cold War, the relations among the major powers have been undergoing significant and profound readjustments. Relations among them are no longer zero-sum games. The major countries are checking on and competing with one another, "while cooperating with and seeking support from each other".[12] Especially since the terrorist attacks against the US on September 11 of 2001, "they have stepped up their coordination and cooperation".[13]

Moreover, China considers its peripheral environment better than that during the Cold War. The end of the Cold War has not only unshackled the relations between China and its neighbouring countries from the confrontation between the two blocs, but also made the elements of ideology and political system irrelevant in their external relations.[14] In October 1992, the report of the 14th National Congress of the CPC stated "China's relations with its neighouring countries are in the best shape after the founding of the PRC". The Chinese government also thinks that, as an area with the greatest economic development vitality in the world, the Asia-Pacific region is "relatively stable" in terms of security, because countries in this region regard economic development as "the most important task", they rely more and more on each other economically, and most of them stand for peaceful settlement of disputes thereby.[15]

The Chinese government is aware that the disappearance of massive military threats "does not mean that there is no longer any problem to China's security".[16] The then General Secretary Jiang Zemin stated in his report to the 15th National Congress of the CPC in September 1997, "the world is not yet tranquil," although "the international situation as a whole is becoming more relaxed". In their eyes, while the end of the Cold War has improved China's military security, it has also brought new and non-traditional challenges to China's security.

In spite of admitting that "military factors still occupy an important position in state security,"[17] China has paid more attention to economic security since the end of the Cold War. The Soviet disintegration has confirmed Chinese political leaders' conviction that "national security depends more upon overall national strength based on a solid economy rather than simply upon military might".[18] The report of the 14th National Congress of the CPC in 1992 states:

> Modern Chinese history and the realities of the present-day world show that so long as a country is economically backward, it will be in a passive position, subject to manipulation by others...If we fail to develop our economy rapidly, it will be very difficult for us to consolidate the socialist system and maintain long-term social stability. Whether we can accelerate economic growth is therefore an important question both economically and politically.

Moreover, as economic competition has become the core of international politics after the Cold War, economic security should become a major composing part of China's security. To quote *China's National Defense* in 1998:

> Economic security is becoming daily more important for state security. In international relations, geopolitical, military security and ideological factors still play a role that cannot be ignored, but the role of economic factors is becoming more outstanding, along with growing economic contacts among nations. The competition to excel in overall national strength, focused on economy and science and technology, is being further intensified; globe-wide struggles centered on markets, natural resources and other economic rights and interests are daily becoming sharper; and the quickening of economic globalization and intensification of the formation of regional blocs render the economic development of a country more vulnerable to outside influences and impacts. Therefore, more and more countries regard economic security as an important aspect of state security. The financial crisis in Asia has made the issue of economic security more prominent, and has set a new task for governments of all countries to strengthen coordination and face challenges together in the course of economic globalization.

After the Cold War, the worldwide trend of national separatism has, in the view of the Chinese government, constituted a new threat to China's national unity. The split-up of the former Soviet Union and some East European countries has created an international environment favourable to the national separatists in China to a certain extent.[19] The growing separatist forces in Taiwan are the greatest concern of China in this respect. After a new generation of leaders who were born in Taiwan took power in the late 1980s, they started to adopt an evasive or even a negative attitude to the reunification of China.[20] Unlike their predecessors who came to Taiwan after their being defeated by the CPC in the civil war, this new generation lacked historical, social and cultural links with the mainland. Throughout the 1990s, Lee Teng-hui, the then Taiwan leader had taken a number of measures to gradually move away from the one-China principle. The last straw was his statement in July 1999 that the cross-strait relationship was a "special state-to-state relation".[21] Separatist forces in Taiwan were strengthened by the fact that the Democratic Progressive Party (DPP), which publicly advocates "independence of Taiwan", won the "elections" consecutively in 2000 and in 2004. Since taking power, the DPP leader Chen Shui-bian has even gone so far as to put forward the proposition of "one country on each side", which means that both China (the PRC) and Taiwan (the Republic of China) are separate countries, as opposed to separate governments within one China.[22] As *China's National Defense in 2002* states, "the Taiwan separatist force is the biggest threat to peace and stability in the Taiwan Straits". Greater concern arises from the American political and military support to the Taiwan authorities. *China's National Defense in 2000* has listed the following actions by the United States that have "inflated the arrogance of the separatist forces in Taiwan":

> The United States has never stopped selling advanced weapons to Taiwan. Some people in the United States have been trying hard to get the Congress to pass the so-called Taiwan Security Enhancement Act. And some are even attempting to incorporate Taiwan into the US TMD system. The newly revised Guidelines for US-Japan Defense Cooperation has failed to explicitly undertake to exclude Taiwan from the scope of "the areas surrounding Japan" referred to in the Japanese security bill that could involve military intervention.

Moreover, the international trend of radical nationalism and activities of the separatists in Taiwan have incited the separatists of the ethnic minority groups in the mainland, "and would thus possibly bring about a danger of domino effect".[23] The separatists have set up their camps abroad and conducted harmful political and even terrorist activities in national minority areas, like Tibet and Xinjiang.[24]

Since the end of the Cold War, China has also attached great importance to the non-traditional security issues. *China's National Defense* in 1998 states, "Terrorism, arms proliferation, smuggling and trafficking in narcotics, environmental pollution, waves of refugees, and other transnational issues also pose new threats to international security". As the 9/11 terrorist attack of 2001 caused worldwide concern regarding the threat of terrorism to national security, China started to accentuate the challenge facing it in this regard. To quote *China's National Defense in 2002*:

> In recent years, terrorist activities have notably increased, and constitute a real threat to world peace and development...China, too, is a victim of terrorism. The "East Turkistan" terrorist forces are a serious threat to the security of the lives and property of the people of all China's ethnic groups, as well as to the country's social stability. On September 11, 2002, the UN Security Council, in response to a common demand from China, the United States, Afghanistan and Kyrgyzstan, formally included the "East Turkistan Islamic Movement" on its list of terrorist organizations.

3.1 (2) A Complex Picture (2002 till the Present)

As the current international situation continues to undergo profound and complex changes, factors of uncertainty, instability and insecurity have increasingly caught China's attention since the world entered the new century.[25] While acknowledging that "peace and development remain the principal themes in today's world," and that China's national security environment has on the whole improved, the Chinese government emphasizes that "uncertainties and the destabilizing factors are on the increase, and new challenges and threats are continuously emerging".[26] In its national defence white paper of 2004, China has listed four elements which will have a major impact on China's security. Apart from the risks and challenges caused by the development of the trends toward economic globalization, China has expressed its deep apprehension for the rapid rise of the 'Taiwan independence' forces, the technological gap resulting from worldwide Revolution in Military Affairs (RMA), and the prolonged existence of unipolarity vis-à-vis multipolarity.[27]

As the Taiwan authorities under Chen Shui-bian markedly escalated their 'Taiwan independence' activities since the DPP took power, the Chinese government has started to consider the Taiwan issue as an immediate as well as the biggest threat to China's national unity. Chen's actions such as advocating his theory of "one country on each side", introducing referendum into Taiwan's political life, promoting the so-called "constitution reform", and purchasing large amounts of offensive weapons and equipment, are regarded by the Chinese government as substantial steps designed to split China. *China's National Defense in 2004* states:

> The separatist activities of the "Taiwan independence" forces have increasingly become the biggest immediate threat to China's sovereignty and territorial integrity as well as peace and stability on both sides of the Taiwan Straits and the Asia-Pacific region as a whole.[28]

China has been closely following the profound reform taking place throughout the world since the end of the Cold War, in the military field led by the development of high-tech weapons. It has noticed that "the form of war is becoming increasingly information-oriented", and that "all major countries have made adjustments in their military strategies and stepped up the modernization by relying on high technologies".[29] As a result, "military imbalance worldwide has further increased".[30] As a developing country, China feels it a challenge to fill the gap vis-à-vis the developed countries in terms of military technology and to keep pace with the ongoing worldwide RMA.[31] Since 2002, this challenge seems to be more serious because China has started to perceive that "the role played by military power in safeguarding national security is assuming greater prominence".[32]

While insisting on the viewpoint that hegemonism and power politics remain the main source of threats to world peace and stability, which was elaborated upon in its previous white papers on national defence, the Chinese government expresses its concern over the US unilateralism for the first time in its 2004 white paper. Viewing the Iraqi War as one of the US "hegemonic endeavors" for strategic points, strategic resources and strategic dominance, China especially has some apprehensions for the following actions by the US in the Asia-Pacific region. First, the United States is realigning and reinforcing its military presence in this region by buttressing military alliances and accelerating deployment of missile defence systems. Second, the United States seems to be encouraging Japan to play a bigger military role in Asia. Japan is stepping up its constitutional overhaul, adjusting its military and security policies and developing the missile defence system for future deployment. It has also markedly increased military activities abroad. Third, the United States keeps playing the Taiwan card to contain China. While reaffirming on many occasions its adherence to the "one China" policy, observance of the three joint communiqués between China and the United States, and opposition to "Taiwan independence", the United States continues to increase, quantitatively and qualitatively, its arms sales to Taiwan.[33]

3.2 China's National Security Strategy

China's national security strategy after the Cold War is qualitatively different from that which prevailed during the Cold War. Thanks to its deepening conviction especially since the early 1990s that economic strength plays a primary role in safeguarding a nation's security in the post-Cold War era, China has formulated a national security strategy centred on a guarantee of the economic development. As factors such as the undercurrent of 'Taiwan Independence', the strengthening US unilateralism and the development of RMA increasingly raised China's eyebrows, China started to seek a more balanced security consideration by including in its focus both the traditional and non-traditional threats. As a result, China has made some new adjustments on its national security strategy since the beginning of the 21st century.

3.2 (1) Objectives of China's National Security Strategy

Since the end of the Cold War, a major shift has come about in the objectives of China's national security strategy. As discussed in Chapter 2, during the most part of the Cold War, national survival and territorial integrity had served as the top aims of China's national security strategy. Overshadowed by immediate war threats, China sought for a stronger military might that would be able to ensure the country's victory in wars against foreign invaders.[34] After the Cold War, with the assessment of a favourable environment that implied no likelihood of massive military invasion in the foreseeable future and the resolve to "make economic development the central task of the entire Party and the whole country", the Chinese government made it very clear that the fundamental objective of China's security strategy would be to safeguard a peaceful security environment for its economic construction.[35] Reports of both the 14th and 15th National Congresses of the CPC state that the major task of China's foreign policy is to "improve the external environment for China's reform, opening up and modernization drive," and that all other work including national defence should be "subordinated to and serve[s]" the central task of economic development.

While safeguarding the country's territorial integrity has always been one of China's objectives for national security, the contents of this task vary in different phases of history. During the Cold War, to defend China's territorial integrity meant that the PRC led by the Chinese Communist Party should be capable of crushing any plot by the Chiang Kai-Shek nationalists in Taiwan to overthrow the new China, on the one hand; and of getting the upper hand in its border conflicts with the adjacent countries, on the other. After the Cold War, however, the essence of this objective shifted from neutralizing Taiwan's subversive activities toward the mainland to preventing Taiwan independence and promoting peaceful reunification. As China has insisted on solving boundary disputes by peaceful means and has respectively reached boundary-related agreements with a number of countries since the end of the Cold War, there are fewer boundary problems for China to deal with today.

As the world enters the 21st century, China affirms that economic construction will remain the central task of the country. *China's National Defense in 2004* states, "the development goal for China to strive for in the first two decades of this century is to build a moderately prosperous society in an all-round way…China needs a peaceful international environment for its own development." Therefore, "securing a long-term and favorable international and surrounding environment" is still a fundamental objective of the present China's national security strategy. As the Taiwan Straits situation became more complicated and grimmer during Chen Shui-bian's tenure, however, the urgency of defending China's territorial integrity has mounted. In the 1990s, with a view to concentrating all of its resources on economic development, China's security objective of defending its territorial integrity, like all other work, was subordinated to that of safeguarding the favourable environment for China's economic construction. In the official document *China's National Defense in 2004*, for the first time since the end of the Cold War, "to stop separation and promote reunification" is put ahead of "to safeguard the interests of national development" on the list of "China's basic goals and tasks in maintaining national security." By emphasizing "China sticks to keeping its development in pace with its security", the two fundamental objectives, one of which is to safeguard a peaceful security environment for China's economic construction, and the other of which is to defend China's territorial integrity, have been provided with the same magnitude of importance.

3.2 (2) China's National Security Interests

In contrast to the Cold War period during which China's security interests were considered only in terms of military and political aspects, the post-Cold War era has witnessed a broader deliberation of national security interests by the Chinese government, with economic security and other non-traditional security being incorporated.

China's economic security interests consist of the following three basic components. First and foremost is to avoid getting involved into any military conflict. In modern world history, the Western countries generally reaped great economic benefits from their victories in the war. On the contrary, China suffered tremendous economic losses in all of the wars it was involved into since the Opium War, no matter whether China was a winner or a loser.[36] During the Cold War, China was involved in six wars or military conflicts including the China-India border conflict of 1962. The frequency of wars diverted China's concentration from its economic construction. Taking lessons from the past, China, which is currently focused on economic development, perceives that wars or military conflicts are bound to damage its economic achievements and delay the process of its four modernizations or "building a moderately prosperous society in all aspects". Moreover, China is still far behind the Western countries in economic development, especially in the sense of GDP per capita, and is aware that it will take scores of years for her to catch up with the developed countries in the world. Therefore, the longer China is capable of shunning wars, the more strategic opportunities China will get for its economic construction.[37]

Second, China should be able to protect its economic rights and interests within its own territory, especially in its territorial waters.[38] The mainland of China has a coastline of more than 18,000 kilometres long, a sea area of 4.73 million square kilometres, and islands of more than 80,000 square kilometres in area.[39] Thanks to its increasing demands for energy, mineral and other raw materials, China's economic activities on the sea have grown rapidly. To guarantee secure and safe exploitation and utilization of its marine resources, therefore, is a basic task for China's economic security.

Third, China must protect its enlarged overseas economic interests. Overseas economic interests involve external trade of commodity and technology, foreign investment, international tourism and external projects and labour service contracts.[40] These external economic activities operate in two directions, i.e. inward and outward, or import-oriented and export-oriented. Being a virtually closed economy, China had few overseas economic interests before its reform and opening up of 1978. In the early stage of China's reform and opening up, China's overseas economic interests rapidly increased in the inward aspect. As China has started to expand its international market and increase its overseas investment in recent years, China's overseas economic interests have enlarged both inwards and outwards. As a consequence of the increasing dependence of China's economic growth on the international supply of energy, energy security has become a prominent overseas economic interest of China.[41]

China's military security interests lie in the ability of the Chinese armed forces to deter war in time of peace, to win wars of self-defence in time of war, and to crush any attempt to split China at any time. In accordance with the needs of the national development strategy, the PLA is first and foremost required to deter "local wars and armed conflicts so as to keep the country from the harm of war".[42] This deterrent derives from the "preparations to win self-defense wars".[43] The PLA, therefore, aims at "winning local wars under modern, especially high-tech conditions".[44] As the danger of the 'Taiwan independence' is rising, the Chinese armed forces are expected to play a larger role in safeguarding the country's unity. China hopes that its unwillingness to renounce the use of force on the Taiwan issue would deter the foreign forces from interfering in China's reunification and the Taiwan separatist forces from "Taiwan independence".[45] Whether this strategy works or not depends on the credibility of the PLA's deterrent capability. Moreover, "should the Taiwan authorities go so far as to make a reckless attempt that constitutes a major incident of 'Taiwan independence'", the Chinese armed forces should be able to 'crush' it.[46]

After the Cold War, the worldwide trend of radical nationalism and political liberalism has constituted a new threat to China's national unity and political stability. China's political security interests, therefore, involve the capacity of the Chinese government under the leadership of the CPC to cope with these threats so as to ensure the endurance of the socialist system and the core values of China.[47] As mentioned before, the international trend of radical nationalism has an agitating effect on the separatists of the ethnic minority groups in China. Their separatist activities not only sabotage China's social stability and national unity but also damage the image of the CPC and challenge the latter's legitimacy of rule in China. Political liberalism has gained momentum since the end of the Cold War, during which multi-party politics has developed in East European nations, former Soviet republics and many Third World countries. 'Export of democracy' has become a strategy of some Western countries to expand their sphere of influence. As one of the several socialist countries left after the Cold War,

China has naturally become a significant target of this strategy. By providing financial and political support for Chinese anti-government individuals and organizations on the one hand, and by accusing the Chinese government of bad human rights records on the other, these Western countries have put a lot of pressure on China and tried to force it to change its domestic policies in regard to family planning, prison management, news and publication regulation and the Tibetan political system.[48]

Apart from economic security, China has many other non-traditional security interests to defend. Lacking experience in this regard, China, like many other developing countries, is facing various challenges in dealing with these new threats. First, non-traditional security threats are no less harmful to China than traditional security threats.[49] For example, international illicit drug trafficking is just like a protracted war against China without gunsmoke. It has not only undermined China's economy but also caused social problems. Second, non-traditional security issues sometimes are intertwined with traditional security issues.[50] The current terror threats facing China derive mainly from the separatist forces both inside and outside China. Third, there are so many forms and types of non-traditional security threats that it takes time to identify, especially when a new form or type has just emerged.[51] The 2003 outbreak of SARS in China has taught the Chinese leaders a lesson that epidemic diseases could pose a threat to national security. Due to the Chinese government's ignorance of the threat from this disease, the disproportionate steps it took during the early stage of this public health accident led to a series of damages, from social panic to economic slowdown and then to losing face in the international community. Fortunately, the Chinese government later adjusted its policy so that it could check the further spread of SARS and bring it under control.[52]

In sum, since the end of the Cold War, China has been seeking "a comprehensive national security in the political, economic, military and social areas".[53] In the re-assessment of China's security environment and re-definition of China's national security objectives, the priority of China's national security interests has also been adjusted. Before 2002, economic security interests preceded military and political security interests as China's top security interests. Since 2002, military security interests have been upgraded to the same level as economic security interests. In other words, economic security interests and military security interests are the dual primary security interests of China, preceding all other security interests.

3.2 (3) China's National Security Policy

China's national security policy of the post-Cold War era has in the main retained the essence of Deng's approaches or theory with regard to safeguarding China's security interests in the 1980s, in spite of some adjustment. Primarily defensive in nature, this policy is represented as a four-in-one combination—a combination of independence, economic cooperation, security dialogue and cooperation, and defence modernization.

Independence means that China adheres to non-alignment and the principle of balance in its foreign policy, seeking friendly relations with all countries, especially with its adjacent countries. With the conviction that "the best policy (for security) is to make peace with others,"[54] since the end of the Cold War, China has not only established various strategic partnerships with all major powers[55] and regional powers,[56] but also cemented good-neighbourly relations with its neighbouring countries. Both the strategic partnerships and the good-neighbourly relationships are different from the "comradeship-plus-brotherhood", a relationship advocated by the Chinese government during the Cold War. While the latter represents a military or political alliance, the former two are a normal state-to-state relationship based on non-alignment.[57] The strategic partnerships and the good-neighbourly relationships are established on the basis of national interest, disregarding the differences in ideology and social system, and not directed against any third party.[58] Since the end of the Cold War, China has also been seeking a balance in its relations with the developed countries on the one hand and with the developing countries on the other. This reflects a departure of the Chinese foreign policy from the Third Worldism during the Cold War. As a result, the developed countries like the US, the neighbouring countries and the other Third World countries have become the three hubs or focal areas of China's current foreign relations.[59]

Like Deng Xiaoping, who promoted the political normalization of China's relations with some of its neighbours and many Western countries by establishing and strengthening economic cooperation in the 1980s, Chinese leaders of the new generation see economic exchange and interaction as "an important avenue to a lasting security".[60] They are convinced that, in a world under globalization, the best way to achieve security is to grow "common interests", i.e. to "seek common security through mutually beneficial cooperation," rather than to pursue the zero-sum and one-sided security that prevailed during the Cold War.[61] The more common security interests countries share, the more interdependent they are for security.[62]

Since the end of the Cold War, China has expanded its economic cooperation at both bilateral and multilateral levels. As China's foreign trade volume enjoyed a nearly 18-fold increase in 17 years, from US$ 115.4bn in 1990 to US$ 2173.8bn in 2007,[63] the role economic cooperation plays in national security has become more and more conspicuous. For example, the huge common economic interests constitute an effective stabilizer in China-US relations, although the US is not satisfied with the large amount of trade surplus in China's favour.[64] In recent years, China has also actively participated in regional economic cooperation of various kinds, like APEC and the ASEAN+3. The development of the mechanism of ASEAN+3 has "not only brought real and tangible economic benefits to the countries concerned, but also enhanced the mutual exchange, mutual trust and cooperation between all parties involved, thus contributing to the security and stability of the region".[65]

Apart from economic cooperation, China regards security dialogue and cooperation as another fundamental approach to security in the era of globalization.[66] First, China insists on the peaceful settlement of disputes. In its five-point proposal for building Asia-Pacific security mechanism, which China put forward at a regional conference held in 1993 on national security and building of confidence among nations in the Asia-Pacific region, it suggested:

> Resolving by peaceful means all international disputes, problems left over by history and problems that might occur in the future. Leaving in abeyance the territorial and boundary disputes which cannot be resolved at this moment until conditions are ripe for their settlement through negotiations. Before the disputes are resolved, countries concerned should take security and confidence-building measures to maintain normal state-to-state relations and economic cooperation.[67]

Under the guidance of these principles, China has resolved the land boundary question with most of its neighbouring countries since the end of the Cold War. It has also signed a Beibu Bay demarcation agreement with Vietnam and the Code of Conduct in the South China Sea with ASEAN. As the 2002 *Position Paper on the New Security Concept* pointed out, "disputes over territorial land and water are no longer an obstacle for China and its neighbours to develop normal cooperation and good-neighbourly relations and jointly build regional security".

Second, believing that "frequent dialogue and mutual briefings on each other's security and defense policies and major operations" may contribute to better mutual trust,[68] China has established various bilateral mechanisms of strategic consultation and dialogue with many countries in recent years. For example, China and Russia have a senior-level meeting mechanism between their political leaders and a consultation mechanism between their armed forces. China and the US have a strategic dialogue at the vice-foreign-ministerial level, the Defence Consultative Talk at the vice-defence-ministerial level, and the maritime military security consultations. China has respectively established such mechanisms of security consultation and strategic dialogue with its neighbouring countries, like India, Pakistan, Japan, Mongolia, Thailand and Australia and other countries, like France, the UK, and South Africa.[69]

Third, China vigorously supports the building of a regional security dialogue and cooperation mechanism in the Asia-Pacific region, believing that "the key guarantee for Asian-Pacific security comes from a regional security framework featuring dialogue instead of confrontation".[70] To this end, China has paid great attention to and taken an active part in the Shanghai Cooperation Organization (SCO) and the ASEAN Regional Forum (ARF). Since the launching of 'Shanghai Five' process in 1996, the SCO has been evolving into an important multilateral security mechanism with "a relatively complete organizational structure" and "a sound legal basis".[71] In this framework, the member states have not only peacefully and properly resolved their border issues, made joint efforts to combat terrorism, separatism and extremism, but also worked steadily for greater regional economic cooperation.[72] China attaches great importance to the role of ARF, the only pan-Asia-Pacific official multilateral security dialogue and cooperation forum at present. To promote its development, China has put forward many suggestions on confidence-building measures and preventive diplomacy. China also supports ARF to "highlight cooperation in non-traditional security fields such as counter-terrorism and combating transnational crimes".[73] Moreover, China has actively participated in other activities for multilateral security dialogue and cooperation, both governmental or non-governmental, like Conference on Interaction and Confidence-Building Measures in Asia (CICA), Council on Security Cooperation in the Asia-Pacific Region (CSCAP), Northeast Asia Cooperation Dialogue (NEACD), Academic Symposium of China, the United States and Japan.

Although growing common interests and mutual trust through dialogue and cooperation are regarded as a fundamental approach to security in the post-Cold War era by the Chinese government, 'active defense' is still 'the basic guarantee' for China's national security and modernization drive.[74] According to the earlier introduction and discussion, the so-called 'active defense' means a sufficient self-defence capability of China to deter the enemy from launching a military attack or keep the flames of war outside China's territory.[75] In light of the increasing military imbalance caused by the worldwide RMA since the end of the Cold War, defence modernization has become the central task of China's active defense strategy. In the 1990s, the guideline for China's defense construction was designated as "building a smaller but better army with Chinese characteristics with a view to raising the quality of the army and reinforcing the country's defense strength".[76] On the basis of the 1980s' demobilization of 1 million servicemen, China has twice downsized its military by another 0.7 million.[77] China wants to maintain the size of the PLA at 2.3 million.[78] Entering into the new century, China has committed itself to the RMA with Chinese characteristics. It has observed building computerized armed forces and being capable of winning IT-based warfare by the mid-21st century as a strategic objective.[79] In his report at the 17th National Congress of the CPC, General Secretary Hu Jintao put it as follows:

> To attain the strategic objective of building computerized armed forces and winning IT-based warfare, we will accelerate composite development of mechanization and computerization, carry out military training under IT-based conditions, modernize every aspect of logistics, intensify our efforts to train a new type of high-caliber military personnel in large numbers and change the mode of generating combat capabilities.[80]

As the Chinese government insisted that economic construction must be taken as the nucleus and believed that economic development was the basic premise of defense modernization, till the 16th National Congress of the CPC of 2002, national defense work had been placed subordinate to and in the service of the nation's overall economic construction, and the armed forces had been required to actively participate in and support the nation's economic construction.[81] As the urgency of defending China's territorial integrity has mounted due to the rising risk of "Taiwan Independence", China has upgraded the significance of defense construction. The report of the 16th National Congress of the CPC, for the first time, accentuated the principle of coordinated development of national defense and the economy, without mentioning the subordinate position of the former to the latter.

Again for the first time, this report put the national support for the defense and army building ahead of army's support for national construction. Moreover, *China's National Defence in 2004* requires the PLA to "step up preparations for military struggle." It is also the first time that the Chinese defense white paper lays stress on the PLA's "war-fighting capabilities".

3.3 China's India Perspective

Since the collapse of the Soviet Union in 1991, among other things, implied the ending of the Indo-Soviet alliance, Deng's perception about India since 1982, that India was one of China's natural and close neighbours rather than an enemy, was reinforced. After the end of the Cold War, in view of the fact that India is both a great neighbour in the southwest of China and a rapidly rising power, the Chinese government under the leadership of new generations has recognized that the relevance of India to China's security is increasing.[82] Based on the Dengist perspective, China started to seek a new-type partnership with India. It defined India as neither an ally nor an enemy but a partner with which China might have both cooperation and competition at the same time.[83] In spite of the brief hiatus after the Pokhran II, the 1998 Indian nuclear tests proved to have little impact on China's perspective of India. Since the world entered the new century, China has been working on the establishment of a strategic partnership with India.

As discussed in Chapter 2, during most part of the Cold War, China had based its perception of "India threat" on the prism of ideology and the two-bloc confrontation. It was Deng Xiaoping who suggested in the 1980s that the China-India relations should be thought out of the box, i.e. India is nothing more than a close neighbour of China and there is no serious problem between China and India. This perception shift happened at a time when the Chinese government was determined to concentrate on its economic modernization. After the Cold War, there appeared to be no further reason for China to treat India as a threat.

On the one hand, China did not consider that India had sufficient capability to constitute a threat to it. Following what Deng Xiaoping said in 1981, the Chinese leaders of new generation believed that India could not be a threat to China by itself. Since the Indo-Soviet quasi-military alliance disappeared due to the disintegration of the latter, the military balance between China and India started to shift in China's favour. Although India had more troops and military equipments than China in the border areas between them, China enjoyed the superiority over India in the general sense.[84] Moreover, as history indicated, the Great Himalayan Ranges could serve as a natural barrier. It would continue to make "large-scale and long-lasting military maneuvers and confrontation in that area impossible".[85]

On the other hand, China did not think that India had the intention to threaten it. First, the ending of the Indo-Soviet quasi-military alliance meant that India was no more under any obligation of international treaty to antagonize China. Second, in light of the fact that economic security has drawn more and more attention of many countries since the end of the Cold War, China noticed that India, being a populous developing country, also needed a peaceful environment including tranquil border areas to develop itself.[86] Third, since the concept of power has greatly changed in today's world, "status and influence is not just made by military capability and economic wealth but also by responsible and respectable roles in international affairs".[87] Therefore, there is reason to believe that India would be very cautious in using force, because "to solve problems and difference by using force or other irresponsible means would obviously damage" its international image.[88] During his 1996 visit to India, the then Chinese President Jiang Zemin repeated to his Indian host what Deng had said 14 years back, "neither of us poses a threat to the other".[89]

Since safeguarding a peaceful security environment has been a primary objective of China's national security strategy in the post-Cold War era, in the opinion of the Chinese government, a friendly and cooperative relationship with India is in the major security interests of China.[90] As the largest neighbour in the southwest of China, India constitutes a significant link in the chain of China's surrounding environment. In view of the fact that there is an undefined border of thousands of kilometres between the two countries, that India is still providing an asylum for the so-called *Tibetan Government-in-Exile*, and that the mutual distrust due to their decades of rivalry cannot possibly disappear overnight, China does have concrete security concerns with regard to India.[91] Moreover, the emergence of India will also bring on China some impact beyond the bilateral level.[92] Therefore, without good relations with India, China cannot really achieve a peaceful environment required by its economic development.[93] During his 1996 visit to India, President Jiang stated that "to develop with India a long-term good-neighbourly friendship and a mutual-benefit and cooperative relationship is an essential part of China's good-neighbourly policy".[94] He also believed that the common interests of China and India far outweigh their differences.[95]

In the opinion of the Chinese government, in addition to their amicable ties in history including the so-called period of 'Hindi-Chini Bhai Bhai', some new grounds for China-India cooperation have come into being since the end of the Cold war.[96] First, as the two largest developing countries in the world, China and India face a common task to develop themselves after the Cold War. This not only implies that "we all need a peaceful environment an many more friends,"[97] but also means more opportunities and demands for bilateral cooperation in the fields of trade, culture, science and technology.[98] Second, China and India share a common stance on many international issues such as the new world order, economic globalization and human rights.[99] During the then Chinese Premier Li Peng's visit to India in 1991, China and India agreed to pursue a new international political and economic order on the basis of the Five Principles of Peaceful Co-existence (i.e. the Panchsheel) and jointly agreed to observe the right to subsistence and development as a basic human right.[100]

Despite the short chill that developed in the bilateral relations after Pokhran II, the Indian nuclear test itself and the allegations of a 'China threat' by the top Indian leaders did not lead China to change its tune. While expressing its outrage against India's "groundless accusations" against China and concerns regarding the damage to the global non-proliferation regime by the test, China maintained that it did not take India as a threat and was still keen on establishing a constructive and cooperative partnership with India.

Indian scholars on their part, admitted that China's initial reaction to the Indian nuclear tests was "relatively muted".[101] On 12 May, the day after the first round of tests, the Ministry of Foreign Affairs (MFA) spokesman only expressed China's "grave concern" over the test's harm to the international process of nuclear disarmament and the peace and stability of South Asia.[102] Yet China's mild response changed after a letter from Prime Minister Vajpayee to President Bill Clinton was leaked in the United States on 13 May (the same day when the second round of tests took place), which cited China as a reason for India's decision to test. In the letter, Prime Minister Vajpayee wrote:

> I have been deeply concerned at the deteriorating security environment, especially the nuclear environment, faced by India for some years past. We have an overt nuclear weapon state on our borders, a state which committed armed aggression against India in 1962. Although our relations with that country have improved in the last decade or so, an atmosphere of distrust persists mainly due to the unresolved border problem. To add to the distrust that country has materially helped another neighbour of ours to become a covert nuclear weapons state. At the hands of this bitter neighbour we have suffered three aggressions in the last 50 years.[103]

Additionally, the then defence minister, George Fernandes, made a statement to the effect that China was India's Enemy No.1 in the weeks before the tests. The Chinese government was infuriated at this "irresponsible" and "immoral" "political tactic" used by India to justify its nuclear adventure.[104] On 14 May, the MFA issued a formal statement to strongly condemn the tests.[105] In the following weeks, China started a barrage of vigorous criticism of India.

Much of the criticism was devoted more to refuting India's groundless accusations against China rather than denouncing the nuclear tests themselves. Vice Premier Qian Qichen said that "the most unacceptable thing" was India's justification that it was conducting the nuclear test in response to China's threat to India.[106] In an interview to the *Newsweek* on 21 June 1998, President Jiang Zemin said, "I was very surprised that they conducted the nuclear tests. I was even more surprised that they cited China as a reason for their nuclear testing."[107] Therefore, China's strong response to the Indian 1998 nuclear tests cannot be assessed in a traditional way, that a country will feel threatened when a neighbour strengthens its military might. The specific cause behind China's outrage must be fully considered in this case. Just as an eminent American China hand noted, China's initial restraint "might have continued…had the Indian government not deflected responsibility for the recent tests onto the China threat".[108]

In mid-July 1998, China started to mellow down its criticism of India. Its ambassador to New Delhi, Zhou Gang, made a series of conciliatory remarks, indicating that China had not changed its perceptions towards India. On 9 July, he told *The Hindu* that Beijing would like India to provide a responsible explanation for the totally "unreasonable and groundless" accusations against China so as to put the bilateral relations back on track. He also stressed that "It was China's set policy to develop a 'constructive and co-operative partnership' with India towards the new millennium".[109] In his speech at the India International Centre on July 25, 1998, Zhou Gang attributed the deterioration in the Sino-Indian relations to "some personalities" in India, and assured that "India's nuclear tests had led to 'temporary difficulties' in Sino-Indian ties, but had not diluted Beijing's commitment to building a long-term friendly relationship with New Delhi".[110] In his later speeches in New Delhi, he further explained China's India perspective as follows:

- There exist extensive common interests between China and India and [our] commonalties far outweigh [our] differences.

- The two countries share similar or identical views on many major issues such as economic development, human rights, environmental protection, combating drug trafficking and crime and population control.
- The outstanding issue between China and India is no more than the boundary dispute left behind by history. The Chinese Government has maintained that while positively seeking a solution to the boundary issue, the two sides should work hard to develop bilateral relations in various fields so as to create a favourable atmosphere for the final solution of the boundary issue.[111]

Some experts attributed China's unchanged threat perceptions and policies toward India after the tests to the former's disrespect for the latter's capabilities.[112] They argued that China did not consider India as a security threat because Beijing viewed New Delhi "as a much less powerful competitor".[113] Taking into account the fact that China had already factored in India's capability to produce nuclear weapons since its first nuclear tests in 1974, Pokhran II "said nothing new about India's capabilities".[114] According to *Jane's Defence Weekly*, the Chinese authorities had assessed that India would take at least 10 years to establish an operational nuclear strike capability and, hence, India did not pose an immediate threat to China's security.[115]

It is evident that these experts have developed their arguments on basis of the more popular and traditional security perspective, i.e. the Cold War mindset as discussed earlier in Chapter 1 and Chapter 2. Although this explanation seems plausible to some extent by emphasizing China's military superiority over India, there are some contradictions even in the traditional sense. In the logic of the Cold War mindset, China must have taken it as a great threat when a neighbour like India, which made hostile remarks against China, strengthened its military build-up. Even though India would pose a real threat to China's security ten years later, China should have taken some preventive steps, such as assuming an active military posture toward India or/and reactivating its traditional alliance with Pakistan. As history has witnessed, China has done neither. China did not move nuclear weapons to Tibet or enhance its launch sites in Gansu, Qinghai, and Yunnan, nor develop tactical nuclear weapons and a missile defence system against India, as some security scholars have expected.[116] Apart from taking an identical stance toward India and Pakistan after their respective nuclear tests in May 1998, calling on both to stop all further nuclear tests and adhere immediately and unconditionally to the NPT and CTBT, China assured the US that it would not provide any assistance to non-safeguarded nuclear facilities in Pakistan or transfer missile technology to it.[117] Moreover, to show its neutrality between India and Pakistan, China reiterated its consistent position on the Kashmir issue. On August 11, 1998, Tang Guoqiang, spokesman of the Chinese Foreign Office, said that "Kashmir is an outstanding issue between India and Pakistan",[118] indicating that China favoured that the issue be solved bilaterally.

By carefully examining the statements and remarks made by the Chinese officials during this period, this author has found that China's determination to continue its friendship with India despite the nuclear tests is in accord with its national security strategy after the Cold War. In other words, the fundamental reason for China's insistence on its positive perception toward India after Pokhran II is that there is no adjustment in its post-Cold War general security perceptions.

First of all, as China gave top priority to economic construction, it was keen to avoid any confrontation with its neighbours. In an interview to the *Al Ahram* of Cairo on July 26, 1998, Prime Minister Zhu Rongji said, "Beijing had no time to threaten or scare other countries, as it is busy with its own economic development".[119] Although this remark aimed at clarifying that there was no China threat to India, it also explained the fundamental cause underlying China's stance of 'tolerance' rather than that of quid pro quo. In his speeches to the Indian businessmen in the following months after the Pokhran II, Zhou Gang expressed China's reluctance to bypass the great economic opportunities that had emerged across its southwest border. He said that "differences between the two countries should not be seen as an obstacle to fostering trade", because expansion of economic relations, trade and technological cooperation between China and India serve the fundamental interests of the two countries.[120]

Second, after the Cold War, China believed that the best way to safeguard a nation's security was to make peace with others or to increase common interests rather than to start arms race. China's good-neighbourly policy is established on basis of this perception. As long as China holds to this framework, it will be firm on its policy "to develop with India a long-term good-neighbourly and constructive partnership of co-operation for the 21st century", which had been repeated by many Chinese officials during this period.

Third, since the end of the Cold War, China has put its strategic focus on its east side. Compared to the potential problems of the possibility of 'Taiwan Independence', the US hegemony and the Japanese miniaturization, the risk of war with India is far lower, given the limited nature of the disagreements between China and India. Therefore, China has been facing more strategic pressure from the east than from the west, and obviously, it is not in China's interests to have a two-front threat.

As China-India relations gradually moved back on track in 1999 as a result of the efforts from both sides to mend fences, China was more confirmed in its post-Cold War perceptions and policies toward India. In his speech at the India International Centre during his second visit to India in January 2001 (this time as Chairman of the Standing Committee of the National People's Congress of China), Li Peng, the No. 2 top leader of China gave his Indian counterparts a comprehensive and unambiguous explanation of China's India perspective, as follows:

- China considered India as an important neighbour rather than a threat.
- Developing good-neighbourly and friendly relations with India was a consistent guiding principle and an essential part of China's foreign policy of peace with surrounding countries.
- China and India had extensive common interests in keeping a peaceful and stable surrounding environment for their respective economic development and building a multi-polar world.
- China agreed that China and India were still lacking in mutual understanding and trust and efforts were required to solve this issue therefore. By preventing the problems and differences between the two sides, such as the boundary dispute, from standing in the way of the growth of the bilateral ties, they could help reach the ultimate resolution of all these difficulties.
- China accepted and welcomed India's emergence as an economically strong and active player in regional and international affairs.[121]

While Deng Xiaoping in 1982 described China and India as natural and close neighbours and Li Peng in 2001 depicted India as an important neighbour of China, the Chinese top leaders have represented India as friends and partners since 2005. In his address at the Indian Institute of Technology on 12 April 2005 in New Delhi, Premier Wen Jiabao told the Indian students, "China and India are friendly neighbors and partners instead of rivals or enemies".[122] During his state visit to India in 2006, President Hu Jintao said that China and India were "true friends and partners".[123] On 22 November 2006, he told his Indian audience at the Vigyan Bhavan convention centre: "To enter into strategic partnership with India is not an expedient. Rather, it's a strategic decision and firm goal of the Chinese government."[124] He also proposed a five-pronged strategy to further expand strategic partnership between the two Asian giants:

- to increase mutual political trust and consolidate the basis of China-India relations;
- to enhance business cooperation and enrich bilateral relations;
- to increase cultural and social exchanges and public support for China-India friendship;
- to step up friendly consultation and work for an early settlement of the boundary issue;
- to develop multilateral cooperation and jointly uphold the legitimate rights and interests of developing countries.[125]

3.4 Nature of the Change in China's Security Perception

According to the foregoing analysis, China's security perception has transformed considerably since the end of the Cold War, and some adjustments are still underway. Compared with the Cold War period, the perspective changes of China have happened in the following respects:

First of all, since the end of the Cold War, China has defined its national security in a much broader sense. During Mao's era, China narrowly confined national security to external military threats. China of this period had been staying in a shadow of an imminent Third World war as well as a possible military invasion by the superpowers, i.e. the United States in the 1950s, both the United States and the Soviet Union in the 1960s, and the Soviet Union in the 1970s. Although Deng Xiaoping in the 1980s tried to dilute China's security concerns by drawing a conclusion that the new world war was avoidable and the external military threat to China's existence was rapidly decreasing, he still looked at national security mainly from a traditional angle. His emphasis on economic modernization as the central task of China originated more from his national development consideration than from a security one. As the Western countries started to increase their political and ideological pressures on China in the late 1980s, Deng warned against the new-type threat of "a third world war without gunsmoke", i.e. the conspiracy of the Western countries to promote a 'peaceful evolution' in the socialist countries. This kind of political threat is still affiliated to the traditional category.

Economic security made a formal appearance in China's national security consideration only after the Cold War. In the light of the fact that the post-Cold War competition among nations is characterized by the integrated national power rather than military strength alone, China attributes its sense of insecurity mainly to its backward economy. This is in vivid contrast to the Cold War period when China regarded its inferior military strength as the main cause of its being threatened. By identifying economic setbacks and underdevelopment, national secessionism, terrorism and other non-traditional issues as the major threats facing China in the post Cold-War era while admitting decreased military pressures beyond its border, China is applying a modern approach to its national security and defines threats in both military and non-military aspects.

The second change of China's security perception is manifested in terms of security categories and priorities. During the Cold War, when China looked at security issues through the prism of "war and revolution", national security fell into two categories: military security and political security, with the former preceding the latter in importance all the time. Strictly speaking, there were no types of security at all at that time, because China, like other countries in the world, took the military and political characters of security for granted. After the Cold War, however, China started to seek a comprehensive national security, including economic security, military security, political security and non-traditional security such as fighting against terrorism, transnational crimes, environmental degradation, drug trafficking and epidemics.

In the first decade of the post-Cold War era, China gave priority to economic security, because it set economic development as the central task of the whole country and required all other work, including national defence, to be subordinated to and serve this strategic objective. When the urgency of defending China's territorial integrity has mounted due to the rising risk of 'Taiwan Independence' since the beginning of the new century, China has made some adjustment in the priorities of its national security. Taking into account the fact that economic construction remains the central task of the country in the 21st century, since 2002, China has upgraded military security to the same level as economic security. In other words, economic security and military security are of equal importance. They are the dual top security concerns of China, preceding all others, like political security and non-traditional security.

Third, China has made a great transformation in its approaches to security since the end of the Cold War. During Mao's era, China adopted alliance security along with self-help security as the major means to safeguard its national security. Believing in the vital role of military strength in the international power games, China concentrated almost all of its resources on building a strong army, including the establishment of its own nuclear arsenal. Meanwhile, China forged alliances with the two superpowers at different periods, as well as exploring a moral alignment with the Third World countries. In 1982, Deng Xiaoping started to drop alliance security on the basis of his new understandings of China's national security. Since the end of the Cold War, this trend has been reinforced when China lays stress on common security. China has been trying to achieve its national security by growing common interests through cooperation, increasing mutual trust through dialogue, and developing strategic partnerships with all major powers and good-neighbourly relations with surrounding countries. In the light of the fact that China has been working for defence modernization since the end of the Cold War, self-help security continues to be an important approach to security for China. As China started to re-emphasize military security in 2002, the importance of self-help security has also been upgraded ever since.

As a consequence of the transformation of its general security perception, China's India perspective has also changed since the end of the Cold War. Apart from the short-lived positive perceptions towards India in the 1950s, China represented India as a threat or a rival in the rest of Mao's era. At a time when Cold War mindset prevailed around the world, India's quasi-military alliance with the Soviet Union, China's then major enemy, as well as the ideological difference between China and India, had contributed to China's protracted negative India perspective. As China under the leadership of Deng Xiaoping was determined to concentrate on economic modernization and implemented an independent foreign policy to create and safeguard a peaceful security environment for its economic construction, China started, in 1982, to regard India as its natural and close neighbour rather than as a threat. Since the end of the Cold War, guided by the new security concept that lays stress on integrated national power and common security, China has believed that a new-type partnership with India is in its fundamental interests. With the good-neighbourly policy becoming an important approach to security, even the Indian 1998 nuclear tests did not change this perspective. Although China started to give equal priority to economic security and military security in 2002, the rising threat in the east has consolidated its determination to strengthen peace and stability in other directions, including the west. Therefore, in recent years, China has started to seek a strategic partnership with India.

Notes

1. Xie Yixian, *Dangdai Zhongguo waijiao sixiang shi* (Contemporary History of China's Diplomatic Thoughts) (Kaifeng: Henan University Press, 2004), p. 413; Zhou Jianming, *'Ya Tai geju yu Zhongguo deDongya zhanlue'* (Asia-Pacific Order and China's East Asian Strategy), in *Zhongguo da zhanlue (The Grand Strategy of China)*, ed. Hu Angang (Hangzhou: Zhejiang renmin chubanshe, 2003), 291-294.
2. National Bureau of Statistics of China, available at http://www.stats.gov.cn/tjgb.
3. Yan Xuetong, 'China's Security after the Cold War', *Contemporary International Relations, Beijing*, Vol. 3, No. 5 (May 1993): 1.
4. Ibid.
5. Zheng Yu, *'Sulian de jieti yu Zhongguo anquan huanjing de bianhua'* (The Soviet Disintegration and the Change of China's Security Environment), *Dongou Zhongya yanjiu (East European & Central Asian Studies)*, Beijing, No.4 (2002), also available at http://www.euroasia.cass.cn/chinese/Magazine/Yanjiu/0204/020409.htm; Qin Yaqing, *'Lengzhan hou Zhongguo de anquan yishi he zhanlue xuanze'* (China's Post-Cold War Security Conception and Strategic Choice), in *Zhongguo waijiao xinlun (New Dimensions of China's Diplomacy)*, eds. Liu Shan, and Hsueh Chun-tu (Beijing: Shijie zhishi chubanshe, 1997), p. 82.
6. Jiang Zemin, 'Accelerating Reform and Opening-Up', report delivered at the 14th National Congress of the CPC on 12 October 1992, available at http://news.xinhuanet.com/ziliao/2003-01/20/content_697148.htm; Jiang Zemin, 'Hold High the Great Banner of Deng Xiaoping Theory for an All-round Advancement of the Cause of Building Socialism With Chinese Characteristics Into the 21st Century', report delivered at the 15th National Congress of the CPC on 12 September 1997, available at http://www.china.org.cn/english/features/45607.htm.
7. *China's National Defence*, Information Office of the State Council of the People's Republic of China, Beijing, July 1998, available at http://www.china.org.cn/e-white/5/index.htm.
8. Ibid.
9. Qin, *'Lengzhan hou Zhongguo de anquan yishi he zhanlue xuanze'*, in *Zhongguo waijiao xinlun*, eds. Liu et al., p. 79.
10. *China's National Defense in 2000*, available at http://www.china.org.cn/e-white/2000/index.htm.
11. Ibid.
12. *China's National Defense in 2002*, available at http://english.people.com.cn/features/ndpaper2002/nd.html.
13. Ibid.
14. Zhang Xiaoming, *'Zhongguo yu zhoubian guojia guanxi de lishi yanbian: moshi yu guocheng'* (The Historical Evolution of China's Relations with Its Neighbours: Model and Process), *Guoji zhengzhi yanjiu (International Political Studies)*, Beijing, No.1 (2006), also available at http://www.coldwarchina.com/zaxz/zgxz/zxm/002059.html.

15. *China's National Defense,* 1998.
16. Yan Xuetong, *'China's Post-Cold War Security Strategy',* Contemporary International Relations, Beijing, Vol. 5, No. 5 (May 1995): 3.
17. *China's National Defense,* 1998.
18. Yan, *'China's Security After The Cold War',* p. 6.
19. Wu Xinbo, *'Lengzhan hou de guojia anquan yu Zhongguo waijiao'* (Post-Cold War National Security and China's External Relations), in Zhongguo waijiao xinlun, eds. Liu et al., p. 225.
20. Ibid, p. 226.
21. 'President Lee's Deutsche Welle Interview', July 9, 1999, available at http://taiwansecurity.org/TS/SS-990709-Deutsche-Welle-Interview.htm.
22. 'Each Side is a Country' Theory Will Push Cross-Strait Relations to Crisis', *People's Daily Online,* August 9, 2002, available at http://english.peopledaily.com.cn/200208/09/eng20020809_101213.shtml.
23. Yan, *'China's Post-Cold War Security Strategy',* p. 3.
24. Zhang Zhirong, *'Zhongguo bianjiang yu minzu wenti'* (China's Border Regions and Ethnic Nationalisms) (Beijing: Peking University Press, 2005), pp. 239-240, 270-274.
25. Jiang Zemin, 'Build a Well-off Society in an All-Round Way and Create a New Situation in Building Socialism with Chinese Characteristics', report delivered at the 16th National Congress of the CPC on 8 November 2002, available at http://www.china.org.cn/english/features/49007.htm.
26. *China's National Defense in 2006,* available at http://www.chinadaily.com.cn/china/2006-12/29/content_771191.htm.
27. *China's National Defense in 2004,* available at http://english.people.com.cn/whitepaper/defense2004/defense2004.html.
28. After Ma Ying-jeou, the leader of Kuomingtang (or the Chinese Nationalist Party), who favoured friendlier relations with mainland China, won the 2008 Taiwan election and took power in May of the same year, a thaw emerged in the cross-strait tension.
29. *China's National Defense in 2002.*
30. *China's National Defense in 2004.*
31. Wang Baocun, *'Shidai cha' de tiaozhan'* (Challenge of the 'Age Gap'), *Renmin ribao (People's Daily),* Beijing, July 9, 2004.
32. *China's National Defense in 2004.*
33. Ibid.
34. Yan, 'China's Post-Cold War Security Strategy', p. 4.
35. Jiang, 'Hold High the Great Banner of Deng Xiaoping Theory for an All-round Advancement of the Cause of Building Socialism With Chinese Characteristics Into the 21st Century', 1997.
36. Yan, 'China's Post-Cold War Security Strategy', p. 4.
37. Wang Yizhou, *'Anquan xin guannian yu Zhongguo de Ya Tai anquan gouxiang'* (New Security Concept and China's Security Consideration in the Asia-Pacific Region), November 1998, available at http://www.irchina.org/xueren/china/view.asp?id=6.

38. Du Gang, *'Lun Zhongguo heping fazhan zhong de junshi liliang xuqiu'* (A Discussion on the Requirement for Military Power in China's Peaceful Development), *Zhanlue yu guanli (Strategy and Management)*, Beijing, No. 3 (2004), also available at http://www.usc.cuhk.edu.hk/wk_wzdetails.asp?id=3248.
39. Chen Degong, *'Xiandai guoji haiyang fa'* (Modern International Law of the Sea) (Beijing: China Social Sciences Publishing House, 1988), p. 449.
40. Yan Xuetong, *'Zhongguo guojia liyi fenxi'* (An Analysis of China's National Interests) (Tianjin: Tianjin renmin chubanshe, 1996), p. 120.
41. Zhang, Wenmu, *'Zhongguo nengyuan anquan yu zhengce xuanze'* (China's Energy Security and Policy Option), *Shijie jingji yu zhengzhi (World Economy and Politics)*, Beijing, No. 5 (2003): pp. 1-9.
42. *China's National Defense in 2002.*
43. *China's National Defense in 2000.*
44. *China's National Defense in 2002.*
45. Jiang, 'Build a Well-off Society in an All-Round Way and Create a New Situation in Building Socialism with Chinese Characteristics', 2002.
46. *China's National Defense in 2004.*
47. *Changqi zhanlue yanjiu xiaozu* (Long-term Group on Strategic Studies), *Guanyu 21 shiji Zhongguo guojia anquan liyi de zhanlue sikao* (Strategic Consideration on China's National Security Interests in the 21st Century), in Zhongguo da zhanlue, ed. Hu, 110.
48. Yan, *'China's Security after the Cold War'*, p. 12.
49. Xiong Guangkai, *'Xieli yingdui fei chuantong anquan weixie de xin tiaozhan'* (Making Joint Efforts to Meet the New Challenge by Non-Traditional Security Threats), *Shijie zhishi (World Affairs)*, Beijing, No.15 (August 1, 2005): 50-51.
50. Tang Yongsheng, *'Chaoyue chuantong de guojia anquan zhanlue'* (A National Security Strategy Beyond Tradition), *'Shijie jingji yu zhengzhi'* (World Economy and Politics), Beijing, No.6 (2004): 35.
51. Wang Yizhou, *'SARS yu fei chuantong anquan'* (SARS and Non-Traditional Security), 2003, available at http://www.iwep.org.cn/zhengzhi/SARSyufeichuantonganquan_wangyizhou.htm.
52. Ibid.
53. *China's National Defense in 2004.*
54. Yan, *'China's Security after the Cold War'*, p. 13.
55. Like the US, Russia and the European countries.
56. Like Brazil, Egypt, India and South Africa.
57. Yan, 'China's Post-Cold War Security Strategy', pp. 12-13.
58. Li Baojun, *'Xin shiji zhi chu Zhongguo duiwai guanxi de jian'gou'* (On China's Diplomacy in the Beginning of the 21st Century), *Waijiao pinglun (Foreign Affairs Review)*, Beijing, No.5 (2005), also available at http://www.cp.org.cn/show.asp?NewsID=879.
59. Jiang, 'Build a Well-off Society in an All-Round Way and Create a New Situation in Building Socialism with Chinese Characteristics', 2002.
60. *China's Position Paper on the New Security Concept*, July 31, 2002, available at http://www.china-un.ch/eng/cjjk/cjjblc/cjlc/t85397.htm.

61. Ibid.
62. Ibid.
63. National Bureau of Statistics of China, available at http://www.stats.gov.cn/tjgb.
64. Chen Baosen, *'Zhong Mei guanxi de wending qi'* (Stabilizer of the Sino-US Relations), *Shijie zhishi (World Affairs)*, Beijing, No.3 (February 1, 2004): 20-23.
65. *China's Position Paper on the New Security Concept.*
66. Ibid.
67. *Wo guo daibiao renwei jianli Ya Tai anquan jizhi ying zunshou heping gongchu wu xiang yuanze* (Our Delegation's Proposal for Establishing Asia-Pacific Security Mechanism According to the Five Principles of Peaceful Coexistence), *Xinhua mei ri dianxun (Xinhua Daily Telegraph)*, Beijing, February 3, 1993.
68. China's Position Paper on the New Security Concept.
69. *China's National Defense in 2004.*
70. *China's National Defense in 2002.*
71. *China's National Defense in 2004.*
72. *China's Position Paper on the New Security Concept.*
73. *China's National Defense in 2004.*
74. Jiang, 'Hold High the Great Banner of Deng Xiaoping Theory for an All-round Advancement of the Cause of Building Socialism With Chinese Characteristics into the 21st Century', 1997.
75. Yan, 'China's Post-Cold War Security Strategy', pp. 8-9.
76. *Zhonggong zhongyang guanyu zhiding di jiu ge wu nian jihua he 2010 nian yuanjing mubiao de jianyi* (The Proposal of the Central Committee of the Communist Party of China for Formulation of the Ninth Five-Year Plan (1996-2000) for National Economic and Social Development and Long-Term Target for the Year 2010), Renmin ribao (People's Daily), October 5, 1995, also available at http://www.people.com.cn/GB/shizheng/252/4465/4466/20010228/405435.html.
77. *China's National Defense in 2004.*
78. Ibid.
79. *China's National Defense in 2006.*
80. Hu Jintao, 'Hold High The Great Banner of Socialism with Chinese Characteristics and Strive for New Victories in Building a Moderately Prosperous Society in all Aspects', report to the 17th National Congress of the Communist Party of China on Oct. 15, 2007, available at http://www.chinadaily.com.cn/china/2007-10/25/content_6204667.htm.
81. Jiang, 'Hold High the Great Banner of Deng Xiaoping Theory for an All-round Advancement of the Cause of Building Socialism with Chinese Characteristics Into the 21st Century', 1997.
82. Han Hua, *'Youhao linbang hai shi anquan weixie—Zhong Yin ruhe kandai duifang'* (Good Neighbour or Threat to Security: How China and India Look at Each Other), *Nanya yanjiu (South Asian Studies)*, Beijing, No.2 (2002), available at http://iap.cass.cn/Bak/nyyj/0202-2.htm.
83. Sun Shihai, 'China-Indian Relations in the 21st Century', in *A Presentation Collection for Conference on India in 21st Century: External Relations*, SIIS

(Shanghai Institute for International Studies) (Shanghai: SIIS Publication, 2002), pp. 152-153, 165.

84. Han, *'Youhao linbang hai shi anquan weixie'.*
85. Ye Zhengjia, 'China-India Relations', in *A Presentation Collection for Conference on India in 21st Century: External Relations,* SIIS, p. 176.
86. Han, *'Youhao linbang hai shi anquan weixie'.*
87. Sun, 'China-Indian Relations in the 21st Century', p. 154.
88. Ibid.
89. Wang Hongwei, *Ximalaya shan qingjie: Zhong Yin guanxi yanjiu* (The Himalayas Sentiment: A Study of Sino-Indian Relations) (Beijing: Zhongguo Zang xue chubanshe, 1998), p. 367.
90. Ye, 'China-India Relations', p. 180
91. Han, *'Youhao linbang hai shi anquan weixie'.*
92. Ibid.
93. Zhao Gancheng, *'Wending Zhong Yin guanxi yu chuangzao zhanlue jiyu chuyi'* (On the Stabilisation of China-India Relations and the Creation of Strategic Opportunities), *Nanya yanjiu (South Asian Studies),* Beijing, No.2 (2003): 19.
94. Lin Liangguang, *'Zhong Yin guanxi de fazhan licheng'* (The Historical Evolution of China-India Relations), in *Zhong Yin guanxi yanjiu (1947-2003) (A Study of Sino-Indian Relation),* in ed. Minqiu Zhang (Beijing: Peking University Press, 2004), pp. 47-48.
95. Ibid, p. 48.
96. Xia Liping, *'China-India Security Relationship: Retrospects and Prospects',* in *A Presentation Collection for Conference on India in 21st Century: External Relations,* SIIS, pp. 110-112.
97. 'India Ready to Work For A Fair and Reasonable Solution to Border Dispute with China,' *UNI,* 1996, available at http://www.rediff.com/news/1996/2811chin.htm.
98. Wang, *'Ximalaya shan qingjie',* pp. 355-360.
99. Du Youkang, *'21 shiji de Zhong Yin guanxi'* (China-India Relations in the 21st Century), Nanya yanjiu (South Asian Studies), Beijing, No. 2 (2001), available at http://iap.cass.cn/Bak/nyyj/0102-2.htm.
100. *Sino-Indian Joint Communiqué,* December 16, 1991, *China Report,* New Delhi, Vol. 28, No. 1 (1992), pp. 89-92.
101. C. Raja Mohan, *Crossing the Rubicon: The Shaping of India's New Foreign Policy* (New Delhi: Penguin-Viking, 2003), p. 146.
102. Susan L. Shirk, 'One-Sided Rivalry: China's Perceptions and Policies toward India', in *The India-China Relationship: Rivalry and Engagement,* eds. Francine R. Frankel and Harry Harding (Oxford: Oxford University Press, 2004), pp. 82-83.
103. Atal Bihari Vajpayee, 'Nuclear Anxiety: India's Letter to Clinton on Nuclear Testing', *New York Times,* May 13, 1998.
104. B. Raman, 'Sino-Indian Relations: A Chronology', South Asia Analysis Group Papers, April 23, 1999, available at http://www.saag.org/papers/paper49.html.
105. Shirk, 'One-Sided Rivalry: China's Perceptions and Policies toward India', in *The India-China Relationship: Rivalry and Engagement,* eds. Frankel et al., p. 83.

106. Ibid.
107. Lally Weymouth, 'Jiang Speaks Out', *Newsweek,* June 29, 1998, also available at http://www.washingtonpost.com/wp-srv/newsweek/interview.htm.
108. Shirk, "One-Sided Rivalry: China's Perceptions and Policies toward India," in *The India-China Relationship: Rivalry and Engagement,* eds. Frankel et al., p. 83.
109. Cited in Raman, 'Sino-Indian Relations: A Chronology'.
110. Ibid.
111. Ibid.
112. Shirk, 'One-Sided Rivalry: China's Perceptions and Policies toward India', in *The India-China Relationship: Rivalry and Engagement,* eds. Frankel et al., p. 93.
113. Ibid, p. 94.
114. Ibid, p. 89.
115. Cited in Raman, 'Sino-Indian Relations: A Chronology'.
116. Shirk, 'One-Sided Rivalry: China's Perceptions and Policies toward India', in *The India-China Relationship: Rivalry and Engagement,* eds. Frankel et al., pp. 89-90.
117. Raman, 'Sino-Indian Relations: A Chronology'.
118. Ibid.
119. Ibid.
120. Ibid.
121. Li Peng, 'Deepening Understanding, Fostering Friendship and Strengthening Cooperation', speech at the India International Center, New Delhi, January 13, 2001, available at http://mea.gov.in/speech/2001/01/13spc01.htm.
122. 'Wen Jiabao Addresses Delhi Institute of Technology', April 12, 2005, available at http://www.chinaembassy.org.il/eng/xwdt/t191998.htm.
123. 'India, China Key to True Asian Century: Hu', *The Times of India,* November 22, 2006.
124. Ibid.
125. 'Hu Makes Five-Point Proposal for Better Ties', Xinhua News Agency, November 22, 2006, available at http://www.chinadaily.com.cn/china/2006-11/22/content_740363.htm.

4

India's Security Perception After the Cold War

Since 1991, state power in India has successively passed to several governments: the Congress-led government under Narasimha Rao (June 1991-May 1996), the Janata Dal-led United Front governments under Deve Gowda (June 1996-April 1997) and I.K. Gujral (April 1997-March 1998), the BJP-led NDA (National Democratic Alliance) government under Atal Bihari Vajpayee (March 1998-May 2004)[1], and the Congress-led UPA (United Progressive Alliance) government under Manmohan Singh (May 2004-till date). Led by different political parties, these governments might have found many divergences in their domestic agendas, but as far as national security and foreign policy are concerned, they have converged in many aspects. Facing a post-Cold War world with various new challenges, each government, though to different extents, chose to respond by introducing new ideas into its security consideration. This gradually led to a major change with regard to India's security perception.

4.1 India's Assessment of its Security Environment

In contrast to China's greatly transformed sense of security after the Cold War, India seemed extremely pessimistic about its security environment in the early days of the post-Cold War era. In the assessment of strategic analysts, the end of the Cold War did not eliminate the traditional threats to its territorial security; "instead it accentuated the Indian security problems".[2] Confronting a radically transformed world order, India foresaw the possibility of being marginalized in world affairs. Since the mid-1990s, however, such apprehensions have been allayed by two events: the recovery of the Indian economy, which started booming after the five-year efforts by the Narasimha Rao government; and then towards the end of the 1990s,

India's going nuclear in May 1998 under the leadership of the NDA government. Since then, a more confident India has looked at its security environment through a much wider prism.

The Indian government considered the early 1990s as a period of "strategic uncertainties".[3] With the end of the Cold War and the disintegration of the Soviet Union, the world has been assessed as having become unipolar in military terms, with the US becoming the power centre, but in terms of technology, natural resources and demography, the world has become multipolar, where new equilibria among the US and the emerging power centres of Western Europe, Russia, Japan and China have not yet stabilized. Issues which dominated international relations during the Cold War period, such as colonialism and imperialism, the ideological struggle between the communist and non-communist states, the economic issues affecting interaction between the industrially advanced countries and the poorer developing countries, have been replaced by concerns about human rights, disarmament and arms control, good governance, management of the global environment and the structuring of the globalized economic order ruled by free market economy principles. The information and technological revolutions and the globalization of the world economy have been eroding the territorial compartmentalization of societies as nation-states. Geopolitical and economic regionalism and regional groupings have replaced the old trans-regional and trans-continental multilateral fora such as the NAM, the UNCTAD and the G-77 that represented the interests of developing countries.[4]

"While the Cold War confrontation has ended," as the Indian annual defence report of 1992-93 states, "the de-escalation of tensions at the global level has so far not had a positive impact in our region."[5] Though there were no overt threats to its territorial integrity and security, covert threats persisted.[6] First of all, Pakistan remained central to India's strategic concerns.[7] To quote:

> Despite these encouraging trends, however, we remained seriously concerned about the political, diplomatic, moral and material support that Pakistan continued to provide to armed militant groups in J&K and Punjab...Pakistan's pursuit of its militarisation programme also continued to outpace, by far, the country's legitimate defence requirements...Pakistan's clandestine nuclear weapons programme also continues to be pursued, despite the strains that have developed in its long standing relations with the US on this point.[8]

Second, as ethnic assertions increased and religious fundamentalism intensified after the Cold War, it led to heightened tension in many areas of the globe.[9] India's national unity as well continued to be threatened by "Pakistan sponsored insurgency in Jammu and Kashmir, the often externally supported subversive activities of militant groups in the North-East, and the proclivities of such extremist groups as the Peoples War Group in Andhra Pradesh and the Naxalites in Bihar and West Bengal".[10]

Third, India's bilateral relations with its immediate neighbours continued to face various difficulties: for example, its water dispute with Bangladesh,[11] the impact of the ethnic conflict in Sri Lanka,[12] and Myanmar's attitude towards Indian insurgent groups in the North-Eastern states.[13] As for China, although the India-China relations continued to improve, "the territorial issue will continue to be the spectre that will haunt...India-China relations until it is finally resolved,"[14] and India maintained "a close watch on China's own military modernisation programmes as well as its military relations with [our] immediate neighbours who have, in the recent past, been beneficiaries of Chinese military supplies in the form of weapons and training".[15]

A number of Indian analysts believe that the end of the Cold War has weakened India's international position in many ways, and this relative political decline has made India "shakier than ever before".[16] The collapse of the Soviet Union, India's de facto military and political ally since 1971, left India with few reliable friends in the new world order dominated by one superpower.[17] Analysts further argue that India came out on the losing side of the Cold War, and was treated by the world as "a regional power locked into a conflict with a hostile smaller neighbour, Pakistan".[18] The post-Cold War marginalization of the Non-Aligned Movement could also be seen as a big blow for the relevance of India, which had for decades seen itself as the leader of the Third World.[19] As developments in West Asia, Central Asia, East Europe and Russia drew increasing international political attention after the Cold War, India was accordingly marginalized as an area of interest.[20] In the meanwhile, the US and other advanced countries continued to be opposed to some essential aspects of India's policies rather than befriend it.[21] As the international non-proliferation regime was strengthened by a series of activities, like the indefinite extension of the NPT and the negotiation of the CTBT, India felt growing global pressures on its nuclear option and missile programmes.[22] Another pressure came from the criticism of India's human rights records by certain quarters in the West. India pointed out that the purpose of the West was to use human rights as a means to "scrutinise India's domestic affairs". [23]

In the early 1990s, the importance of the domestic situation in determining India's overall national security was especially salient. Apart from the above-mentioned 'subversive activities', which had been threatening India's unity for decades, the economic crisis and internal riots deepened India's sense of insecurity. Along with the disappearance of the military and political support of the former Soviet Union, the economy which was considerably weakened by the external payments crisis of 1990-91,[24] appeared to make India more vulnerable in the new world order. As India started its economic reform, the speed and direction of its liberalization and modernization plans became new areas for the West to intervene in India's domestic affairs.[25] Destruction of the Babri Masjid in Ayodhya by Hindu extremists on 6 December 1992 also affected India's international credibility. It created an impression that "the Government of India was weak"[26] and "the country's principles of secularism, religious tolerance and rule of law" were under "an unprecedented threat".[27]

The economic revival and the nuclear tests changed the way the Indian elite thought about national security.[28] The fact that an emerging India was becoming "an inexorable reality"[29] eradicated India's earlier concern about being marginalized in world affairs and allowed India to look at its post-Cold War security environment with a sense of confidence that had not been much in evidence earlier. The annual defence report of 2007-2008 states, "India's rapidly growing economy, relative size and strategic location in the region thus brings the country into prominence in the world geopolitics".[30] On the occasion of the 60th anniversary of India's independence, Prime Minister Manmohan Singh told the nation:

> As I have often said, the world today wants India to do well. The world community wishes us well. Our external situation is benign and favourable. Our challenges are at home.[31]

Non-military challenges and energy security were listed for the first time as separate items in India's annual defence report of 1997-1998. Since then, India has adopted "a more comprehensive approach to security".[32] During the 2004 national electoral campaign, the Congress party stated in its *Security Agenda* that national security "has political, economic, social and developmental dimensions" and should not be perceived "within the narrow prism of the purely military context".[33]

Drawing lessons from the collapse of the Soviet Union and its own economic setback, India started to pay attention to economic security in the mid-1990s. The collapse of the Russian economy was a warning to all nations, including India, of the risk of pursuing power through the barrel of a gun. Although the Soviets had armed themselves to the teeth to fight NATO on every possible battlefield, they lost the Cold War due to their poor performance on the economic front. Some analysts also saw some relevance in the notion of *Comprehensive National Power,* which was formulated by the Chinese scholars. They believed that "power in the modern world was based as much on economic competitiveness and political resilience of a country as it was on military capability".[34] As India received much greater respect from the world due to its economic performance and liberalization since 1991, it started to put economic interests, in place of high politics, at the centre of its foreign policy.[35] It was in this context that India began to attach importance to the relevance of the economic factor in national security and the economic dimension of its external environment. This has also motivated India to keep a closer watch on situations in its extended neighbourhood in the Gulf and Central Asia, because these are the two energy-rich areas on which India's economic development is heavily dependent, as also arenas of intense international competition for access.[36] When looking at its maritime environment, India lays more stress on the security of its economic interests, including its rights to the maritime resources and the safety of the sea-lanes.[37]

Apart from economic security, India has also started to pay attention to other new security challenges since the mid-1990s. As India's annual defence report of 1994-95 states:

> Simultaneously, new sources of tension and potential conflict are emerging in today's world involving availability of resources such as oil, gas, food and water. There are anxieties regarding population migration, new concerns over ecological degradation and its effect on health and quality of life, the peddling of drugs and its links with terrorism, and the proliferation of small arms and their linkages with both state and non-state actors.[38]

The 1997-98 report explains further that "the linked problems of drugs trafficking, terrorism and organised crime" are the major non-traditional threats facing India in the post-Cold War era. Located between two of the world's leading narcotics producing and exporting regions—North West Pakistan and Afghanistan on one side and Myanmar on the other, India is particularly concerned about the "involvement of insurgent and criminal groups in the drug trade".[39] The September 11, 2001 terrorist attack against the United States was instrumental in forging an international convergence on the fact that terrorism had become the major non-traditional threat to nations in the post-Cold War era. India gave its own view regarding the threat of terrorism to its national security. Its 2003-2004 annual defence report states that "terrorism is India's primary and most immediate security threat," because India is located "at the centre of the arc of extremist activism and terrorism".[40] Since the end of the Cold War, India has been a victim of terrorist attacks, such as the Mumbai bomb blasts of 1993 and of 2003. By emphasizing the "crossborder and state-sponsored" nature of terrorism faced by India, however, it is clear that India sees Pakistan using terrorism as an instrument to de-stabilize India.[41]

Since the late 1990s, India has also been keeping a close watch on the implications of "new technologies" for its national security. "Adequate concern is being focused towards information and space technology, advanced materials and bio-technology," as these are shaping a country's national strength "in a far more significant manner than is commonly realised".[42] The Indian national defence especially faces a new challenge of the worldwide RMA driven by the development of new technologies.[43] The 1999-2000 annual defence report observes:

> The future battlefield scenario would be vastly different from its traditional version. Technological superiority, weapon effectiveness and force mix, capabilities for rapid response and precision strike will be more important than conventional numerical superiority. There is already a transformation in warfare towards the utilisation of high technology weapons and systems, advanced command and control networks, electronic and information warfare, as well as enhanced administrative efficiency and logics support.[44]

In spite of the fact that India's security environment has improved considerably due to positive developments in relations with its two largest neighbours, India's traditional two-front security concerns seem to be persisting. In January 2004, India and Pakistan started the peace process with President Musharraf assuring India that Pakistani territory would not be used to support terrorism in any manner and Indian Prime Minister Vajpayee's commitment to a purposeful discussion of the Kashmir issue. Since then, a number of initiatives have been taken to ease tensions, normalize and improve relations between India and Pakistan. At the level of the government, the Composite Dialogue was initiated with the resumption of Foreign Secretary level talks in June 2004. At the level of the armed forces, a number of CBMs were exchanged. At the level of the people-to-people contacts, major steps were taken to start bus services and restore rail links.[45] Despite these positive elements in the India-Pakistan relations, India was not convinced that it meant "any discernible change of heart, or action, by the Pakistani authorities," because "there was no evidence of any significant Pakistani effort to dismantle the infrastructure of terrorism".[46] Meanwhile, India accused Pakistan of pursuing a policy of acquiring military superiority by taking advantage of the war against terrorism to procure sophisticated weapons and platforms like the F-16s, P3C Orion maritime surveillance aircraft, etc.[47] Although China-India relations were continually improving and entered into "a phase of comprehensive all-round development supported by high-level exchanges and dialogue", concerns about China's military modernization and its "close defence relationship with and military assistance to Pakistan" were of a serious nature.[48] India's 2002-2003 annual defence report states, "the India Armed Forces have a two-front obligation, which requires them to safeguard the security of our borders with Pakistan as well as with China".[49]

4.2 India's National Security Strategy

4.2 (1) Objectives of India's National Security Strategy

The objectives of India's national security strategy after the Cold War are not in essence different from that of the Nehru's era, though the backdrop on which they are based has transformed. As discussed in Chapter 2, the first two decades after Independence witnessed the two-fold strategic objectives set by Nehru for India: to preserve India's independence and maintain its national unity and territorial integrity, on the one hand; to play a leading role in world affairs, on the other. The post-Cold War security strategy of India also has a two-fold objective. To safeguard the territorial security and integrity remains the primary task. To emerge as a major power or an important pole—along with the United States, Europe, Russia, China and Japan—in the new international system is a continuing effort by India to recover "the lost space in the global arena".[50] This is a goal that has been pursued by India for decades.

India, in the post-Cold War period, unlike in the Nehru era, was confident that its existence as an independent nation-state was under no threat. However, covert threats to its territorial integrity and security persisted after the Cold War, and India has listed "defending the country's borders as defined by law and enshrined in the Constitution and protecting the lives and property of its citizens against terrorism and insurgencies" at the top of its national security objectives.[51] The Bharatiya Janata Party (BJP) and the Congress party, the two biggest political parties in the contemporary Indian political arena, appear to share a consensus in this regard. The BJP claims that it "has always attached the highest importance to national security"[52] and dedicated itself to "preserving the honour and territorial integrity of [our] motherland".[53] In its manifesto for the general elections of 2004, the Congress party stated that "safeguarding India's territorial integrity and unity against overt or covert external aggression is the supreme responsibility of the Government...keeping the nation armed forces fully prepared, backed up by necessary resources is important".[54]

In the early 1990s, when India felt the pressure of being marginalized in the world arena and bogged down in South Asia, it was clear that to recover India's relevance and position in world affairs, at least to the level during the Cold War, was obviously another major strategic objective of the then Indian political leaders. In the view of strategic thinkers, "[R]egaining the psychological parity with Beijing, reasserting a role in the Asian balance of power and getting out of the subcontinental box" were the concrete targets.[55] The vision of India did not just stop here, however. As it has turned out since the late 1990s, the 'Indian Renaissance' or 'India's rise' is actually a more ambitious agenda.[56] In 1998, the then Indian Prime Minister Vajpayee put it simply that "our aim is to be a strong nation".[57] In 1999, the NDA government made a commitment to "build a resurgent, modern India" and to "obtain for India its rightful place in the comity of nations".[58] In 2004, the NDA which was seeking a renewed mandate under the leadership of Vajpayee set a goal to make India a developed nation and a great power by 2020. This means to "secure for India a steadily broadening role in international affairs"[59] and a status of "economic superpower"[60] as well.

Compared with Nehru's aspirations, there is nothing new in the post-Cold War objective of India's national security strategy. Independent India always had the sense of a manifest destiny to be resurgent. Like Nehru, the current Indian leaders base this destiny on India's greatness. They are proud of India's 5,000 year-old civilization and long for the pre-colonial era when India, along with China and Europe, was one of the three poles of equal power.[61] What makes a difference in the present context, is a distinct possibility of achieving this goal. Since Independence, "it was only in the 1990s that India seemed able to grasp that destiny".[62] The new turn in India's economic performance due to the economic reforms since the early 1990s and the Pokhran-II blasts in 1998 have, for the first time, shaped the basis for India's re-emergence.[63] Today, even the world recognizes India as an emerging power.[64]

4.2 (2) India's National Security Interests

Like China, post-Cold War India has broadened the parameters of its definition of national security interests. While China's consideration in this regard has experienced a shift from emphasizing the antecedence of economic interests to equalizing the significance of economic interests and military interests, India has taken a converse route by continuing its focus on military interests and then gradually incorporating economic interests. Generally speaking, a stronger defence, rapid economic growth, and multipolarity are the three major national security interests of India in the post-Cold War era, reflecting an even hand of India in dealing with its respective security in military, economic and political dimensions.

Guided by the above-mentioned security objectives of India after the Cold War, a consensus that a "stronger defence"[65] is a fundamental requirement of India's national security, has been built among India's political forces. Each government sees strengthening India's defence capability and preparedness as a paramount duty.[66] Believing its national unity and territorial integrity to be still under threat, India finds it imperative to "maintain a high level of defence vigilance and preparedness to face any challenge to its security".[67] It is also apparent that India would find it impossible to attain the status of a major power without credible strategic and military capabilities. As Atal Bihari Vajpayee, the then Indian Prime Minister, argued in September 2000, "our experience has taught us that peace[68] lies in strength".[69] Since the aim of his argument was to justify India's decision to go nuclear in 1998, the word 'strength' should be comprehended here as military and strategic capabilities. This view appears to be shared by other mainstream political parties in India.

In the light of the changed world military scenario since the end of the Cold War, a stronger defence of India cannot just be interpreted in the traditional sense as more troops and weapons. It means "a credible nuclear weapons programme",[70] "a secure, effective and credible minimum deterrent against the use or the threat of use of weapons of mass destruction against India," the ability to defy the international sanctions by indigenous research, development and production of material, equipment and technologies that have a bearing on India's security, and the ability to catch up with the worldwide RMA, including technological innovation and management reform.[71]

While Vajpayee accentuated the significant consequences of the military and strategic capabilities for national security, he also admitted that "the strength of a nation flows primarily from the strength of its economy".[72] Based on this kind of understanding, since the mid-1990s, India has started to see enduring and rapid economic growth as another security interest, as significant as a stronger defence. Analysts have argued that to regain its pre-eminent place in the global arena, "India must ensure faster paced economic growth...Unless the Indian economy becomes more competitive and is more globally engaged, unless the economic well-being of all Indians is assured, unless the financial health of the Government improves, India will not be able to sustain itself as a major power".[73] India's improved economic performance will have strategic consequences on its national security, both internal and external. A more equitable and efficient growth process will reduce domestic social and political tensions. The new relationships of economic interdependence, due to its better economic engagement with the world, will "have benign consequences for international relations".[74] Moreover, rich fiscal resources will empower the Indian government to invest more in strategic capabilities.[75]

Therefore, accelerating the growth rate of the economy has become a central task for each Indian government since the 1990s. The NDA government (March 1998-May 2004) successfully reached the goal of an annual growth rate of 7-8%. The UPA government (May 2004-till date) which succeeded it is committed to the same growth rate. To quote:

> The UPA government supported by the Left Parties will have six basic principles for governance...to ensure that the economy grows at least 7-8% per year in a sustained manner over a decade and more and in a manner that generates employment so that each family is assured of a safe and viable livelihood.[76]

Thanks to India's confidence in its potential to re-emerge as an important pole in the international system, it appeared that "the creation of a multipolar world was in the interest of India".[77] India's annual defence report of 1997-98 states, "India's long-term and immediate security interests lie in encouraging the evolution of the international community towards greater multi-polarity".[78] The objective of preventing world domination by the sole superpower achieved national consensus after the end of the Cold War. During the national elections of 2004, both the Congress party and the BJP, along with their respective partners, expressed strong support for the idea of a multipolar world and made multi-polarity a major theme of their respective external agendas.

In its *Common Minimum Programme,* the Congress-led UPA undertook to "promote multi-polarity in world relations and oppose all attempts at unilateralism".[79] The BJP-led NDA promised to "work for the creation of a cooperative multi-polar world order, with India as one of the poles"; to further raise India's standing in the world; and to secure for India a meaningful and steadily growing role in international affairs.[80] In the opinion of the Indian political leaders, the multipolar world should be fashioned according to the following principles: it will be composed of six poles, including India, China, United States, Europe, Russia, and Japan; rising powers like China and India should secure their emergence "within their legally defined borders"; major powers should interact with each other out of "a position of mutual benefit, mutual respect and equality";[81] "the United States will continue to be the pre-eminent power but will have to accommodate the aspirations of many other nations;"[82] "the legitimate aspirations of developing countries" should be taken into account.[83]

4.2 (3) India's National Security Policy

With a broadened definition of its national security interests since the end of the Cold War, India has adopted a comprehensive and multi-dimensional national security policy, which features a combination of military and technological self-reliance, new partnership, security dialogue and cooperation, and economic diplomacy.

Although self-reliance has been an important principle of India's national security policy since Independence, it was after the Cold War that it became more imperative than ever before. The 'idealist' Nehru paid too much attention to moral strength. The 'realist' Indira Gandhi felt a diminished urgency due to the de facto military and political alliance with the Soviet Union, the then superpower. The disintegration of the Soviet Union left India with few reliable friends, however. As analysts put it, when alliance security became history, "the importance of self-help in managing its national security was coming to the fore with greater clarity".[84] Moreover, the decades-long international restriction on the transfer of such items as material, equipment and technologies that have a bearing on India's strategic and military programmes, the intensifying global pressures on India's nuclear option and missile development, and the international backlash and sanctions after Pokhran II, have reinforced India's belief in self-reliance. Prime Minister Vajpayee told the nation in 1999 that a resurgent India must stand on its own feet: "In a rapidly changing security environment, India cannot depend on others to defend her. We have to develop our own indigenous capabilities".[85]

Since the end of the Cold War, India has taken a series of concrete steps in this regard. First and foremost, India conducted five successful nuclear tests at Pokhran from May 11 to 13, 1998, achieving nuclear weapon capability. The preparation for Pokhran II was started by the Narasimha Rao government. It was stopped in December 1995 by the United States when the latter noticed that the former was getting ready to test. In the second week after he took office, Prime Minister Vajpayee chose to act.[86] Second, India started to accelerate its missile programmes. India has expedited the development of the Agni series of ballistic missiles with a view to increasing their range and accuracy.[87] On April 11, 1999, India successfully test-fired *Agni-II*, a nuclear capable missile with a range of 2,000-2,500 km. Eight years later, *Agni-III* was successfully test-fired on April 12, 2007. With a strike range of over 3,000 km, it catapulted India into the league of nations with IRBM (intermediate range ballistic missile) capability. Third, India has paid more attention to space technology. A series of successful launches of INSAT satellites has taken India into a new orbit of world-class satellite communication. It is also promoting the *Chandrayan* programme, which aims to send India's first space mission to the moon as early as in 2008. Fourth, more emphasis has been put on the indigenous development of defence-related technology. "Abundant budgetary support"[88] or "special allocations"[89] were promised by the successive governments. The Defence Research and Development Organisation (DRDO) has launched a number of major programmes for the development of critical technologies and systems. As a result, "several major systems have been indigenously developed and led to production".[90] The Department of Defence Production has set self-reliance as a major goal in key areas of defence production.[91]

Nevertheless, "*Swadeshi* does not mean an inward looking policy."[92] As the world has become a global village, interdependence requires India to walk on two legs: ensuring military and technological self-reliance, on the one hand; engaging proactively with the world, on the other. As mentioned in Chapter 2, since independence, non-alignment had been India's fundamental approach to world affairs. Formulated as a way to shun the two-bloc confrontation, non-alignment made India stress multilateralism more than bilateralism, stand with the Third World vis-à-vis the West, and become in essence a revisionist power in the then world system. After the Cold War, the altered world and especially the fact that India was becoming a major player of the post-Cold War 'polycentric order'[93], motivated India to pursue a national security policy beyond non-alignment. Throughout the 1990s, successive Indian governments gradually deviated from non-alignment by introducing 'new partnership'[94] as a significant approach to safeguarding India's security interests.

In contrast to non-alignment, the 'new partnership' has the three following features: First, it attaches equal importance to bilateralism and multilateralism. Since the end of the Cold War, India has shifted its focus from multilateral diplomacy in the NAM to "the creation of strategic partnerships with pivotal states in the region and beyond".[95] Meanwhile, India also began to promote greater regional relationship.[96] India showed a growing interest in making effective the South Asian Association for Regional Cooperation (SAARC) and expected to establish a South Asian Parliament. India also made purposeful efforts to strengthen its relations with other regional groups, like ASEAN and APEC.[97]

Second, this implied a strategy of omnidirectional diplomacy. With no bias, India, like China, worked for strengthening and expanding good relations with countries all over the world, irrespective of whether they were major powers or neighbouring countries, Western countries or developing countries. Since the end of the Cold War, India has improved its relations with all major powers including the United States, the European countries, the Russian Federation, China and Japan. With regard to its immediate and small neighbours, India tried to promote a positive neighbourhood policy by replacing the Indira Doctrine with the Gujral Doctrine. This doctrine essentially sought to transform India's approach towards its smaller neighbours by discarding the principle of reciprocity and being more accommodating and generous to Nepal, Bangladesh, Bhutan, Maldives and Sri Lanka.[98] Keeping in mind the special relevance of its extended neighbours in Central Asia, West Asia and the Gulf, India made continuing efforts to enhance cooperation in political, economic and technological spheres with them.[99] Through the 'Look East' policy,[100] India's relations with South East Asian countries and countries in the South Pacific region have made considerable progress in recent years.[101] As for countries in Africa, South America and Latin America, India promised to continue its traditional friendship with them.

Third, new partnership can be assessed as genuine non-alignment. As discussed in Chapter 2, India's policy of non-alignment was not in the literal sense of the term as such, especially when Nehru "sought and received American, British and Canadian military equipment on concessionary terms" in the early 1960s.[102] Moreover, it had lived with an Indo-Soviet alliance for decades. The post-Cold War new partnership laid emphasis on independence, non-alignment and compatibility. Even though Vajpayee went so far as to proclaim that India and the United States were "natural allies"[103], and a strategic trilateral cooperation seemed to emerge among India, Russia and China, neither of them appears to be based on a zero-sum pattern of alliance. With its aspiration to be a pole in the new international system India is unlikely to become "a satellite or a junior partner" of any power of the world, including the United States.[104] Neither is it possible for an India-Russia-China triangular alliance, when all of them "value their relations with the United States".[105] The annual defence report of 2003-2004 put it clearly that "any military alliance or strategic grouping" was not consistent with India's interests.[106] In this context, India's partnership with the United States is only a part of its multidirectional engagement with the major powers. It does not exclude India developing new partnerships with other individual powers. As K. Subrahmanyam, India's leading strategic analyst, put it:

> In this balance of power system each power tries to develop strategic partnerships and relationships with other individual powers in order to optimize its own economic, political and strategic advantages. In pursuance of this strategy, India has developed partnerships with the US, the European Union and Russia and strategic relationships with China and Japan.[107]

India sees security dialogue and cooperation as another important approach to security in the post-Cold War era. As challenges of international terrorism, concerns about the proliferation of weapons of mass destruction, and threats to the security of transport, travel and the sea lanes, have brought countries closer to "cooperate for their mutual security", India has developed and expanded its security dialogue and defence cooperation with major powers and key partners.[108] Since the 1990s, India and the US have developed a number of mechanisms for security and strategic dialogue on global, regional and bilateral issues. These institutionalized dialogues include bilateral nuclear talks, Asian Security Dialogue (bilateral), Joint Working Group on Counter-terrorism, the Defence Policy Group, and the Joint Technical Group on R&D cooperation, etc.[109] India's strategic ties and defence cooperation with Russia are manifest in various mechanisms including a tradition of annual summits, security dialogue at the level of heads of National Security Councils, mechanisms to deal with specific challenges such as terrorism and Afghanistan, and the only ministerial-level mechanism for defence-industrial cooperation, i.e. the Indo-Russian Inter-Governmental Commission on Military Technical Cooperation.[110] With other countries, India has various institutionalized security dialogues and defence consultative mechanisms at the Defence Secretary's level, such as the India-UK Defence Consultative Group, the India-France High Committee on Defence Cooperation, the India-Italy Joint Defence Committee, the India-Vietnam Security Dialogue, and the India-South Africa Joint Defence Committee.[111] To enhance mutual understanding, India has also sought security cooperation with a large number of countries in the form of military training exchanges, joint and combined exercises and port calls.

With neighbouring countries, India observes confidence building and dialogue along with defence preparedness as effective ways to improve its periphery security environment and commits to solving all disputes and differences peacefully.[112] In spite of the Kargil War of 1999 and constant tensions with Pakistan, India has continued the bilateral contacts at different levels. Apart from the Lahore Summit (1999), the Agra Summit (2001), and the New Delhi Summit (2005), top leaders from the two sides regularly meet on the sidelines of the international fora. Based on the framework of a "composite and integrated dialogue" unveiled in September 1998, India and Pakistan initiated the Peace Process in January 2004, as mentioned earlier. The eight issues listed on the agenda are as follows: peace and security including confidence-building measures; Jammu and Kashmir; Siachen; Tulbul navigation project; Sir Creek; terrorism and drug trafficking; economic and commercial cooperation; and promotion of friendly exchanges.[113] Since 2004, the two sides have held four rounds of the Composite Dialogue and produced a number of positive results in terms of agreements on nuclear confidence-building measures and normalization of diplomatic relations.[114] With Myanmar, India has a regular institutional dialogue on border management-related matters.[115] With Sri Lanka, "cooperation in operational matters of mutual interest continued through institutionalized consultations such as the Operational Review Talks".[116]

At the multilateral level, India has an increasing interest in regional security cooperation. It is engaging in cooperative security initiatives, such as the ASEAN Regional Forum (ARF).[117] As a member of the ARF, "India sees the ARF as an experiment for fashioning a new pluralistic, cooperative security order in tune with the diversity of the Asia-Pacific region, and in consonance with the transition away from a world characterized by poles built around military alliances".[118] In addition, India became an observer of the Shanghai Cooperation Organization in 2005. In the same year, India joined the East Asian Summit as a founding member. While the thrust of this new pan-Asia forum "is on building free trade area, eventually, its aim is to help evolve an Asian community that will cover strategic (political and security) and cultural aspects of the 'regional architecture'".[119]

Despite the cautious pace and domestic 'knee-jerk resistance', economic diplomacy has become a complementary element of India's national security policy in the post-Cold War era.[120] The aim of India's economic diplomacy is to ensure India's rapid economic growth and safeguard other economic security interests like energy security. There appears to be a national consensus on laying new stress on economics in the making of foreign policy. In its manifesto of 1998, the Congress party stated: in the new situation, "economics, commerce and trade are the new languages of diplomacy. [Our] foreign policy and foreign service...will be refashioned to suit the contemporary world".[121] The BJP also committed "to re-orient Indian diplomacy to [our] economic and commercial goals and to ensure that [our] missions abroad play a more active and supportive role in meeting these".[122] In practice, Indian diplomats are actively engaged in "promoting India as a business destination globally, especially to access foreign investment and key technologies".[123]

India's interest in regional economic cooperation is also growing. India has shown more enthusiasm for such initiatives as the South Asian Free Trade Agreement (SAFTA), the BIMST-EC (Bangladesh, India, Myanmar, Sri Lanka and Thailand Economic Cooperation), IOR-ARC (Indian Ocean Rim Agreement for Regional Cooperation), the Ganga-Mekong Group (including India, Myanmar, Thailand, Laos, Cambodia and Vietnam) and the ASEAN-India dialogue.

Bearing in mind the vital impact of energy security on its entire developmental process, India also observes energy diplomacy as a significant and integral part of its economic diplomacy. The Indian annual defence report of 1999-2000 set several principles for energy diplomacy as follows: (i) working for "mutually beneficial arrangements with India's eastern neighbours as well as Nepal for long-term energy exploitation and sharing"; (ii) promoting cooperation "with other interested parties in protecting the sea-lanes of communication"; (iii) seeking "greater involvement in exploration projects overseas pertaining to oil and gas resources".[124]

4.3 India's China Perspective

In contrast to China's explicit stance towards India, India's post-Cold War perspective on China is ambivalent and complex, much resembling Rajiv Gandhi's era. While a positive and realistic view of China, and a sense that China is not hostile to India but desirous of good relations, have started to gain momentum, the 'China threat' is still haunting India's thinking about China. There are hot debates domestically on how to look at China, therefore, and most Indians seem to drift between two ends: representing China as an ancient sister civilization or as a perennial threat to India.[125] Although such kind of debate has a bearing on India's decision-making with regard to China policy, this book focuses on the official perspective, which reflects the mainstream Indian perceptual position on China in recent years.

In the early days of the post-Cold War era, India saw China as an 'inward looking' power which did not pose an immediate threat to India and with which India should maintain 'a good working relationship'.[126] According to J.N. Dixit, who served as Foreign Secretary of India from 1991 to 1994, India tried to maintain its relations with China "on an even keel".[127] On the one hand, "there is no Indian desire for the revival of any emotional closeness of the type with China which [we] presumed in the late 1940s and early 1950s", nor are there "possibilities of any grand strategic equation between India and China to counter the West or other important centres of power".[128] On the other hand, "competition or confrontation are not elements of [our] policy towards China and they should not be".[129]

As a country with a feeling of being marginalized in world affairs and suffering from both economic crisis and internal riots, India kept alert to China's increasing national strength in all aspects. India was aware that "it is a powerful China in transition that [we] are dealing with". Already being seen as a great political power, "China is firm on nurturing its great power status in economic and military terms". [130] Against this backdrop, the post-Cold War India continued to have a number of security concerns with regard to China, mainly related to China's military build-up and its military relations with Pakistan. As listed in the India's annual defence report of 1997-1998, these concerns include:

- India is conscious of the fact that China is a nuclear weapon state and continues to maintain one of the largest standing armies in the world;
- Its military modernisation programme is rapidly transforming the technological quality and force projection capabilities of its armed forces in all aspects;
- China's assistance to Pakistan's nuclear weapons programme and the sale of missiles and missile technology to Pakistan also directly affect India's security;
- India is aware of military collaboration between China and Myanmar, including the development of strategic lines of communication.[131]

Despite this negative impression, India also noticed that, in order to fully concentrate on its programme of modernization and economic restructuring, China was pursuing a good-neighbourly policy to ensure a peaceful and stable environment in its neighbourhood and in the Asia-Pacific region.[132] Therefore, "While China remains a great and nuclear weapon power, it is perhaps a more inward looking China that [we] are dealing with".[133] China would not be a threat to India at least in the short term, because it desired a "normal stabilised relations" with India to ensure that "developments in the subcontinent or in Tibet do not affect China's stability and security".[134]

On India's part, it was also in the interest of New Delhi to maintain good relations with Beijing. Since the early 1990s, "India too has embarked upon a more liberalised economic programme…(and therefore) needs a peaceful environment in which faster economic growth can be achieved".[135] The Indian annual defence report of 1994-1995 put it in the following way: "Both our nations are concentrating on economic development; hence, peace and tranquility on our common borders is important for both".[136]

Furthermore, along with the evolving international situation, certain parallel interests with regard to various world issues emerged between China and India. According to the then Indian Prime Minister Narasimha Rao, "there are international fora where India and China are working together more or less on the same themes, on the same lines and, therefore, the prospect on that score seems to be quite encouraging".[137] These shared attitudes provided the basis for cooperative and positive relations between them.[138]

In 1996, the Indian President Shankar Dayal Sharma told the visiting Chinese President Jiang Zemin, "India seeks a relationship of constructive co-operation with…China". He said, "friendship between India and China was dictated by the logic of history and the needs of the present". It would not only serve the fundamental interests of both sides but also contribute to the peace and stability both at the regional level as well as the international level. While expressing his satisfaction with the latest trend in India-China relations, he urged to "give a renewed impetus to [our] bilateral trade, economic co-operation and technological collaboration". He also suggested that India and China strengthen cooperation in world affairs and play an active role in the evolution of the international situation. As to the boundary dispute and "other issues on which their positions differed", he insisted on peaceful resolutions through dialogue.[139]

India's annual defence report of 1997-1998 states, "India will continue to engage China through bilateral discussions in a spirit of good neighbourly relations to address all outstanding differences with a view to enhancing mutual understanding and building a relationship of constructive cooperation based on a recognition of India's legitimate security concerns".[140] Along with the speech of Indian President Shankar Dayal Sharma, this statement reflected the then India's perception on China.

What happened during the days of Pokhran II, however, seemed to reflect a dramatic change of India's China perspective. In early May 1998, just a week before the Indian nuclear test, Defence Minister George Fernandes made a series of statements against China. In an interview broadcasted on May 3 by a private television channel, he declared that China was the number one threat to Indian security, greater even than Pakistan. He accused China of implementing a defence strategy that intended to encircle India. To support his argument, he listed several 'facts' as follows:

- China has provided Pakistan with both missile as well as nuclear know-how;
- China has its nuclear weapons stockpiled in Tibet right along India-China borders;
- China has expanded military airfields in Tibet;
- On the eastern frontier, the Chinese have trained and equipped the Myanmarese Army;
- China has also been building a naval base in Myanmar's Coco Islands near the Andamans.

He concluded that China must be perceived as a bigger threat than Pakistan by "any person who is concerned with India's security". In the following days, he indicated the possibility of an antagonistic stance toward China by saying that "our past experience has shown that talks are not enough". His statement, that "[we] need to strengthen [our] borders with China…and there will be no cut in the strength of [our] armed forces in those areas", completely moved away from the spirit of the 1993 and 1996 agreements with China.[141]

The sign of a perception change appeared to be reinforced by the above-mentioned letter of Prime Minister Atal Vajpayee to US President Bill Clinton. The letter was leaked to *The New York Times*, which had it published on May 13, 1998. To quote again:

> I have been deeply concerned at the deteriorating security environment, especially the nuclear environment, faced by India for some years past. We have

> an overt nuclear weapon state on our borders, a state which committed armed aggression against India in 1962. Although our relations with that country have improved in the last decade or so, an atmosphere of distrust persists mainly due to the unresolved border problem. To add to the distrust that country has materially helped another neighbour of ours to become a covert nuclear weapons state. At the hands of this bitter neighbour we have suffered three aggressions in the last 50 years.[142]

George Fernandes' statements and Atal Bihari Vajpayee's letter caused a hot debate both inside and outside India. Different people gave different interpretations. How to read them became a key to define whether there was a perception change or not on the Indian side. Although some still disagree, subsequent developments indicate that, against the backdrop of Pokhran II, they are meant for justifying the nuclear tests rather than amounting to a declaration of perspective change.

Evidence suggested that Fernandes spoke more for himself than for the BJP-led government. Given his sympathies for the movement for Tibetan independence and his long anti-China record, "some sources said that Fernandes was acting to further his own anti-China agenda". Although maintaining a "stoic silence" on his remarks, Prime Minister Vajpayee did rebut Fernandes' earlier claims that China had built helipads on Indian soil. According to officials in the Prime Minister's Office, that initial refutation of Vajpayee "made it clear that the Minister was not speaking for the Government". By criticizing Fernandes' statements as "irresponsible and unfortunate", the opposition parties in India also doubted that it was an official stance and demanded that the BJP-led government "put an end to the confusion the Defence Minister is creating".[143] It also indicated a lack of national consensus on the view expressed by Fernandes.

It is widely believed that the BJP-led government deliberately kept silent, however, because Fernandes' arguments would serve to justify the upcoming nuclear tests. Although it is not clear if Fernandes was informed about the nuclear decision,[144] "it is evident that his aggressive stand helped in shaping a climate in which the decision could be legitimised".[145] As mentioned earlier, after the Cold War, India faced a tightening international non-proliferation regime. The successive Indian governments knew quite clearly what the cost was if India went nuclear. Narasimha Rao eventually withdrew his nuclear decision in 1995 mainly because he feared that the resurgent Indian economy could not afford the inevitable international sanctions.[146] But it might be different if India has a significant and immediate nuclear threat from China.

Viewed in this context, the silence of the BJP-led government appeared to be "part of a well-thought-out strategy of using Fernandes as a signal flare".[147]

Indian Prime Minister Atal Bihari Vajpaypee's letter further displayed the tactical gamble he was playing. As discussed earlier, the major impetus of India's nuclear tests was its dream of becoming a pole in the new world system. The preparations for the nuclear tests were almost through during the leadership of Narasimha Rao, under whom the India-China relations achieved major improvements. If Vajpayee's argument had reason and logic, Narasimha Rao should have taken some position regarding a 'China threat'. There could be two explanations of the contradiction here. One is related to the possibility that Narasimha Rao covertly observed China as an enemy but overtly disguised himself as a friend of China. The other more plausible interpretation is that he did not see any link between India's nuclear weapon programme and China. He regarded both the nuclear programme and good relations with China as effective approaches to India's national security in the post-Cold War era. Therefore, the ostensible links built by Vajpayee between his nuclear decision and the "China threat" do not have a substantial base. As a Chinese analyst said on May 18, 1998, India was just trying to "lessen the blow of sanctions" by demonizing China.[148] What happened in the following months and years has proved that Vajpayee's letter and Fernandes' arguments were only temporary expedients rather than a result of perception change.

Indirectly responding to the confusion caused by Fernandes' anti-China statements and his letter to Clinton, Prime Minister Vajpayee elaborated his stance towards China during his testimony to Rajya Sabha, the upper House of the Indian Parliament, on the nuclear tests on May 29, 1998. It was the first time since Pokhran II that he had made an effort to clarify his China perspective. In his speech, he avoided mentioning the China factor in India's nuclear tests. He just repeated India's traditional concerns regarding territorial security and China's defence cooperation with Pakistan. He urged China to speedily address these concerns of India. To quote him:

> But we have some concerns. We would like the Chinese side to appreciate that our concerns need to be addressed in a meaningful manner with a view to finding early resolution. There are issues relating to India's sovereignty, territorial integrity and security that have been reflected at various levels, including highest levels…On the boundary question, we recognise that a resolution requires time and patience. But progress can, and should, be made…Given Pakistan's approach to India, assistance in the defence field to Pakistan affects India's security directly and adversely. The Chinese side should pay attention to the depth of feeling on the Indian side.[149]

Though Vajpayee's tone was not soft, he admitted the improvement in India-China relations achieved in recent years, especially the significant growth of bilateral trade and economic cooperation. He also said, in the same speech, "we do not seek a confrontation with China...We remain committed to the process of dialogue to resolve outstanding differences and to the development of friendly, cooperative, good neighbourly and mutually beneficial relationship with China".[150]

Two months later, Vajpayee further softened his words on China. He gave a more definite clarification of his China perspective by saying that he did not regard China as an enemy of India. In a statement in the Lok Sabha, the lower House of the Indian Parliament, on August 4, 1998, Vajpayee said India was keen on improving its relations with China and asserted that his government had never dubbed China as an enemy or a threat. In the following months, this stance was reinforced by other official statements at different levels. At the end of 1998, in his first press conference after taking office, Foreign Minister Jaswant Singh stated that India was committed to improving its ties with China so that all outstanding issues were resolved in accordance with the five principles of peaceful co-existence. On February 22, 1999, President K.R. Narayanan told the Indian Parliament that India "seeks to strengthen and deepen its historic and friendly relations with China" and "is looking forward to continuing the dialogue with that country".[151] The annual defence report of 1998-99 released on April 16, 1999, in its section on Sino-Indian relations, observes:

> China is India's largest neighbour. India's relations with China have improved in recent years. India has expressed its interest time and again in resolving the boundary dispute with China peacefully and through bilateral negotiations as quickly as possible. China's assistance to Pakistan's nuclear weapons programme and the transfer of missiles and missile technology to Pakistan affect the security situation in South Asia. India does not regard China as an adversary but as a great neighbour with which it would like to develop mutually beneficial and friendly relations.[152]

In his speech at Peking University during his visit to China in June 2003, Prime Minister Vajpayee stressed the benefits of an India-China partnership. He said, "No objective analysis can deny the combined strength and complementarity of an India-China partnership". As the two most populous countries and the two fastest growing economies in the world, India and China had similar advantages and problems in terms of development. Their strengths in information technology complemented each other. They had overlapping positions on globalization and multilateralism. The two countries had greatly expanded their bilateral trade and economic cooperation and "have made good progress" in "increasing mutual trust and understanding". Their dialogue "already transcends bilateral relations to encompass international issues such as terrorism, security, environment and sustainable development". Calling for a closer cooperation between the two countries, he said, "We should focus on the simple truth that there is no objective reason for discord between us, and neither of us is a threat to the other. These simple, but profound principles should form the bedrock of the future India-China partnership".[153]

Representing India as a friend of China, Indian Prime Minister Manmohan Singh told the press after his meeting with the visiting Chinese President Hu Jintao in New Delhi on November 21, 2006, as follows:

> Following my talks with President Hu today, I am reassured that as India and China move forward towards all-round national progress, friendship will be the underlying theme of our cooperation. We will take strength from our cooperative endeavours. President Hu and I are in full agreement that the prospects are bright for the simultaneous development of India and China. There is enough space for the two countries to develop together in a mutually supportive manner while remaining sensitive to each other's concerns and aspirations, as befits good neighbours and partners for mutual benefit.[154]

4.4 India's Security Perception in Transformation

Much like the development with regard to China since the end of the Cold War, India's security perception has also experienced a great change in the past decade or so. Though commencing somewhat later, advancing in a more gradual manner and bearing unique features, India's perception change has happened in areas similar to that of China's, viz. the definition of threat has been broadened, the security structure has been reorganized and the security approaches have been renewed.

During the Cold War, the successive Indian leaders observed the threats facing India within a narrow prism of purely military and political contexts. Though Nehru did not see any prospect of direct military invasion by the superpowers, he was still convinced that the two-bloc confrontation as well as colonialism and imperialism posed a strategic threat to the newly independent India. This kind of threat carried on both political and military elements. While the remnant political influence of the colonial forces and the political pressure of the superpowers challenged India's independence and sovereignty in a 'soft' way, the military alliances like the SEATO and CENTO pacts constituted an indirect 'hard' threat to India due to the possibility of its responsibility-related interference in the Indo-Pak disputes. With Pakistan being the major military threat to India since Partition, after 1962, China was added to India's top lists of direct threats. During Indira Gandhi's era, India was haunted by a sense of being encircled when it found new threats emerged while old ones strengthened. It believed that the two-front threat was enhanced by the Sino-Pak collaboration since the mid-1960s; the Sino-US alliance in the 1970s and 1980s had a strategic bearing on the India-China disputes; the smaller regional states attempted to counterbalance India by developing military cooperation with the major powers. All these threats, whether old or new, were also affiliated to military and political categories. Trapped in the subcontinent, Rajiv Gandhi still focused on the military and political consequences of the unrest in its neighbourhood, although he noticed the decreasing strategic pressures on India by China in particular and by the Cold War structure in general.

As discussed above, in the early stage of the post-Cold War era, India's threat perception was still confined to the political and military dimensions. As the traditional threats implicitly persisted, what concerned India most after the Cold War was the danger of being marginalized on the world stage. This was a political threat in essence. It was in the mid-1990s that India started to introduce other new-type threats into its security consideration. Recovering from the economic crisis, India realized the implications of economic strength for its national security. In the post-Cold War era, an economically weak country does not have a say in world affairs. At the same time, India also started to pay attention to other non-traditional problems like drug-trafficking, terrorism and organized crime. In recent years, the threats posed by them to India's national security has become more salient, especially when they were combined with those traditional threats facing India.

With a broader definition of threat, the security structure perceived by India has changed considerably. During the Cold War, India, like China and many other countries in the world, proceeded on the assumption that national security had only military and political dimensions. While Nehru and Rajiv Gandhi seemed to view military security and political security with equal importance, Indira Gandhi obviously believed that military security should come ahead of political security. This came as a result of the fact that, during most of her tenures, Indira Gandhi thought India was under intensified two-front military threats from both China and Pakistan. In the early 1990s, India laid more stress on political threat than military threat, because the latter turned into covert from overt while the political marginalization became the primary threat to India. Since the mid-1990s when India started to define threat in a broader sense, new components have been brought into India's security structure. Like China, nowadays, India views national security as a comprehensive issue that includes military, political, economic and other non-traditional elements. What differentiated India from China was the understanding of the sequence of these security categories. As mentioned in Chapter 3, after according priority to economic security in the 1990s, China has upgraded military security to the same level as economic security in recent years. In contrast to China, India has never downgraded the significance of military and political security, but since the mid-1990s it has gradually realized that economic security is just as important as military and political security in the contemporary world.

As the definition of threat was broadened and the security structure was reorganized, the approaches adopted by India to deal with its national security issues have also been expanded since the end of the Cold War. As discussed in Chapter 2, during the most part of the Cold War, India, just like Mao's China, was heavily dependent on alliance security and self-help security to safeguard its national security. After the Cold War, however, India started to adopt comprehensive approaches to security. By emphasizing military and technological self-reliance, India still regards self-help security as a significant approach to security for India in the post-Cold War era. This has been especially manifested in India's decision to go nuclear in defiance of the strong international opposition. A new partnership, which has been gradually replacing non-alignment as another important security approach of India, should be attributed to common security, because it aims at cooperation and dialogue with countries all over the world, including major powers and neighbouring countries, Western countries and the Third World. India's security dialogue and cooperation with major powers, neighbouring countries and regional organizations is a typical instance of cooperative security, which is characterized by various confidence- and security-building measures (CSBMs) including joint training exercises, demilitarization of common borders, exchange programmes of military personnel, etc. Representing a dimension beyond military, economic diplomacy is a comprehensive security adopted by India as a new way to deal with its security problems since the end of the Cold War. As India's quasi-military alliance with the Soviet Union became history due to the latter's disintegration and these new approaches started to gain momentum, alliance security has basically been deleted from the list of India's approaches to security.

As its security perception has transformed in general, India's China perspective has changed in particular since the end of the Cold War. Except the brief India-China 'honeymoon', when Nehru regarded China as a friend, the lengthy Cold War witnessed the fact that China was dubbed as a major enemy of India. Haunted by the humiliation of its defeat in the 1962 war with China, India thought that China's proximity to Pakistan, its later alliance with the United States, and its pursuit of nuclear weapons and missile capacities, were all India-directed. India even believed that there was a Chinese 'conspiracy' to seek China's dominance in Asia by reducing India's position to a state of subordination. It was Rajiv Gandhi who started to reconsider India's China policy during his tenure. Against the backdrop of Sino-Soviet rapprochement and China's dedication to economic reform, Rajiv Gandhi narrowed down the prediction of an India-China confrontation but saw a prospect of both cooperation and competition between them.

In the early 1990s, India viewed China as an inward-looking power which did not pose an immediate threat to India. A good working relationship with China was thought to serve the interests of the similarly inward-looking India at that time. As it started to take a more comprehensive security perception in the mid-1990s, India saw more opportunities than challenges in its relations with China. It expected a constructive cooperation with China, both at the bilateral level and on the multilateral fora. Although some Indian top leaders, such as then Defence Minister and Prime Minister warned against the 'China threat' in 1998, it was not a manifestation of a return of India to its negative China perspective in the Cold War period but a tactical attempt to justify India's nuclear tests. As history has witnessed, shortly after the Pokhran II, the Vajpayee government reiterated India's commitment to the development of a friendly, cooperative, good neighbourly and mutually beneficial relationship with China. Entering the 21st century, India regards China as a partner rather than an adversary. Although there are still some old security concerns regarding China, such as its military build-up and its military relations with Pakistan, India is adopting approaches beyond military confrontation towards solving these outstanding differences with China.

Notes

1. At the end of 1998, the BJP-led coalition NDA government collapsed due to the AIADMK, one of the coalition partners, pulling out. It proceeded to win the 1999 elections with a greater majority and new alliances. It formed a new government with Atal Bihari Vajpayee again as Prime Minister.
2. C. Raja Mohan, *Crossing the Rubicon: The Shaping of India's New Foreign Policy* (New Delhi: Penguin-Viking, 2003), p. 11.
3. *Annual Report 1992-93* (New Delhi: Ministry of Defence, Government of India, 1993), p. 1.
4. J.N. Dixit, *India's Foreign Policy 1947-2003,* updated edition (New Delhi: Picus Books, 2003), pp. 223-224.
5. *Annual Report 1992-93*: 8.
6. Dixit, *India's Foreign Policy* 1947-2003, p. 225.
7. *Annual Report 1991-92* (New Delhi: Ministry of Defence, Government of India, 1992), p. 3.
8. Ibid, pp. 3-4.
9. *Annual Report 1994-95* (New Delhi: Ministry of Defence, Government of India, 1995), 1.
10. *Annual Report 1996-97* (New Delhi: Ministry of Defence, Government of India, 1997), 7.
11. India and Bangladesh had had a dispute on the sharing of the waters of the Gangetic basin for decades. Stress and strain arose in the Indo-Bangladesh relations when the Ganges water issue was internationalized and raised at the UN General Assembly by Bangladesh prior to its being amicably settled in 1996. See Padmaja Murthy, 'India and Its Neighbours: The 1990s and Beyond', *Strategic Analysis,* New Delhi, Vol. XXIV, No. 8 (November 2000), also available at http://www.ciaonet.org/olj/sa/sa_nov00mup01.html. For details, also see (MEA) *Annual Report (1993-94)* (New Delhi: Ministry of External Affairs, Government of India, 1994).
12. After the withdrawal of the Indian Peace Keeping Force (IPKF) from the island-nation of Sri Lanka early in 1990, the ethnic conflict between Tamil and Sinhalese continued. The instability in Sri Lanka continued to put India in a dilemma since India had to take the sensitivities of its own Tamil population into consideration. Moreover, due to the prevailing Tamil insurgency, Sri Lanka "has developed some sort of reservation with respect to India". R.S. Siwach, 'The Strategic Environment of South Asia and India's Security', in *India's Security in 21st Century: Challenges & Responses,* ed. Rajendra Prasad (New Delhi: Dominant Publishers and Distributors, 2002), 315; J.N. Dixit, *India's Foreign Policy and its Neighbours* (New Delhi: Gyan Publishing House, 2001), pp. 271-304.
13. According to Indian annual defence report of 1991-92, some reports indicated that there were "growing links between the Myanmar Army and some insurgent organisations in the North Eastern part" of India. *(Annual Report 1991-92: 7)* The annual defence report of 1994-95 stated, "Indian insurgent groups in the North-Eastern states continue to use the border areas of Myanmar for

sanctuary, training and import of arms." *(Annual Report 1994-95:* 4*)*

14. Mira Sinha Bhattacharjea, *China, the World and India* (New Delhi: Samskriti, 2001), p. 390.
15. *Annual Report 1991-92*: 5.
16. Mohan, *Crossing the Rubicon,* p. 3.
17. Lalit Mansingh, 'Foreign Policy Imperatives for a Post-Nuclear India', in *Emerging India: Security and Foreign Policy Perspectives,* eds. N.S. Sisodia and C. Uday Bhaskar (New Delhi: Institute for Defence Studies and Analyses, 2005), p. 43.
18. Mohan, *Crossing the Rubicon,* p. 12.
19. Ibid, pp. 30, 38.
20. Dixit, *India's Foreign Policy 1947-2003,* p. 226.
21. M.S. Rajan, *India and International Affairs* (New Delhi: Lancers Books, 1999), p. 133.
22. *Annual Report 1995-96* (New Delhi: Ministry of Defence, Government of India, 1996), pp. 2-3.
23. *Annual Report 1994-95*: 2
24. "In early 1991 a crisis engulfed India. A high fiscal deficit, overdue payments to the International Monetary Fund, and Gulf War-precipitated soaring oil prices reduced India's foreign currency assets to $1 billion, barely enough to cover two weeks of imports." Tarun Khanna, *Billions of Entrepreneurs* (New Delhi: Penguin-Viking, 2008), p. 94.
25. Dixit, *India's Foreign Policy 1947-2003,* pp. 225, 237.
26. Ibid, p. 230.
27. Mohan, *Crossing the Rubicon,* p. 59.
28. Mansingh, 'Foreign Policy Imperatives for a Post-Nuclear India', p. 45.
29. C. Uday Bhaskar, 'Concept Note', in *Emerging India: Security and Foreign Policy Perspectives,* eds. Sisodia et al., p. xx.
30. *Annual Report 2007-2008* (New Delhi: Ministry of Defence, Government of India, 2008), p. 2.
31. Manmohan Singh, "Prime Minister's Speech on the Occasion of 60th Anniversary of India's Independence," August 15, 2007, New Delhi, available at http://pmindia.nic.in/speeches.htm.
32. *Annual Report 2000-2001* (New Delhi: Ministry of Defence, Government of India, 2001), p. 7.
33. Congress (Indian National Congress), 'Security Agenda: Security, Defence and Foreign Policy', *Congress* Sandesh, May 2004, available at http://www.congresssandesh.com/may-2004/securityagenda.html.
34. Sanjaya Baru, *Strategic Consequences of India's Economic Performance* (New Delhi: Academic Foundation, 2006), p. 26.
35. Yashwant Sinha, *Facets of Indian Foreign Policy: Statements and Media Interaction (February-November 2003),* Vol. II (New Delhi: Ministry of External Affairs, Government of India, 2003), pp. 480, 492-494.
36. *Annual Report 1999-2000* (New Delhi: Ministry of Defence, Government of India, 2000), p. 10.
37. Ibid, pp. 6, 10-11.

38. *Annual Report 1994-95*: 1.
39. *Annual Report 1997-98* (New Delhi: Ministry of Defence, Government of India, 1998), p. 7.
40. *Annual Report 2003-2004* (New Delhi: Ministry of Defence, Government of India, 2004), p. 7.
41. Ibid, pp. 6-8.
42. *Annual Report 2001-2002* (New Delhi: Ministry of Defence, Government of India, 2002), p. 13.
43. *Annual Report 2004-2005* (New Delhi: Ministry of Defence, Government of India, 2005), p. 8.
44. *Annual Report 1999-2000*: 11.
45. As a result, bus services between Srinagar and Muzaffarabad and between Amritsar and Lahore commenced respectively on 7 April 2005 and 20 January 2006. The Khokrapar-Munabao rail link resumed on 18 February 2006. The Poonch-Rawalakot bus service began on 20 June 2006.
46. *Annual Report 2004-2005*: 10.
47. Ibid.
48. Ibid, p. 13. Also see *Annual Report 2006-2007* (New Delhi: Ministry of Defence, Government of India, 2007), pp. 5-6.
49. *Annual Report 2002-2003* (New Delhi: Ministry of Defence, Government of India, 2003), p. 10.
50. Baru, *Strategic Consequences of India's Economic Performance*, p. 27.
51. See India's annual defence reports since 1997-98.
52. Bharatiya Janata Party, *Vision Document 2004,* March 31, 2004, available at http://www.bjp.org/Press/mar_3104a.htm.
53. National Democratic Alliance, *For A Proud, Prosperous India: An Agenda,* 1999, available at http://www.bjp.org/manifes/manifest99.htm.
54. Congress, *'Security Agenda: Security, Defence and Foreign Policy'.*
55. Mohan, *Crossing the Rubicon,* p. 12.
56. Bharatiya Janata Party, *Vision Document 2004.*
57. Atal Bihari Vajpayee, 'Address by Prime Minister Atal Bihari Vajpayee at the India Economic Summit-1998', organised by the World Economic Forum and the Confederation of Indian Industry, November 29, 1998, available at http://www.indianembassy.org/special/cabinet/Primeminister/pm(indiaeconomicsummit).htm.
58. National Democratic Alliance, *For A Proud, Prosperous India: An Agenda.*
59. Bharatiya Janata Party, *Vision Document 2004.*
60. National Democratic Alliance, *An Agenda for Development, Good Governance, Peace, and Harmony,* April 8, 2004, available at http://www.bjp.org/Press/NDA Agenda.htm.
61. Baru, *Strategic Consequences of India's Economic Performance,* p. 26.
62. Mohan, *Crossing the Rubicon,* p. 53.
63. Baru, *Strategic Consequences of India's Economic Performance,* p. 27.
64. Bharatiya Janata Party, *Vision Document 2004.*

65. Congress (Indian National Congress), 'Salient Points of Previous Manifestos', 1991-1996, available at http://www.aicc.org.in/documents-detail.php?id=2.
66. National Democratic Alliance, *For a Proud, Prosperous India: An Agenda;* Congress, 'Security Agenda: Security, Defence and Foreign Policy'.
67. *Annual Report 2002-2003*: 2.
68. Read it as security here.
69. Atal Bihari Vajpayee, 'India's Experience has taught that Peace Lies in Strength', *International Herald Tribune,* September 21, 2000, also available at http://www.iht.com/articles/2000/09/21/edvajpay.t.php.
70. Congress (Indian National Congress), 'Manifesto-2004', *Congress Sandesh,* April 2004, available at http://www.congresssandesh.com/manifesto-2004/17.html.
71. *Annual Report 1999-2000:* 3, 11-12.
72. Vajpayee, 'Address by Prime Minister Atal Bihari Vajpayee at the India Economic Summit-1998'.
73. Baru, *Strategic Consequences of India's Economic Performance,* pp. 26-27.
74. Ibid, p. 27.
75. Ibid.
76. United Progressive Alliance, *National Common Minimum Programme of The Government of India,* May 2004, available at http://pmindia.nic.in/cmp.pdf.
77. 'CPI(M) for Wider India-China-Russia Cooperation', *The Hindu,* September 18, 2005, also available at http://www.hinduonnet.com/2005/09/18/stories/2005091807080800.htm.
78. *Annual Report 1997-98*: 2.
79. United Progressive *Alliance, National Common Minimum Programme of The Government of India,* p. 22.
80. Bharatiya Janata Party, *Vision Document 2004;* National Democratic Alliance, *An Agenda for Development, Good Governance, Peace, and Harmony.*
81. *Annual Report 1997-98*: 2.
82. Baru, *Strategic Consequences of India's Economic Performance,* p. 27.
83. Manmohan Singh, 'Prime Minister's Address to the Nation', June 24, 2004, New Delhi, available at http://pmindia.nic.in/speech/content.asp?id=3.
84. Mohan, *Crossing the Rubicon,* p. 11.
85. Atal Bihari Vajpayee, 'Address to the Nation by Prime Minister Vajpayee on the Launching of Agni-II', New Delhi, April 11, 1999, available at http://www.indianembassy.org/special/cabinet/Primeminister/pm_apr_11_1999.htm.
86. George Perkovich, *India's Nuclear Bomb: The Impact on Global Proliferation,* (New Delhi: Oxford University Press, 2000), pp. 353-354, 404.
87. Bharatiya Janata Party, *BJP Election Manifesto '98,* Chapter 8, 1998, available at http://www.bjp.org/manifes/manifes.htm.
88. Ibid.
89. Congress, 'Security Agenda: Security, Defence and Foreign Policy'.
90. For details, see *Annual Report 1999-2000:* 11. Also see *Annual Report 2007-2008:* 80-97.

91. *Annual Report 2003-2004:* 72.
92. Atal Bihari Vajpayee, 'Prime Minister's Independence Day Address', New Delhi, August 15, 1998, available at http://pib.nic.in/focus/foyr98/fo0899/fo1508983.html.
93. K. Subrahmanyam, 'Partnership in a Balance of Power System', Strategic Analysis, New Delhi, Vol.29, No.4 (Oct-Dec 2005): 551.
94. Manmohan Singh, 'Prime Minister's Address to the Nation'.
95. Mohan, *Crossing the Rubicon,* p. 47.
96. Bharatiya Janata Party, *BJP Election Manifesto '98,* Chapter 7.
97. Congress, 'Manifesto-2004'.
98. I.K. Gujral, *A Foreign Policy for India* (New Delhi: Ministry of External Affairs, 1998), pp. 74-75.
99. Congress, "Manifesto-2004".
100. The 'Look East' policy was launched by the then Narasimha Rao government in 1992. Initially, this policy was aimed at increasing India's economic and political interaction with the so-called economic 'tigers' of South East Asia. Later, it was extended to encompass the entire Asia-Pacific region and became a vital part of India's foreign policy. According to Prime Minister Manmohan Singh, the 'Look East' policy "was not merely an external economic policy, it was also a strategic shift in India's vision of the world and India's place in the evolving global economy". See Manmohan Singh, 'Prime Minister Manmohan Singh's Speech Inaugurating The Asia Society's 16th Asian Corporate Conference', Mumbai, March 18, 2006, available at http://inhome.rediff.com/money/2006/mar/18asoc.htm.
101. *Annual Report 2000-2001*:12.
102. Surjit Mansingh, *India's Search for Power: Indira Gandhi's Foreign Policy 1966-1982* (New Delhi: Sage Publications, 1984), p. 16.
103. Atal Bihari Vajpayee, 'India, USA and the World: Let Us Work Together to Solve the Political-Economic Y2K Problem', Prime Minister Atal Bihari Vajpayee's Speech at the Asia Society, New York, September 28, 1998, available at http://www.indianembassy.org/special/cabinet/Primeminister/pm(asiasociety).htm.
104. Lalit Mansingh, 'Indo-US Strategic Partnership: Are We There Yet?' *IPCS Issue Brief 39* (October 2006): 5, available at http://www.ipcs.org/countIssueBrief.jsp?issue=39.
105. Amit Baruah, 'A Chance to Take Centre Stage', *The Hindu,* May 13, 2005.
106. *Annual Report 2003-2004*: 14.
107. Subrahmanyam, 'Partnership in a Balance of Power System', pp. 551-552.
108. Ibid, p. 184.
109. Ibid, pp. 198-199; *Annual Report 1999-2000*: 14.
110. *Annual Report 2003-2004*: 196.
111. Ibid, pp. 185-186.
112. Ibid, p. 2.
113. B. Muralidhar Reddy, 'India, Pakistan Exchange Proposals', *The Hindu,* February 17, 2004.

114. For details, see MEA *Annual Report since 2005.*
115. *Annual Report 2000-2001*: 11.
116. *Annual Report 2003-2004*: 191.
117. *Annual Report 1997-98*: 2.
118. *Annual Report 2000-2001*: 16.
119. S.D. Muni, 'East Asia Summit and India', *ISAS Working Paper,* No.13 (October 3, 2006), available at http://www.isn.ethz.ch/pubs/ph/details.cfm?lng=en&id =25443.
120. Baru, *Strategic Consequences of India's Economic Performance,* p. 70.
121. Congress (Indian National Congress), *Election Manifesto for the 1998 Lok Sabha Elections,* 1998, available at http://www.aicc.org.in/manifesto-1998.php.
122. Bharatiya Janata Party, *BJP Election Manifesto '98,* Chapter 7.
123. Sinha, *Facets of Indian Foreign Policy,* p. 274.
124. *Annual Report 1999-2000*: 10.
125. Some within the Indian strategic community have argued that China did not have the intention to antagonize India but desired good relations and a strategic partnership with India. The Sino-Pakistan relations, including the security and nuclear arrangements in the past, should be seen more as strategic responses of China to the then Sino-Soviet rivalry and other challenges to its internal security than as India-directed moves. The most important lesson learnt from the past was that the two neighbours must make peace not war. Cooperation between India and China was indeed a historical necessity. For further details about the positive view of China, please refer to Bhattacharje, *China, the World and India;* Ranganathan et al., *India and China: The Way Ahead; Giri Deshingkar, Security and Science in China and India* (New Delhi: Samskriti, 2005). However, some others within the same community argued that China was a country determined to seek hegemony in Asia and to therefore keep India confined to South Asia. China was definitely practicing strategic encirclement of India and enabling Pakistan to threaten India. Clearly, China was a long-term strategic threat to India. India should develop adequately military strength and powerful leverages to deter China from continuing its 'mischief'. For details about the negative view of China, please refer to Brahma Chellaney (ed.), *Securing India's Future in the New Millennium* (New Delhi: Orient Longman, 1999), pp. 141-222, 313-336; Bharat Karnad, *Nuclear Weapons & Indian Security: The Realist Foundations of Strategy* (New Delhi: Macmillan, 2002); Gurmeet Kanwal, 'India's National Security Strategy in a Nuclear Environment', *Strategic Analysis,* New Delhi, Vol. XXIV, No. 9 (December 2000): 1591-1628.
126. Dixit, *India's Foreign Policy and its Neighbours,* pp. 227, 223.
127. Ibid, p. 239.
128. Ibid, pp. 243, 223.
129. Ibid, p. 239.
130. Ibid, p. 243.
131. *Annual Report 1997-98*: 2. Also see the annual defence reports from 1991 to 1997.

132. Dixit, *India's Foreign Policy and Its Neighbours,* pp. 226, 243.
133. Ibid, p. 227.
134. Ibid, p. 239.
135. V.P. Dutt, 'India-China: Promise and Limitation', in *Indian Foreign Policy: Agenda for the 21st Century,* Vol. II, eds. Lalit Mansingh et al., (New Delhi: Konark Publishers and Foreign Service Institute, 1998), p. 235.
136. *Annual Report 1994-95*: 3.
137. P.V. Narasimha Rao, *Selected Speeches 1992-93,* Vol. II (New Delhi: Publications Division, Ministry of Information and Broadcasting, Government of India, 1994), p. 402.
138. Dixit, *India's Foreign Policy and Its Neighbours,* p. 224.
139. 'India Ready to Work For A Fair and Reasonable Solution to Border Dispute with China', *UNI,* 1996, available at http://www.rediff.com/news/1996/2811chin.htm.
140. *Annual Report 1997-98*: 2.
141. Praveen Swami, 'A Hawkish Line on China', *Frontline,* Vol.15, No.11 (May 23-June 5, 1998), also available at http://www.hinduonnet.com/fline/fl1511/15111050.htm.
142. Atal Bihari Vajpayee, 'Nuclear Anxiety: India's Letter to Clinton on Nuclear Testing', *New York Times,* May 13, 1998.
143. Swami, 'A Hawkish Line on China'.
144. Some accounts claimed that he was informed of the decision just 10 minutes before the Prime Minister made the announcement. See Swami 'A Hawkish Line on China'; Mohan, *Crossing the Rubicon,* pp. 292-293.
145. Swami, 'A Hawkish Line on China'.
146. Mohan, *Crossing the Rubicon,* pp. 6-7.
147. Swami, 'A Hawkish Line on China'.
148. Cited in B. Raman, 'Sino-Indian Relations: A Chronology', *South Asia Analysis Group Papers,* April 23, 1999, available at http://www.saag.org/papers/paper49.html.
149. Atal Bihari Vajpayee, 'Prime Minister's Reply to The Discussion in Rajya Sabha on Nuclear Tests', May 29, 1998, available at http://www.indianembassy.org/pic/pm(rs).htm.
150. Ibid.
151. Raman, 'Sino-Indian Relations: A Chronology'.
152. *Annual Report 1998-99* (New Delhi: Ministry of Defence, Government of India, 1999), p. 2.
153. 'Speech by Prime Minister of India Shri Atal Bihari Vajpayee at Peking University, 23 June 2003," *China Report,* Vol. 39, No.4 (November 2003): pp. 583-586.
154. 'PM's Statement at Press Interaction with Chinese President', New Delhi, November 21, 2006; also see 'India and China in the 21st Century', Speech by Prime Minister Dr. Manmohan Singh at the Chinese Academy of Social Sciences, Beijing, January 15, 2008, available at http://www.meaindia.nic.in/.

5

Perception Change and the Transformation of China-India Relations Since 1991

Treating each other as new partners rather than adversaries and acknowledging the need for comprehensive approaches to national security, both China and India have accordingly adjusted their respective policies toward each other since the end of the Cold War. Irrespective of their specific expectations from this relationship, both countries converged on the understanding that a stable and cooperative relationship between them would best serve their respective national interests in the post-Cold War era. Therefore, since 1991, the China-India relationship has experienced an impressive transformation, from normalization to partnership.

The last decade of the 20th century witnessed the two countries emerging from their three-decade cold relationship and replacing it with a normal one. Normal relations mean no war or military tension between two countries. Since the end of the Cold War, the China-India border areas have enjoyed continuous peace and tranquility. Both have been committed to solving their differences through dialogue. Normal relations also mean regular contacts and stable links in political, economic, cultural and social aspects, which would exempt their relationship from tension. Frequent exchange of high-level visits and increasing economic and cultural contacts since 1991 have demonstrated the degree of normalization of China-India relations.

In spite of the brief hiatus after Pokhran II, the Indian nuclear tests did not derail the China-India relations. This provides a strong verification of this book's major hypothesis that perceptions construct relations. If there were no perception changes in China or India, there would be no change of their relationship, and vice versa. Walking out of the shadow of India's nuclear tests, China-India relations have entered a new stage of comprehensive cooperation and the establishment of a strategic partnership.

5.1 Perceptible Improvements in China-India Relations Preceding Pokhran II (1991-April 1998)

5.1(1) China's India Policy

Against the backdrop of the perception change on its national security in general and with respect to India specifically, China has adopted unwavering efforts to promote more friendly and stable relations with India since the end of the Cold War. From 1991 to the eve of India's nuclear tests, China undertook a series of steps in this regard. These were: promoting political proximity between China and India by virtue of the bilateral economic cooperation and cultural exchange; exploiting CBMs and security dialogues to increase mutual trust and to create a congenial atmosphere for the resolution of the China-India boundary dispute; maintaining even-handedness in its relations with Pakistan and India; and, urging India to keep its promises on the Tibet issue through low-level political pressure.

As mentioned in Chapter 2, it was Deng Xiaoping's belief that economic cooperation could promote political normalization. This was manifested in his proposal to de-link the improvement in China-India relations from their border dispute. During his talk with the Indian delegation in 1982, he suggested, "[E]ven if the border question cannot be resolved for the time being, we can leave it as it is for a while. We still have many things to do in the fields of trade, the economy and culture and can still increase our exchanges so as to promote understanding and friendship between us".[1] India, however, did not accept this proposal until 1988. After the Cold War, according the priority to economic security and seeking a peaceful environment for its economic development, China was keen on good relations with India. In view of the slight possibility of solving their boundary problem immediately, the Chinese leadership of the new generation upheld Deng Xiaoping's approach. They preferred to shelve the border dispute and promote China-India friendship by establishing economic, technological and cultural interactions. Great achievements in this regard during Li Peng's 1991 visit to India included the reopening of border trade, cooperation on space research, and India's commitment to "a dynamic increase and diversification of exchanges in the economic field, including trade".[2]

To shelve the China-India boundary dispute has reflected the principles China has observed towards the international disputes since the end of the Cold War. As discussed in Chapter 3, these principles include resolving all international disputes by peaceful means, preventing normal state-to-state relations from being held hostage to disputes, postponing the resolution of the disputes till conditions are ripe for peaceful settlement, and taking security and confidence-building measures to increase mutual trust. However, this did not mean that China wanted to freeze its border talks with India. On the contrary, China was convinced that more efforts should be made to create the right atmosphere for an early resolution of its boundary dispute with India. During Li Peng's 1991 visit to India, China agreed that the Sino-Indian Joint Working Group on the Boundary Question (JWG) should step up its work in search of "an earliest-possible solution", on the one hand; and that both sides should explore certain CBMs in the area along the LAC pending a final settlement in order to avoid any crisis caused by misunderstanding, on the other.[3]

As a part of its omnidirectional and good-neighbourly policy, China has adjusted its South Asian policy as well and tried to take a more even-handed approach in its relations with Pakistan and India. During the Cold War, the Sino-Pakistan 'all-weather friendship' and the Sino-Indian antagonism made China usually take a pro-Pakistani position on issues related to the Indo-Pakistan confrontation.[4] After the Cold War, as China replaced the 'comradeship-plus-brotherhood' with the new-type partnership as the basis of its national security policy, China started to move away from its Pakistan-preferred stance and to take a more neutral position on issues such as Kashmir.

During his 1991 visit to New Delhi, Premier Li Peng told reporters, "China is willing to maintain and develop friendly relations with India, Pakistan, and all countries in South Asian on the basis of the Five Principles of Peaceful Coexistence".[5] The real message here was that China wanted Sino-Pakistan and Sino-Indian relations to be independent of each other. In other words, better ties between China and India should not affect China's links with Pakistan, and China's existing friendship and cooperation with Pakistan should not block the improvement of Sino-Indian relations, nor should it be seen as directed against any third country, i.e. India. During his visit to Pakistan after he concluded his Indian trip in December 1996, President Jiang Zemin told the Pakistani Senate that if the Kashmir issue could not be resolved immediately, then it should be put on the back burner and South Asia should concentrate on economic cooperation. This was read by India as a great shift of the Chinese position on Kashmir, "from an aggressively pro-Pakistani position on self-determination for Kashmiris in the 1970s to an emphasis on Indo-Pakistani bilateralism in the 1990s."[6]

The Tibet issue has been a significant element in China-India relations. India's constant support for Tibetan 'autonomy' and its explicit or implicit support since 1959 for the Dalai Lama and the so-called *Tibetan Government-in-Exile,* the Tibetan 'splittists' in Chinese eyes, have been a great concern of

China in its relations with India. As a result, "[T]he essence of Beijing's policy toward India regarding Tibet has been to apply pressure to compel India to desist from policies and actions that work counter to China's control over Tibet".[7] During the era when the two countries antagonized each other, the major modalities of pressure included strong diplomatic protests and military deterrent. To stop "an Indian effort to turn Tibet into a buffer" was perceived as a major cause of China's involvement in the 1962 war.[8]

After the Cold War, as China was keen on a good relationship with India and saw security dialogue as an effective approach to its national security, China started to confine itself to low-level political pressure on India with regard to the Tibet issue. Article Six of the 1991 *Sino-Indian Joint Communiqué* reflected the key points of the new China's India policy regarding Tibet. First, China declared that "it was firmly opposed to any attempt and action aimed at splitting China and bringing about 'independence of Tibet'". Second, the expressions of their respective stance on this issue were a manifestation of China's tolerance toward the China-India difference on the Tibet issue. As long as India did not challenge China's sovereignty over Tibet, China would not allow the Tibet issue to stand in the way in the improvement of China-India relations. From 1991 to the eve of Pokhran II, although China kept the Tibet issue on the agenda of every high-level meeting between top leaders of the two countries, China shunned public protests about actions which it perceived as a violation of its commitments by India.

5.1(2) India's China Policy

As discussed in Chapter 4, although India continued to adhere in many ways to its traditional approaches to national security in the early 1990s, it saw China in positive terms due to the latter's inward-looking inclination. Suffering multifaceted challenges both externally and internally, India expected a practical and stable, i.e. a good working relationship with China. Bearing this objective in mind, India made the following adjustments in its China policy: trying to ensure that the improvement of bilateral relations would lead to the resolution of the boundary dispute; keeping a low profile on the Tibet issue; leaving the door open for discussion of each other's security concerns; and "emulating China"[9] in order to restore the balance with China.

For years during the Cold War, New Delhi refused to normalize relations with Beijing before they had settled the boundary question. It insisted that a border agreement had to precede the restoration of bilateral relations. As mentioned earlier, it was Rajiv Gandhi who chose to "end India's unrealistic

China policy" and "moved towards a normalization of relations with China and found a framework to accelerate the negotiations on the boundary dispute at the same time".[10] After the Cold War, while the successive Indian governments continued Rajiv Gandhi's policy towards China, i.e. moving ahead with cooperation elsewhere despite the unresolved boundary question, they emphasized the imperative of tackling the issue as early as possible. Despite the awareness that the resolution of the difficult boundary question would take time, India now and then showed some uneasiness about the 'slow' process. As J.N. Dixit warned, the lack of "tangible results" might remove the credibility of the boundary discussions "in both Indian and Chinese public opinion".[11] The Indian leaders also conceived that the development of bilateral relations should not be totally de-linked from the border dispute. However, the former should lead to the latter. "The expectation being that multifaceted and contentful relations will generate mutual trust and educate public opinion in both countries, which will enable the resolution of the complex boundary question. The question has been shelved for practical purposes, but it has to be tackled. It cannot be wished away," J.N. Dixit argued.[12]

From the Indian perspective, articles, relating to stepping up the process to resolve the border issue, in the three significant documents signed with China in the 1990s represented the major achievements of India in its interaction with China.[13] These agreements are: *Sino-Indian Joint Communiqué* signed on 16 December 1991, *Agreement Between the Government of the People's Republic of China and the Government of the Republic of India on the Maintenance of Peace and Tranquility Along the Line of Actual Control in the China-India Border Areas*[14] signed on 7 September 1993, *Agreement Between the Government of the People's Republic of China and the Government of the Republic of India on Confidence-Building Measures in the Military Field Along the Line of Actual Control in the China-India Border Areas*[15] signed on 29 November 1996. Article 5 of the 1991 Joint Communiqué states:

> The leaders of the two countries reiterated that efforts would be made to arrive at an early and mutually acceptable solution to the boundary question through friendly consultations. Both sides believed that the talks held so far by the Sino-Indian Joint Working Group on the Boundary Question had enhanced mutual understanding and agreed that the group should step up its work in search of an earliest-possible solution to the boundary question.

Article X of the 1996 Agreement stipulates:

> Recognizing that the full implementation of some of the provisions of the present Agreement will depend on the two sides arriving at a common understanding of the alignment of the line of actual control in the China-India border areas, the two sides agree to speed up the process of clarification and confirmation of the line of actual control. As an initial step in this process, they are clarifying the alignment of the line of actual control in those segments where they have different perceptions. They also agree to exchange maps indicating their respective perceptions of the entire alignment of the line of actual control as soon as possible.

Viewing Tibet as an area affecting India's security, India provided an active support for Tibetan 'autonomy' during the Cold War. Three distinct periods of policy can be identified as follows: (i) From 1947 to 1951, New Delhi attempted to boost the international status of the local Tibetan government and pressured Beijing not to move militarily into Tibet; (ii) From 1954 to 1958, New Delhi tried to persuade Beijing to grant Tibet a substantial degree of autonomy and to minimize its military presence in Tibet by convincing Beijing that there was no need to do otherwise and that India-China friendship would thereby prosper;(iii) From 1959 to the mid-1980s, New Delhi openly supported Tibetan rebellion and mobilized international pressure on China in Tibet.[16] In hopes of fostering better relations with China, Rajiv Gandhi agreed to restrain anti-China activities by Tibetans in India during his 1988 visit to Beijing.

After the Cold War, although successive governments in New Delhi were convinced that keeping a low profile on the Tibet issue would best serve the national interests of India, the different perceptions regarding Tibetan 'autonomy' continued to exist between India and China.[17] As a result, India tried to find a balance between accommodating Beijing's demands to restrict Tibetan exile activities and condoning exile efforts to mobilize international pressure on Beijing to reach a political settlement of the Tibet issue.[18] On the one hand, during the bilateral high-level exchanges since 1988, the Indian government kept repeating its commitments that Tibet was an autonomous region of China and that anti-China political activities by Tibetan elements were not permitted on Indian soil. On the ground, the *Tibetan Government-in-Exile* in India felt that "restrictions imposed by the Indian government increased as Beijing and New Delhi maneuvered to improve ties in the 1980s and 1990s".[19] On the other hand, as some Indian scholars pointed out, "it is not possible for India" to completely accommodate China's wishes.[20] It was convinced that the best result for India "would be a dialogue between Beijing and the Dalai Lama leading to his return and that of his followers to Tibet to a life of dignity, safety, religious and cultural freedom, with His Holiness enjoying the respect and status which are his due".[21]

As mentioned in Chapter 4, in the early 1990s, although India no longer considered China as an immediate threat, it continued to uphold traditional security concerns regarding China's military build-up and the military cooperation between China and Pakistan. During Mrs. Gandhi's era, India laid stress on both self-help and alliance in dealing with these security problems. After the Cold War, as its security perception gradually changed, India started to see security dialogue and cooperation as an important approach to security. Since India expected a good working relationship with China, dialogue with China became the best way for India to address these concerns without sacrificing the bilateral relations. As J.N. Dixit argued, "[O]ur relations should be mature and balanced enough for both sides to be able to candidly articulate concerns about each other's policies and attitudes on specific usuals like Tibet, Sino-Pak defence cooperation, and to see how they can be overcome. We should be able to caution China about the negative implications of its arms supplies to and nuclear cooperation with Pakistan. The Chinese should be able to voice their concerns about Tibet without getting impatient or offended about it."[22]

In the early days of the post-Cold War era, while India was embarrassed by the fact of being marginalized in the international system, China continued to progress on the way which led to the world power status. Consequently, India appeared to be left far behind. In order to effectively safeguard its territorial security and fulfill its decades-long aspiration to be a major power, India chose to emulate China, and "restoring the balance with China became an unstated national strategic objective for India during the 1990s".[23] In other words, India expected that this emulation would not only help narrow the gap of national strength between India and China but also enable India to acquire an international standing equal to China. As a result, focusing on economic modernization and keeping a low international political profile became the central themes of security policy of Narasimha Rao's government.[24]

5.1(3) Perceptible Improvements in China-India Relations

From 1991 to the eve of India's nuclear tests in 1998, there was"a steady and substantial improvement in India-China relations".[25] Frequent exchange of high-level visits helped reinforce understanding and expand cooperation between the two countries. A series of Confidence-Building Measures were instituted and contributed to peace and tranquility in the China-India border areas. Increasing bilateral contacts in various areas such as trade, technology and culture provided China-India relations with a multifaceted character.

High-level Sino-Indian exchanges became routine during this period. Three landmark visits among them were: Chinese Premier Li Peng's visit to India in December 1991, Indian Prime Minister Narasimha Rao's visit to China in September 1993, and Chinese President Jiang Zemin's visit to India in November 1996. Apart from these three visits at the top level, exchange of visits at the ministerial level totalled almost 20.[26] (See Table 5.1)

Table 5.1: Sino-Indian High-Level Exchange Visits, 1991-1997

Date	Action
February 1991	Indian External Affairs Minister Vidya Charan Shukla visited China.
December 1991	Chinese Premier Li Peng visited India.
May 1992	Indian President R. Venkataraman visited China.
July 1992	Indian Defence Minister Sharad Pawar visited China.
January 1993	Indian Lok Sabha Speaker Shivraj Patil visited China.
September 1993	Indian Prime Minister Narasimha Rao visited China.
November 1993	Li Ruihuan, Chairman of the Chinese People's Consultative Committee, visited India.
July 1994	Chinese Vice Premier and Foreign Minister Qian Qichen visited India.
September 1994	Chinese State Councilor and Defence Minister Chi Haotian visited India.
October 1994	Indian Vice President K.R. Narayanan visited China.
July 1995	Indian Home Minister S.B. Chavan visited China.
November 1995	Qiao Shi, Chairman of the Chinese People's Congress, visited India.
March 1996	Chairman of the Chiefs of Staff Committee and Chief of the Naval Staff of India visited China.
November 1996	Chinese President Jiang Zemin visited India.
December 1997	Wei Jianxing, Secretary of the Chinese Communist Party Secretariat, visited India.

Li Peng's visit was a reciprocation of Rajiv Gandhi's 1988 visit to China. It was also the first visit by a Chinese Premier since 1960. The *Joint Communiqué,* signed during this visit, echoed the spirit of the 1988 *Sino-Indian Joint Press Communiqué,* which aimed at restoring, improving and developing Sino-Indian good-neighbourly and friendly relations, and further provided all-around and concrete guidelines for the development of the bilateral relations in the 1990s. While stressing joint efforts to expand their cooperation in fields such as trade, agriculture, energy, health, and education, they also expressed their willingness to strengthen coordination of their stances on major international and regional issues including how to construct a new international order. On the boundary dispute, as mentioned earlier, they agreed to step up the work of the Sino-Indian Joint Working Group on the Boundary Question and solve the problem as early as possible. Pending a final settlement of the boundary question, the two sides would maintain peace and tranquility in the area along the Line of Actual Control. On the Tibet issue, they tried to narrow down the difference between them. They also stated that "the improvement and development of Sino-Indian relations was not directed against any third country, nor would it affect their existing friendly relations and cooperation with other countries".[27]

Prime Minister Narasimha Rao's 1993 visit to China was notable for the *Agreement on the Maintenance of Peace and Tranquility along the LAC in the China-India Border Areas, while President Jiang Zemin's 1996 visit to India, for the Agreement on Confidence Building Measures in the Military Field along the LAC.* These two agreements were considered as evidence of the continuation of qualitative improvement in the China-India relations since 1988. Besides the three most important documents, many other agreements were signed by the two countries during this period to increase bilateral trade, foster cultural and technology exchanges and military-to-military links, and promote other cooperative projects.

The China-India border registered a tension-free decade since 1988. The Joint Working Group on the boundary question, a new mechanism initiated during Rajiv Gandhi's visit to Beijing, met regularly and achieved a set of agreements on the maintenance of durable peace and tranquility in the border areas. Between 1989 and 1997, the Joint Working Group held 10 rounds of talks. Till 1993, a number of measures had already been set up for the purposes of increasing mutual trust and avoiding mutual misunderstanding. The two defence establishments agreed to exchange visits. Meetings of the border personnel were arranged regularly. Telecommunication links were established at two points along the LAC.[28]

The aforementioned 1993 Agreement on border issue laid down a more comprehensive framework for maintenance of peace and tranquility along the LAC between China and India. Under the Agreement, the two sides have reiterated their commitment to resolve the boundary question peacefully through consultations and "strictly respect and observe" the LAC pending an ultimate resolution. Provisions in this regard are as follows:

- Neither side shall use or threaten to use force against the other by any means;
- No activities of either side shall overstep the line of actual control;
- When there are differences on the alignment of the LAC, the experts from two countries shall jointly check and determine where the LAC lies;
- References to the LAC in the Agreement are, however, without prejudice to the respective positions of the two countries on the boundary question.

Under the Agreement, China and India have also agreed to work out a series of confidence-building measures along the LAC, including the reduction of their military forces along the LAC "in conformity with the principle of mutual and equal security".[29] As part of the implementation of this agreement, China and India agreed, at the 8th meeting of the Joint Working Group held in August 1995, to pull back four posts, two on each side, located in immediate proximity to each other in the Sumdorong Chu Valley in the eastern sector. The disengagement of the posts was carried out in October-November 1995, without prejudice to the respective positions of the two sides on the alignment of the LAC in the area.[30]

The 1996 agreement on CBMs was built on the foundation of the 1993 agreement on border peace and tranquility. It provided for a number of important CBMs to preserve peace and tranquility in the China-India border areas. While reiterating that "neither side shall use its military capability against the other side," the two militaries committed to:

- limiting the number of field-army troops, border-defence forces, paramilitary forces, and major categories of armaments along the LAC;
- avoiding holding large-scale military exercises near the LAC and to give the other side prior notification of exercises involving one brigade (five thousand troops) or more;
- preventing air intrusions across the LAC;
- preventing dangerous military activities along the LAC including discharging firearms, causing biodegradation, using hazardous chemicals, setting off explosives, and hunting with firearms within two kilometres of the LAC;
- increasing and expanding their service-to-service contacts.[31]

The two sides also reached a consensus on the urgency and imperative of "arriving at a common understanding of the alignment of the line of actual control in the China-India border areas" and agreed to "speed up the process of clarification and confirmation" of the LAC.[32]

As the political atmosphere between China and India was greatly improved due to frequent exchange of high-level visits and visible peace and tranquility in the border region, bilateral contacts surged in various areas and at different levels after a gap of nearly three decades. Increasing varied interactions between China and India in turn promoted mutual trust and confidence that were necessitated by the ultimate resolution of their long-standing political problems. While Chinese and Indian cultural festivals were successfully held in each other's countries, this period witnessed a set of agreements for cooperation between China and India in the spheres of space-related technologies, education, civil services, public administration, social welfare, radio and television, environmental management, and combating narcotics-traffic. Among these rapidly growing interactions, however, their bilateral economic engagement had been "the most visible part".[33]

The economic relations between China and India might have been the least significant element in their bilateral relations during the Cold War. The 1962 war and the subsequent chill in bilateral political relations "effectively eliminated much trade and other economic relations between the two countries".[34] Although in 1984 the two sides signed their trade protocols to grant each other the most favoured nation (MFN) status and set up a joint working group to promote mutual trade and commerce, their economic engagement registered an impressive growth only after the Cold War. In 1991, the total volume of China-India bilateral trade was only US $264 million. By 1997, it touched US $1.83 billion, with an increase of nearly 6 times in a relatively short period of six years. (See Table 5.2) The commodity structure of bilateral trade covered a range from agricultural products, industrial raw materials, to seafood, textiles and machine tools. Although the bilateral trade between China and India was still on the margins of their respective foreign trade, the continuous and rapid growth since the early 1990s indicated "their rising enthusiasm in building strong economic engagement"[35] and "a vast potential which needs to be tapped".[36]

Apart from the commodity transfers, the two countries also started to explore opportunities for mutual or third country investments and joint ventures. In January 1993, the first China-India joint venture—between China Metallurgical Import & Export Corporation and India's Mideast Integrated Steel Limited—was commissioned in Orissa.[37] Indian companies, like Ranbaxy and Hero Motors also established joint ventures in China around the same period. While Chinese investments were concentrated on India's mining and manufacturing sectors, India's investments were directed at services, information technology education and pharmaceutical sector in China.[38]

Table 5.2: China-India Bilateral Trade 1991-1999 (Unit US$ million)

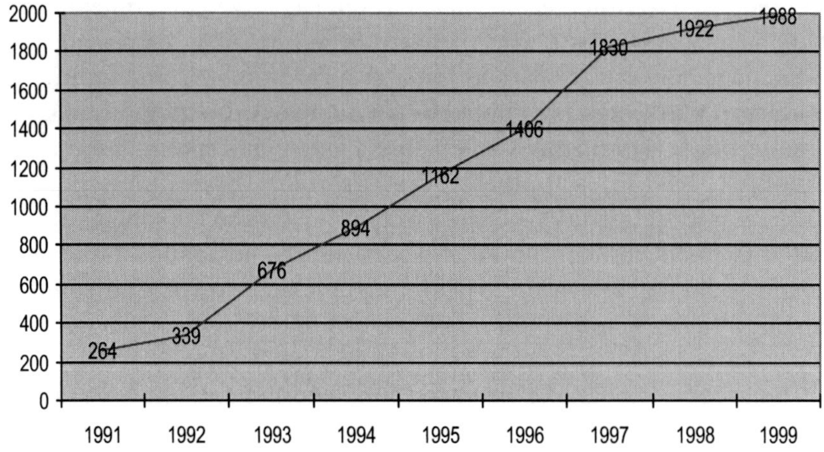

Source: China Customs Statistics, various years.

5.2 Post-Pokhran II Hiatus and Fence-Mending Efforts (May 1998-June 1999)

As discussed in Chapters 3 and 4, Pokhran II did not lead to any fundamental change in their mutual perceptions of each other. Nevertheless, the aftermath of Pokhran II saw a brief hiatus in China-India relations. Apart from the exchanges of vigorous criticism between them, the positive trends of high-level contacts developed in the previous years were totally suspended. The meeting of the Joint Working Group on the Boundary Question, scheduled for October 1998, was postponed. The bilateral trade, which registered an impressive growth since the early 1990s, lost momentum. Bilateral contacts in other spheres were also affected to a certain extent. Irrespective of these setbacks, the impact of Pokhran II on China-India relations was limited and brief. As history witnessed, the border areas between China and India remained quiet when tension arose in the political field. In other words, neither China nor India decided to antagonize each other due to the nuclear tests and the subsequent discordance. On the contrary, both of them not only reiterated their respective commitments to a friendly China-India relationship but also took some concrete steps to mend fences for this sake.

First of all, both China and India observed a certain self-restraint and tried to avoid extremes during their critical exchanges. Since neither of them wanted to see a break-up of the bilateral ties, the purpose of this self-restraint was to limit the damage and ensure that continued engagements would clear the tensions. On its part, as mentioned earlier, China attributed the setback of Sino-Indian relations to "some personalities" in India during this period. In December 1998, when Ram Jethmalani, the then Indian Urban Affairs Minister, publicly suggested that India should recognize Taiwan as an independent country, China protested against "certain Indian politicians" rather than the Indian government. The Chinese *People's Daily* wrote on 31 December 1998: "We strongly urge certain Indian politicians to stop interfering in China's internal affairs and work towards improving rather than damaging the bilateral ties. Jethmalani's remarks have further hurt the feelings of the Chinese people."[39] At the same time, the Chinese government made efforts, mainly through the Chinese Embassy in New Delhi, to explain its policy towards India, especially regarding those issues about which India was rather concerned. As explored in Chapter 3, Zhou Gang, the then Chinese ambassador to India, provided a series of explanations in this regard. Apart from expressing China's strong willingness to develop a constructive and cooperative partnership with India, he reiterated the assurances that Sino-Pak relations were normal and non-India-oriented.

On India's part, irrespective of Fernandes' assertion of the 'China threat' and Vajpayee's secret letter to Clinton, the Indian government endeavoured to avoid publicly building any links between the China factor and its nuclear tests. When referring to the Indian official literature of this period, the relevant remarks all stopped at the point of calling for more Chinese sensitivity to India's security and strategic concerns. The Vajpayee government also attempted to distance itself from any anti-China statements, especially after the nuclear tests. When the director-general of the Indo-Tibetan Border Police (ITBP) Gautam Kaul stated in October 1998 that the Chinese were amassing troops along the LAC, the Indian government termed it as "inaccurate" later on.[40] Following Jethmalani's remarks on Taiwan, the Government of India, through the Indian Embassy in Beijing as well as through its press spokesman in New Delhi, promptly assured China that there was no change in India's policy on Taiwan.[41] Furthermore, as mentioned in Chapter 4, a number of official statements at different levels, including several from the Prime Minister himself, were made in succession to clarify that there was no change of India's China perspective and that India was also keen on a good relationship with China.

Second, both countries kept the door open for dialogue despite the suspension of exchanging high-level visits. What irked China in 1998 were not the nuclear tests themselves but India's attempt to justify these tests by selling the 'China threat'. Although China, after Pokhran II, insisted that India should sign the NPT and in effect roll back its nuclear programme, Beijing did not set this as a pre-condition for resumption of the bilateral relations. On the contrary, China soon made it very clear that what Beijing wanted was for India to retract its assertions about the China threat. Addressing a seminar on Sino-Indian relations in New Delhi on 25 February 1999, Ambassador Zhou Gang said that the attribution of a Chinese threat to justify India's nuclear tests by some personalities was "the main cause upsetting Sino-Indian relations". Two weeks later, he told the audience of another seminar that "strict adherence to the five principles of peaceful co-existence…and shedding a threat image of each other were the key for laying a credible foundation for a healthy Sino-Indian relationship". Through its ambassador to New Delhi, China also demanded that India should take the lead in mending relations. Ambassador Zhou Gang told the national daily *The Hindu* on 9 July 1998, that, "it is up to the doer to undo the knot".[42] As events transpired, India took these demands seriously and definitely responded through various official statements.

Apart from this sort of indirect interaction, direct diplomatic engagement between China and India continued, though at a lower level. Despite the postponement of the meeting of the Joint Working Group on the Boundary Question, a June 1998 bilateral meeting of military experts went ahead. On 27 July 1998, the Chinese Foreign Minister Tang Jiaxuan met the Indian prime minister's special representative, Jaswant Singh, on the sidelines of the ASEAN Regional Forum meeting in Manila. They "conducted frank discussions on the Indian nuclear explosions and Sino-Indian relations," as a Chinese spokesman put it later. On 15 December 1998, the Chinese Foreign Minister Tang Jiaxuan wrote to Jaswant Singh to congratulate him on his taking over as the Minister for External Affairs. In this letter, Tang Jiaxuan hoped that Sino-Indian relations could be consolidated and further developed during Singh's tenure. Jaswant Singh replied in the following words: "India remains committed to the process of dialogue to address and resolve outstanding issues," and he looked forward to "continuing [our] interaction to further mutual understanding, co-operation and friendship, so essential for [our] two countries and peoples." In February 1999, a team of officials of India's Ministry of External Affairs visited Beijing and held consultations with their Chinese counterparts in preparation for the JWG. The two sides discussed India's nuclear tests and their impact on Sino-Indian ties and expounded their respective positions on the issue. They agreed to "work for the restoration and improvement of bilateral relations".[43] In April 1999, the long-delayed JWG meeting was held in Beijing.

Third, there was a joint attempt to keep the bilateral economic relations on track and let it "facilitate revival of China-India interactions in the wake of India's nuclear tests".[44] Compared with the average growth rate of 40 per cent during the preceding six years, the China-India bilateral trade did suffer a visible setback due to Pokhran II, with an increase of only 5 per cent for the whole of 1998. (See Table 5.2) In this period, especially during those months around the tests, some of their economic interactions were cancelled or postponed. These negative trends were neutralized by other bilateral economic engagements, however. India signed agreements for 5 joint ventures in China during 1998 involving an investment of US $8 million and other 6 joint ventures during 1999 involving investment of US $1.9 million.[45] Notwithstanding the symbolic cancellation of the China Commodity Fair in Mumbai during August-September 1998 and China's visibly low-profile presence during the Indian International Trade Fair of November 1998, China National Chemicals Import and Export Corporation, one of China's largest state-run corporations, went ahead with its decision to expand its business of exports of natural gas, crude oil, etc. to India.[46] The 1998 positive rather than negative growth rate of bilateral trade itself, in the view of some analysts, indicated that the impact of Pokhran II on Sino-Indian economic relations was "not only short-lived but also very marginal".[47] Moreover, quick revival of trade and commerce links after the nuclear tests helped pave the way for the political engagement between the two sides.

In June 1999, Indian External Affairs Minister Jaswant Singh visited China. During his meeting with the Chinese Foreign Minister Tang Jiaxuan, the two sides agreed that neither side regarded the other as a threat. China appeared to be satisfied that the prerequisite for the resumption of relations (i.e. India's retraction of its assertions about the China threat) upon which it had been insisting was met finally and firmly by the Indian government. On its part, India also expressed satisfaction that China agreed to commence a dialogue on security matters.[48] Jaswant Singh's visit to Beijing re-commenced the high-level contacts between the two countries after a gap of over one year. Since then, China-India relations had been brought back on track with the resumption of all bilateral interactions in various fields.

5.3 New Stage of China-India Relations (July 1999-till Date)

Coming out of the shadow of India's nuclear tests, China-India relations have entered into a new stage since mid-1999. Irrespective of their specific expectations from this relationship, as the twin rising powers, China and India converged at the point that stable and cooperative relations between them would best serve their own national interests in the new century. If the last decade of the 20th century represented the initial stage of the transformation of China-India relations, in which the two countries re-engaged with each other after a gap of nearly three decades, the first years of the 21st century witnessed a steady consolidation of their cooperation for the purpose of establishing a strategic partnership.

5.3 (1) China's India Policy

Given the fact that even the Indian nuclear tests were not able to shake China's resolve to befriend India, China unwaveringly continued its India policy that had been fashioned since the end of the Cold War. As China-India relations were put back on track after Jaswant Singh's Beijing visit, China started to introduce some new steps into its efforts to strengthen mutual ties. In sum, China's India policy in this stage was characterized by the following features: to show flexibility on the nuclear issue; to put focus on economic cooperation; to explore new fields of cooperation; and, to maintain an even-handed approach towards India and Pakistan.

Although their differences on the nuclear issue itself were not the main cause for the deterioration of China-India relations after Pokhran II, they have become a new challenge to the bilateral ties anyhow. As far as China was concerned, it appeared to be very difficult to work out a balance between China's position that India should sign the NPT and CTBT and India's request to be accepted as a nuclear weapon state. To walk out of this dilemma, China reasserted Deng Xiaoping's initiatives in the early 1980s and the consensus reached between China and India in 1988 which suggested the two sides to set contentious issues aside and concentrate on improving the relationship in other areas. During Indian President K.R. Narayanan's visit to China in 2000 and Li Peng's visit[49] to India in 2001, China chose to avoid any reference to the unpleasant memory of the recent past. In fact, there was no mention of the nuclear issue at all.[50] This was seen as "the Chinese approach that nothing would be allowed to mar the general air of goodwill and the future prospects of the relationship."[51] Another significant gesture by China was its mild reaction to the Agni II missile test which India conducted just prior to the conclusion of Li Peng's India visit. In a "rather cautiously worded" statement by the Chinese Foreign Ministry, there was no direct criticism of this intermediate range ballistic missile test but warning against an arms race in the region.[52]

Three months after India clinched a nuclear deal with the United States in July 2005, *People's Daily*, the Chinese official media, accused the US in a commentary of "double standards" on nuclear proliferation and warned of its "negative impact" on the global nuclear order.[53] This was read by the Indian side as China's official disapproval of the Indo-US nuclear deal. Since China's vote in the International Atomic Energy Agency (IAEA) and the Nuclear Suppliers' Group (NSG) would be of great importance to move the deal forward, India is very sensitive to the Chinese position on this issue. As an Indian columnist put it in his article, if China denied the deal, it "could reopen New Delhi's many past grievances against Beijing".[54] To avoid its emerging as a new irritant in its relationship with India which had just overcome the difficulties due to the Pokhran II, China responded to India's sensitivity with flexibility, although it did not withdraw from its stance on safeguarding the effectiveness of international non-proliferation principles and still kept an eye on the intentions behind the deal. According to Articles 27 and 39 of the *Joint Declaration* signed during President Hu Jintao's visit to New Delhi in November 2006, the two sides pledged to promote cooperation in the field of nuclear energy and agreed that "international civilian nuclear cooperation should be advanced through innovative and forward-looking approaches".[55] These were interpreted by the Indian government as an endorsement of the Indo-US nuclear deal by China.[56] It seemed that Prime Minister Manmohan Singh got the same message again from his Chinese counterpart during his visit to Beijing in January 2008 when he told the Indian media aboard *Air India One* as follows:

> I cannot say that I got a firm and definitive answer, but my own feeling is that the Chinese, when the issue comes up before the IAEA Board of Governors and, if subsequently, before the NSG, would not be an obstacle. But I can't say that I have that assurance today.[57]

After mid-1999, China started to lay more stress on its economic engagement with India. It was evident that China expected economic cooperation to be the engine and the stabilizer of China-India relations pending the final solution of the border problem which would take more time. In each high-level contact since 2000, China made economic cooperation a focus of the bilateral talks. On the occasion of Narayanan's

China visit in 2000, China suggested that the two countries should expand their economic cooperation from bilateral to the regional level. During Narayanan's short stay in Kunming, the capital of China's south-western province of Yunnan, the provincial authorities formally sought India's support to the so-called 'Kunming Initiative'.[58] The *Kunming Initiative* was originally put forward by scholars at Kunming's Institute of South Asian Studies in 1999. It called for sub-regional cooperation among south-western China, north-eastern India, Myanmar and Bangladesh. Accompanied by a large trade and business contingent, Li Peng made it a major focus of his 2001 visit to India to "explore new avenues for increasing economic exchanges and trade in the new century".[59] By visiting Hyderabad and Bangalore, India's major IT centres, Li Peng conveyed China's keenness on cooperation with India in such fields as IT sector and software where India had made great strides. During Chinese Premier Zhu Rongji's visit to India in 2002, it became clear that China "preferred to concentrate on the business of strengthening bilateral economic ties".[60] Five Memoranda of Understanding and contracts worth more than US $100 million were signed during this visit. According to Hua Junduo, the then Chinese Ambassador in New Delhi, China believed that "the orientation of future relations between the two countries would depend on the level of economic interaction".[61]

In order to move bilateral trade and economic ties to a new high, China also displayed its keenness on the establishment of a free trade area (FTA) between the two countries. To push for such an agreement with India was obviously a priority item during Premier Wen Jiabao's visit to New Delhi in April 2005. He told the Indian media just ahead of his visit: "I hope the two sides will soon begin their feasibility study of FTA".[62] During his India visit of 2006, President Hu Jintao also suggested that the two sides "actively discuss trade liberalization". He said:

> China and India are highly complementary in terms of economy and enjoy great potentials for cooperation. The two countries have basic conditions ready for the establishment of free trade relations. Establishing the free trade area between China and India will lift the bilateral business relations to a higher level and drive regional economic integration in Asia.[63]

Apart from strengthening economic cooperation, China also continued to explore the routes for building diversified cooperation with India. The two major fields in which China showed great interest were bilateral cooperation on non-traditional security issues and coordination in multilateral fora. As

China attached greater importance to the non-traditional security issues such as terrorism, transnational crimes, environmental degradation and drug trafficking, it started to explore the possibility of cooperation with India in this field. During Narayanan's visit, China for the first time brought up the subject of international terrorism and the need for India and China to cooperate at the global level to combat it. In 2001, in a conversation with the Indian media, Li Peng made "the most forthright statement" of China's desire for cooperation with India to combat terrorism.[64] Since then, the need for combating terrorism has become a routine topic of the bilateral talks.

Moreover, China expected a joint contribution by China and India in fashioning a new world order. In his Four-Point Proposal on Sino-Indian relations, which was put forward during his meeting with his Indian counterpart Narayanan, the Chinese President Jiang Zemin called for strengthening the bilateral "coordination and cooperation in international affairs, and make(ing) joint efforts for the establishment of a just and reasonable new international political and economic order".[65] During Li Peng's 2001 visit to India, he again expressed China's desire to join hands with India to promote multipolarity for world peace and "ride the tide" of globalization for common development, in order to bring about a "just and fair" new political and economic order.[66] During Zhu Rongji's 2002 visit to India, it was announced that the two countries would hold regular dialogue on this subject and constitute an anti-terror consultation mechanism.[67]

Since 2005, China has been pushing for a strategic cooperation with India. In an interview with the Indian media ahead of his visit of April 2005, Premier Wen Jiabao suggested that China and India should handle their relations "from a strategic high ground bearing in mind the larger picture".[68] In 2006, President Hu Jintao also committed to promote strategic cooperation between the two countries. According to a Chinese India hand, this strategic cooperation should be viewed in the following three tiers: (i) on the bilateral level, China-India ties should go beyond the boundary issue, and the areas of cooperation should be expanded from trade to other aspects like energy and security; (ii) on the regional level, China and India should join hands in safeguarding peace and stability of the region, which are fundamental to their respective developments; (iii) on the international level, China sees India as a major partner on issues like multipolarity and safeguarding the overall interests of developing countries.[69]

This period also witnessed China's firm adherence to its even-handed approach to the region since the end of the Cold War. In the Indo-Pak Kargil War of 1999, "many Indians were surprised to find that China did not stand by Pakistan".[70] After the terrorist attack of 13 December 2001 on the Indian Parliament, the Chinese government strongly condemned it, though it cautiously avoided echoing India's complaint of the cross-border terrorism sponsored by the Pakistani state. While military tensions between India and Pakistan went on the boil later on, the Chinese Premier Zhu Rongji paid a visit to India as planned in the second week of January 2002. During the visit the two sides discussed the crisis. Zhu Rongji reiterated the Chinese position that the India-Pakistan dispute should be resolved through negotiations. He also said that the January 12 speech of President Pervez Musharraf reflected the resolve of the Pakistani government to combat terrorism.[71]

These reactions by China further manifested the contour of China's current policy towards the India-Pakistan dispute: keeping neutral on the India-Pakistan problem; supporting Indo-Pakistani bilateralism rather than any third-party mediation; reacting if necessary according to the ground realities; not allowing tensions between India and Pakistan to apply brakes to China's respective relations with both countries. In Prime Minister Manmohan Singh's visit of 2008, it was reported that the unfolding situation in Pakistan[72] even "figured majorly in the deliberations between the two leaders" and China expressed its appreciation of India's efforts to improve ties with Pakistan.[73]

5.3 (2) India's China Policy

Taking a more comprehensive security perception since the mid-1990s, India saw more opportunities than challenges in its relations with China after the bilateral ties came back on track in mid-1999. India was convinced that a constructive cooperation with China would serve its national interests at the juncture of the new century. India's China policy in this period reflected its comprehensive approaches to its national security. With territorial security still top of its security agenda, India tried its best to keep the border talks at the core of its bilateral contacts with China. Having upgraded economic security to the same level as military and political security, India was committed to solving its difference with China through dialogue in order to keep a peaceful and stable relationship with its largest neighbour. As a result, India initiated a security dialogue with China, hoping that most of its security concerns regarding China could be discussed and solved under such a mechanism. At the same time, India made serious efforts to establish and develop new partnerships with other major powers which could be construed in terms of balance-of-power politics and thereby counterbalance China. The Indian government also believed that the improving bilateral ties made it possible to seek China's support for the great power status of India.

From India's perspective, "the border continues to be the centrepiece of the relationship" before the final solution is reached, although "it is no longer a stumbling block to further progress".[74] The sooner a final settlement is reached, the earlier would considerable military and financial energies of India be released for other more purposeful activities.[75] Dissatisfied with the "static" nature of the border talks till then and suspicious that China might not be "very forthcoming or desirous of accelerating the pace of the discussions"[76], India has invested more efforts since mid-1999 to keep the border issue at the centre of its interaction with China. In each high-level contact between India and China, the border issue was always one of the first things brought up by the Indian side. During his 2000 visit to China, Indian President K.R. Narayanan told his Chinese counterpart Jiang Zemin that, although it was nobody's case that the contentious border could be easily resolved given the extremely complex dimensions, it ought not for that reason be left to later generations to tackle.[77] To speed up the border talks, India worked for more political initiative and intervention at the highest level on both sides. The appointment of special political representatives in 2003 could be seen as an achievement of India's efforts in this regard.

The Manmohan Singh government has repeatedly emphasized that an early boundary settlement should be pursued by the two sides "as a strategic objective".[78] In the joint press conference held during President Hu Jintao's visit to India in 2006, Prime Minister Manmohan Singh said, "Such a settlement will invest our strategic partnership with further strength and dynamism".[79] This indicates that India still regards the unsettled boundary issue as a major hurdle in the bilateral ties. At the same time, the Manmohan Singh government has also ordered a comprehensive review of India's crumbling border infrastructure and initiated a plan for its rapid modernization. Days after returning from China, Manmohan Singh became the first Indian Prime Minister who visited Arunachal, a disputed boundary area with China, after a gap of nearly nine years. There he announced a development package worth Rs. 67,000 crore, including a two-lane 1,840-km long Trans-Arunachal highway, and a railway project which will link Arunachal to Assam, a neighbouring Indian state. He also promised to upgrade its connectivity to the rest of the country in the coming years.[80] By integrating Arunachal physically, these transport projects may help New Delhi strengthen its negotiating position in the border talks with Beijing.[81]

As India's security concerns regarding China went beyond the pending boundary question and the overlapping areas of their security interests were broadening in the process of their simultaneous emergence, India felt the necessity of starting a formal security dialogue with China in order to dispel its security concerns and prevent tensions caused by misunderstanding. In the 1990s, such a dialogue on security issues took place mainly between the top leaders of the two countries. In meetings of the Sino-Indian Joint Working Group on the boundary question, both sides also informally exchanged their views on security matters. As mentioned earlier, it was during Jaswant Singh's 1999 visit to China that the two countries agreed to establish a specific institutional arrangement for security dialogue which would be independent of the JWG.

This formal annual security dialogue was inaugurated in March 2000 when Indian and Chinese delegations of the Joint-Secretary level met in Beijing. During this round of dialogue, the Indian side "did convey [our] concerns that China's assistance to Pakistan's nuclear and missile programme had an adverse impact on regional stability to which we have been obliged to respond in a responsible and restrained manner."[82] In other words, this mechanism in fact "provided a forum for India to raise its concerns on China's nuclear and missile cooperation with Pakistan as well as broader questions of nuclear arms control."[83] As J.N. Dixit put it, "[T]he bilateral exchange of views could also serve the purpose of removing misunderstandings about India's nuclear and missile weaponisation and structuring a political and strategic understanding on non-proliferation and arms control issues. The dialogue would also serve the purpose of evolving an understanding between India and China on issues affecting South and South East Asian security in general, and perhaps in reducing tensions between India and Pakistan."[84] India's keenness on developing a formal mechanism on security dialogue with China is again in accord with its post-Cold War comprehensive approaches to security, which observes security dialogue and cooperation as a significant component of it. As China and India launched their strategic dialogue at the vice-ministerial level in January 2005, the security dialogue has been integrated into the new mechanism since then.

To cope with the rise of China, at another level, India kept the traditional game of balance-of-power as an option. In India's perspective, its new partnership policy since the end of the Cold War best served this purpose. Unlike the alliance security prevalent in the Cold War period, the new partnership policy could play a role of counterbalancing China without sacrificing the improvement in its relations with China. In other words, India's post-Cold War great power diplomacy and 'Look East' policy were designated to safeguard its national security in general and counterbalance China in particular.

By the turn of the century, when India tried to expand its ties with the United States and deepen its relationship with the ASEAN countries, it obviously bore China in mind, hoping that these relationships could provide it more strategic space in its relations with China.[85] Since then, India has also extended its Look East policy to get Australia, Japan and South Korea involved. It has laid more stress on the strategic and geopolitical dimensions of its cooperation with these countries. On 25 May 2007, US, India, Japan and Australia kicked off the *Quadrilateral Initiative,* when their officials at the rank of assistant secretary of state secretly held their first security dialogue on the sidelines of the ASEAN Regional Forum gathering in Manila.[86] Three months later, this group plus Singapore held a five-day joint naval exercise in the Bay of Bengal. Although the Indian government has assured China that these activities do not have any anti-Chinese connotation, some Indian strategists asserted that they were essential to counter China's might in Asia.[87]

As the emergence of India moved onto a rapid but stable track at the turn of the new century, the Indian government felt it imperative to play a more active role in the global arena. In the past, India had believed that China was a stumbling block in this regard. As discussed in earlier chapters, during the Cold War, especially in Indira Gandhi's era, India thought China attempted to dominate Asia by eclipsing India's international standing and prestige. After the Cold War, now that China did get ahead of India in many ways, it seemed to India that China was less desirous to accept its emergence. Therefore, in the early 1990s, India started to emulate China in hopes of correcting the imbalance with China. It believed that China was unlikely to take India's global prospects seriously until it was both economically and militarily as strong as China.

India's efforts in this regard bore fruit in the late 1990s, when its comprehensive national strength started to grow noticeably. As a result, India resolved to continue this strategy. At the same time, as India and China extended their cooperation to the global level, India felt the positive side of the China factor. Its cooperation with China at the global level itself had positive effects on upgrading India's international position. In spite of their differences on the nuclear issue and some mutual suspicions thereby, India was clear that China's acceptance and acknowledgement were imperative for its legal status of nuclear weapon state. Furthermore, since India started to press its claim for a UNSC seat in the late 1990s, it has been seeking China's support in this respect.

5.3 (3) New Stage of China-India Relations

Emerging from the above discussion of their policies towards each other since mid-1999, it is clear that the respective expectations of China and India about this relationship were not always identical. With the consensus and resolve to maintain stable and cooperative relations between them, however, they tried to maximize their own interests only within the framework of friendship. This meant that sometimes they would accommodate their requirements to the concerns of the other, for instance, China's attitude toward the Indo-Pak tensions and India's stance on the Tibet issue. Not everybody was satisfied with the pace of the development of China-India relations, but no one could deny that this relationship forged ahead and entered a new stage of comprehensive cooperation during this period. The following are striking manifestations of this transformation: a new boom in high-level visits, a new consensus on the orientation of this relationship, a new leap forward in their economic cooperation, new progress in border talks, and new efforts in terms of trust building.

This period first witnessed a new boom of exchange of high-level visits. Almost in each year, there was a state-level visit between them. (See Table 5.3) Apart from their significance in an overall sense to mutual trust and close cooperation between the two countries, each of these visits made a specific contribution to the improvement of China-India relations.

Table 5.3: Sino-Indian High-Level Exchange Visits, 2000-2008

Date	Action
May 28-June 3, 2000	Indian President K.R. Narayanan visited China.
January 9-16, 2001	Chinese National People's Congress Standing Committee Chairman Li Peng visited India.
January 13-17, 2002	Chinese Premier Zhu Rongji visited India.
June 22-7, 2003	Indian Prime Minister Atal Bihari Vajpayee visited China.
April 9-12, 2005	Chinese Premier Wen Jiabao visited India.
November 20-23, 2006	Chinese President Hu Jintao visited India.
October 25-29, 2007	Indian Congress President Sonia Gandhi visited China.
January 13-15, 2008	Indian Prime Minister Manmohan Singh visited China.

Narayanan's visit closed the Pokran II chapter in their bilateral relations and started a new chapter. Li Peng's visit reinforced the positive trends in this relationship since Narayanan's visit. He also made a three-point proposal[88] regarding the promotion of cooperation between the two parliaments, on the basis of which a Parliamentary Friendship Group was established. Zhu Rongji's visit especially gave a boost to bilateral trade and economic relations, as well as tourism. Vajpayee's visit produced a joint declaration and as many as nine agreements on cooperation in the economy, law and justice, science and technology, and culture. The two sides agreed to establish a Special Representative mechanism to address the border issue.

Wen Jiabao's visit bore fruit as follows: a consensus on building a strategic partnership between the two countries, a guideline for the solution of border issue, and a five-year plan for economic and trade cooperation. Hu Jintao's visit yielded a 'ten-pronged strategy' aiming at substantiating and reinforcing their strategic and cooperative partnership. The significance of Sonia Gandhi's visit lay in her political status and the timing of her visit. Being the Congress president and the chairperson of the ruling UPA in the Lok Sabha, Sonia Gandhi was perceived as the most powerful political leader of India. Since her visit took place just days after the conclusion of the 17th National Congress of the CPC, she became the first leader of a foreign country received by the newly elected Chinese leadership. During Manmohan Singh's visit, the two sides reached *A Shared Vision for the 21st Century,* which represented "an important milestone in the evolution of [our] relations".[89]

Through these high-level contacts, a new consensus was reached on the orientation of China-India relations in the new century. As mentioned earlier, the objective set for the China-India relationship by the 1988 *Sino-Indian Joint Press Communiqué* and the 1991 *Sino-Indian Joint Communiqué* was to restore, improve and develop friendly and good-neighbourly relations. After the mid-1990s, the two countries attempted to upgrade it. Since then, top leaders from both sides had been talking about their "constructive cooperation" or "cooperative and constructive partnership" during their bilateral contacts. However, it was not formally contracted until 2003. *The Declaration on Principles for Relations and Comprehensive Cooperation between the Republic of India and the People's Republic of China,* signed during Vajpayee's China visit, set up a new orientation for this relationship on the basis of their normalization efforts in the 1990s. In this joint declaration, both sides not only affirmed that they would "promote a long-term constructive and cooperative partnership" but also drew a blueprint for "comprehensive cooperation", including regularization of political contacts, expansion of economic cooperation, and broadening of defense exchanges.[90]

During Wen Jiabao's visit to India in 2005, the two sides agreed to "establish an India-China Strategic and Cooperative Partnership for Peace and Prosperity," since their bilateral relations "have now acquired a global and strategic character".[91] The *Joint Statement* issued during this visit stated:

> Such a partnership is based on the principles of Panchsheel, mutual respect and sensitivity for each other's concerns and aspirations, and equality; provides a sound framework for an all-round and comprehensive development of bilateral relations based on mutual and equal security, development and prosperity of the two peoples; and contributes to jointly addressing global challenges and threats. It reflects the readiness of the two sides to resolve outstanding differences in a proactive manner without letting them come in the way of the continued development of bilateral relations.

This period also witnessed impressive new achievements in the bilateral economic cooperation. As their political relations moved back on track, their economic relationship leaped forward at a pace it had never had. At the most visible level, the bilateral trade increased by 18 times in 8 years, from US$ 1.99 billion of 1999 to US$ 38.7 billion of 2007. (See Table 5.4) Compared with the average growth rate of 40% during the period between 1991 and 1997, the annual growth rate of this period reached 45.8%, and this was achieved on basis of a much huger volume. China is already the second largest trading partner of India while India is one of the top ten trading partners of China.

Table 5.4: China-India Bilateral Trade 1991-2007 (Unit US$ million)

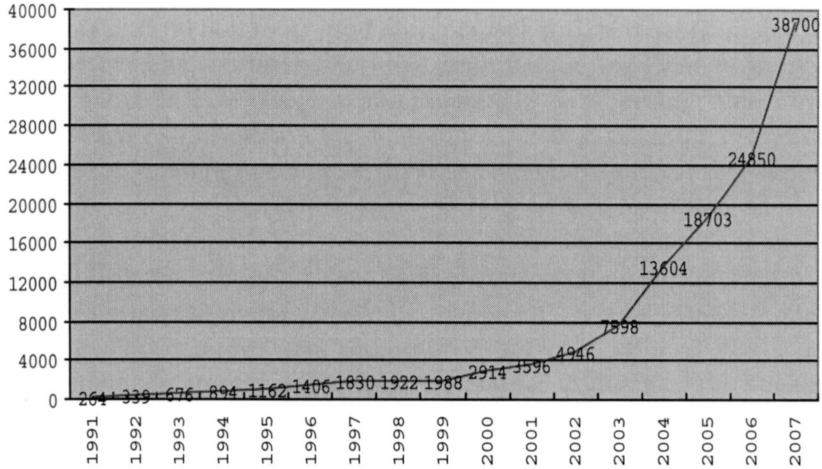

Source: China Customs Statistics, various years.

While commodity transfers dominated the bilateral trade between China and India, many new sectors, like border trade and trade in high-tech products, were also explored.[92] Meanwhile, two-way flow of investments continued to grow steadily. At the current juncture, there are more than 150 Indian companies in China and 50-60 Chinese companies in India.[93] According to Nirupama Rao, Ambassador of India to China, there was "a growth in the quantum of Indian investments in China which is present currently in a range of operations including manufacturing (pharmaceuticals, refractories, laminated tubes, auto-components, wind energy) and IT-enabled services (including IT education, software solutions and specific software products), trading, and the banking sector".[94] For example, India's Ranbaxy Pharmaceuticals and National Institute for Information Technology dominated China's scene in pharmaceuticals and IT education. India's Tata Group, one of the largest conglomerates in Asia, were expanding its business in China by increasing investment in software and launching new joint-venture projects in other sectors like automobiles and steel.[95] India has become a major destination for Chinese projects abroad. By 2008, Chinese firms have contracted projects in India worth over 12 billion US dollars.[96] These projects include those at airports, laying of gas pipelines, and building power plants.[97] China's home electric appliance makers TCL and Haier also established joint ventures in India.[98]

In March 2004, China and India also launched talks to evolve a bilateral free trade area (FTA) agreement. By 2008, a Joint Task Force has finalized its report on the feasibility of a China-India Regional Trading Arrangement (RTA), which is perceived as a precursor to the FTA. Moreover, the two countries have strengthened their cooperation in WTO on many trade-related issues. They have agreed to work together to support the establishment of an "open, fair, equitable, transparent and rule-based" multilateral trading system.[99] They have been cooperating closely at the bilateral level as well as within the group of 20 in the Doha Development Round of the WTO negotiations which commenced in 2001. In the recent past, Beijing and New Delhi have also strengthened their energy cooperation. The oil companies of the two countries have carried out successful cooperation in a third country, like in Sudan and Syria. In December 2005, China National Petroleum Corp (CNPC) and India's Oil and Natural Gas Corp (ONGC), the two largest oil companies in the respective countries, won a joint bid to buy Petro-Canada's 37% stake in Syrian oilfields for US $573 million.[100] In January 2006, China and India signed 5 memoranda on energy cooperation, including plans for joint bidding for third-country oil assets by national oil companies of the two countries.[101]

Although the border negotiation did not advance at the desired speed, no one can deny that it did achieve some new and steady progress till 2008. From mid-1999 to 2003, China and India had conducted three rounds of JWG meetings and 4 rounds of Expert Group[102] meetings. During the 8th Expert Group meeting which was held in November 2000, the two sides completed the exchange of maps of actual positioning of troops and control on the least controversial 'middle sector' of their border areas. Then a new mechanism came into being. During Vajpayee's visit in 2003, India and China agreed to "appoint a special representative each to explore, from the political perspective of the overall bilateral relationship, the framework of a boundary settlement".[103] Immediately thereafter, China named Dai Bingguo, the seniormost vice minister in the Chinese Ministry of Foreign Affairs, as its Special Representative, and India nominated Brajesh C. Mishra, National Security Adviser and Principal Secretary to the Prime Minister of India. The two special representatives held the first round of talks in October 2003 in New Delhi. The institution of Special Representatives on the boundary question was welcomed in both countries as a 'breakthrough'.[104] This decision "marks the first public acknowledgement of the imperative of seeking eventual solutions based primarily on *political* considerations, something which has been privately talked about for many years."[105] Having the full confidence of their Prime Ministers, the two special representatives could provide inputs and political will reflecting the objectives of the leaderships at the highest level. Therefore, it would overcome the limits which the former border talks and JWGs had reached, and then hopefully lead to a speedy resolution.

Till January 2008, twelve rounds of talks have been held between the two special representatives. A major outcome of the mechanism has been the *Agreement on the Political Parameters and Guiding Principles for the Settlement of the India-China Boundary Question,* which was signed by the two governments during Wen Jiabao's visit in 2005. This is the first political document of its kind since 1981, when the bilateral border talks started. According to both sides, this agreement "is truly a major milestone on the way to the settlement of the boundary question",[106] "laying a good foundation for the ultimate resolution of border issues".[107] It was learnt that in the 12th round of the talks between Special Representatives, each side presented on the table its own draft on a possible framework agreement involving territorial concessions. A working group has therefore been set up by the two special representatives to look at these two alternative drafts and work out an agreed framework to permanently settle their boundary dispute.

It was also exposed that both sides were willing to set the contentious Tawang issue aside "for the moment" and look to concentrate on areas where there was "least disagreement".[108]

As the border areas remained peaceful and tranquil and the border talks steadily moved forward, other new efforts were introduced in trust building between the two countries. Each made gestures of goodwill to relieve some of the concerns of the other. On China's part, for instance, it finally accepted Sikkim as a part of India. During the days when China and India were antagonistic towards each other, the PRC's official position was that the Chinese government "absolutely does not recognise India's illegal annexation of Sikkim".[109] Since the 1990s, however, China had been obsessed with competing interests: adhering to its traditional opposition to any infringement of state sovereignty, and promoting its friendship with India. At the beginning of the new century, China decided to make a compromise with regard to the former in order to provide a guarantee for the latter. During Vajpayee's visit of 2003, through the memorandum on border trade involving Sikkim and Tibet, China extended de facto recognition to the accession of Sikkim to India. This memorandum designated Changgu of Sikkim state and Renqinggang of the Tibetan Autonomous Region as the venue of border trade and Nathu La as the pass of entry and exit. In early October of the same year, the Chinese Ministry of Foreign Affairs removed the page of Sikkim (as an independent country) from its website. The China-India *Joint Statement* of 2005 referred to "Sikkim State of the Republic of India". According to the Indian Prime Minister Manmohan Singh, the Chinese Premier Wen Jiaobao stated, during their meeting in New Delhi, that China regarded Sikkim as an "inalienable part of India", and that Sikkim was no longer an issue in China-India relations. China has also officially handed over to India a revised map showing Sikkim as within the international boundaries of India.[110]

On India's part, in the joint declaration of 2003, it "recognizes that the Tibet Autonomous Region is part of the *territory* (emphasis added) of the People's Republic of China and reiterates that it does not allow Tibetans to engage in anti-China political activities in India". The terminology, which India applies to Tibet, has changed thrice since the 1950s. In 1954, India referred to the "Tibet region of China".[111] In the 1988 *Sino-Indian Joint Press Communiqué* and the 1991 *Sino-Indian Joint Communiqué,* India recognized that "Tibet is an *autonomous* (emphasis added) region of China". Taking into account the Chinese position that "Tibet is an inalienable part of Chinese territory," it is evident that the 2003 terminology by India is the closest to China's stance.

Moreover, defence exchanges between the two countries were strengthened during this period. The two sides reached a consensus that broadening and deepening of the bilateral defence exchanges "was of vital importance in enhancing mutual trust and understanding between the two armed forces, and to ensuring a peaceful environment in which they could pursue their respective national development objectives".[112] There were regular and frequent exchanges of high-level defence delegations including their Defence Ministers. Naval ships of both sides exchanged visits regularly and some of India's mid-level officers attended courses in Chinese institutions. The first ever India-China naval exercise was held off Shanghai in November 2003, while the first ever joint Army training exercise was held in Kunming in December 2007. Since September 2004, Indian officers have also participated as observers in several military exercises held by the PLA in the Chinese territory. During the visit of India's Defence Minister to China in May 2006, the two sides signed the *Memorandum of Understanding for Exchanges and Cooperation in the Field of Defence.* The MoU envisaged regular and institutional contacts between armed forces and defence officials and experts of the two countries. It is also expected to serve as an instrument for a regular and sustained dialogue on defence issues between the two countries.[113] The mechanism for an Annual Defence Dialogue (ADD) was initiated in November 2007.

Notes

1. *Deng Xiaoping wenxuan* (Selected Works of Deng Xiaoping), Volume III (Beijing: Renmin chubanshe, 1993), pp. 19-20.
2. *Sino-Indian Joint Communiqué,* December 16, 1991, China Report, New Delhi, Vol.28, No.1 (1992), pp. 89-92.
3. Ibid.
4. Wang Hongwei, *Ximalaya shan qingjie: Zhong Yin guanxi yanjiu* (The Himalayas Sentiment: *A Study of Sino-Indian Relations)* (Beijing: Zhongguo Zang xue chubanshe, 1998), pp. 268-271.
5. FBIS, DRC, December 16, 1991, cited in John W. Garver, *Protracted Contest: Sino-Indian Rivalry in the Twentieth Century* (New Delhi: Oxford University Press, 2001), pp. 221.
6. C. Raja Mohan, *Crossing the Rubicon: The Shaping of India's New Foreign Policy* (New Delhi: Penguin-Viking, 2003), pp.144-145.
7. Garver, *Protracted Contest,*p. 33.
8. Ibid, p. 59.
9. Mohan, *Crossing the Rubicon,* p.142.
10. Ibid, p.143.

11. J.N. *Dixit, India's Foreign Policy and Its Neighbours* (New Delhi: Gyan Publishing House, 2001), p. 225.
12. Ibid,p. 226.
13. Ibid,pp. 225-226.
14. *Agreement Between the Government of the People's Republic of China and the Government of the Republic of India on the Maintenance of Peace and Tranquility Along the Line of Actual Control in the China-India Border Areas,* Beijing, September 7, 1993, available at http://www.fmprc.gov.cn/eng/topics/wzlcflyeng/lsbjyd/dindia/t15915.htm.
15. *Agreement Between the Government of the People's Republic of China and the Government of the Republic of India on Confidence Building Measures in the Military Field Along the Line of Actual Control in the China-India Border Areas,* New Delhi, November 29, 1996, available at http://www.fmprc.gov.cn/eng/topics/wzlcflyeng/lsbjyd/dindia/t15914.htm.
16. When the Dalai Lama fled to India following the Lhasa revolt of March 1959, he was welcomed as an honoured guest by the Indian government. New Delhi also accorded refugee status to tens of thousands of Tibetans who followed the Dalai Lama. In 1963, the Indian government did not prohibit the Dalai Lama from promulgating a new 'constitution' for Tibet. Throughout the 1960s, the Research and Analysis Wing (RAW) pilots dropped supplies and arms to insurgents inside Tibet. In November 1962 India established a substantial Tibetan military force, which was formally named the Special Frontier Force (SFF). India also began supporting efforts to raise the Tibet issue in the United Nations. For further evidence of India's active support for Tibetan 'autonomy' during the Cold War, see Garver, *Protracted Contest,* pp. 43-66; Wang Hongwei, *'Zhong Yin guanxi zhong de Xizang wenti'* (The Tibet Issue in China-India Relations), in *Zhong Yin guanxi yanjiu: 1947-2003 (A Study of Sino-Indian Relations:* 1947-2003), ed. Zhang Minqiu (Beijing: Peking University Press, 2004), pp.156-175.
17. C.V. Ranganathan, and Vinod C. Khanna, *India and China: The Way Ahead,* second edition (New Delhi: Har-Anand Publications, 2004), p.178.
18. Garver, *Protracted Contest,* p. 43.
19. Ibid, p.74.
20. Ranganathan and Khanna, *India and China: The Way Ahead,* p.176.
21. Ibid, p.178.
22. Dixit, *India's Foreign Policy and its Neighbours,* p. 244.
23. Mohan, *Crossing the Rubicon,* pp.149-150.
24. Ibid, p.154.
25. *Annual Report* 1995-96 (New Delhi: Ministry of Defence, Government of India, 1996), p.4.
26. *Zhang, Zhong Yin guanxi yanjiu: 1947-2003,* Appendix, pp. 358-364.
27. *Sino-Indian Joint Communiqué* (1991).
28. *Annual Report 1993-94* (New Delhi: Ministry of Defence, Government of India, 1994), p. 4.
29. *Agreement on the Maintenance of Peace and Tranquility Along the LAC in the China-India Border Areas (1993).*

30. *Annual Report 1995-96,p. 4.*
31. Susan L. Shirk, 'One-Sided Rivalry: China's Perceptions and Policies toward India', in *The India-China Relationship: Rivalry and Engagement,* eds. Francine R. Frankel and Harry Harding (Oxford: Oxford University Press, 2004), p.81.
32. Agreement on Confidence Building Measures in the Military Field Along the LAC in the China-India Border Areas (1996).
33. *Swaran Singh, China-India Economic Engagement: Building Mutual Confidence,* CSH Occasional Paper (New Delhi: Centre de Sciences Humaines, 2005), p. 85.
34. T.N. Srinivasan, 'Economic Reforms and Global Integration', in *The India-China Relationship: Rivalry and Engagement,* eds. Frankel et al., p. 220.
35. Singh, *China-India Economic Engagement,* p. 85.
36. Ranganathan and Khanna, *India and China: The Way Ahead,* p.174.
37. Singh, *China-India Economic Engagement,* p.101.
38. Ibid, pp.102-103.
39. Cited in B. Raman, 'Sino-Indian Relations: A Chronology', *South Asia Analysis Group Papers,* April 23, 1999, available at http://www.saag.org/papers/paper49.html.
40. Alka Acharya, 'Sino-Indian Relations since Pokhran II', *Economic and Political Weekly,* Mumbai (June 5, 1999): 1398.
41. Raman, 'Sino-Indian Relations: A Chronology'.
42. Ibid.
43. Ibid.
44. Singh, *China-India Economic Engagement,* p.107.
45. Ibid, p.109.
46. Acharya, *'Sino-Indian Relations since Pokhran II',* p.1399.
47. Singh, *China-India Economic Engagement,* p.108.
48. Ranganathan and Khanna, *India and China: The Way Ahead,* p.176.
49. Li Peng, Chairman of the National People's Congress of the PRC, was then the No. 2 political figure in China. It was the second time that he had visited India. The first happened in 1991 when he visited India as the Chinese premier.
50. Alka Acharya, "'Irresistible Attraction' and Implacable Reality: The President's China Visit", *Economic and Political Weekly,* Mumbai (June 17, 2000): 2093; Alka Acharya, 'Li Peng's India Visit: Ritual and Reality', *Economic and Political Weekly,* Mumbai (February 3-10, 2001): 437-438.
51. Acharya, *'Li Peng's India Visit',* p.438.
52. Ibid, p.437.
53. Xin Benjian, 'Who's Pushing Nuclear Proliferation: Commentary', *People's Daily Online,* October 27, 2005, available at http://english.people.com.cn/200510/27/eng20051027_217234.html.
54. C. Raja Mohan, 'Delhi's Comrades Slam India, Beijing's Slam US for N-deal', *The Indian Express,* November 4, 2005.
55. *Joint Declaration by the Republic of India and the People's Republic of China,* New Delhi, November 21, 2006, available at http://www.meaindia.nic.in/.

56. 'China Has "Endorsed" Indo-US Nuke Deal: Pranab', *The Times of India,* November 27, 2006.
57. Diwakar, 'Hope China Backs Us at IAEA', *The Times of India,* January 16, 2008.
58. Acharya, "Irresistible Attraction" and Implacable Reality: The President's China Visit', pp. 2094-2095.
59. Acharya, 'Li Peng's India Visit', p. 438.
60. John Cherian, 'Zhu Rongji in India', *Frontline,* Chennai, Vol.19, No. 3 (February 2-15, 2002), available at http://www.hinduonnet.com/fline/fl1903/19031220.htm.
61. Ibid.
62. 'Free Trade is Inevitable: Wen', *Hindustan Times,* April 5, 2005.
63. 'Hu Jintao Attends China-India Economic, Trade and Investment Cooperation Summit and Delivers an Important Speech', November 23, 2006, available at http://www.fmprc.gov.cn/eng/wjdt/zyjh/t281852.htm.
64. Acharya, 'Li Peng's India Visit', p. 438.
65. Acharya, "Irresistible Attraction" and Implacable Reality: The President's China Visit', 2095.
66. Acharya, 'Li Peng's India Visit', p. 439.
67. Cherian, 'Zhu Rongji in India'.
68. Anil K Joseph, 'Let's Take Strategic High Ground: Wen', *The Indian Express,* April 4, 2005.
69. Li Bo, *'Yindu wenti zhuanjia Sun Shihai: Zhong Yin zhanlue hezuo huoban guanxi de neihan'* (Connotation of the China-India Strategic Partnership: Sun, An India Expert), *21 shiji baodao (The 21st Century Report),* April 15, 2005.
70. Jaideep Saikia, and Wang Hongwei, 'Giants at Peace: India and China', *Swords and Ploughshares,* Vol. XV, No. 3 (Winter 2003-04), available at http://www.acdis.uiuc.edu/Research/S&Ps/2003-04-Wi/S&P-Wi-2003/india_china.html.
71. Cherian, 'Zhu Rongji in India'.
72. At the time, the situation in Pakistan was very complex due to the shocking assassination of the Pakistan People's Party leader Benazir Bhuto and the subsequent postponement of the national election which was originally due on 8 January 2008.
73. Diwakar, 'Pak Figures Prominently in Manmohan-Wen Talks', *The Times of India,* January 15, 2008.
74. Alka Acharya, and G.P. Deshpande, 'Talking of and with China', *Economic and Political Weekly,* Mumbai (July 12, 2003): 2941.
75. This point was made by Indian Prime Minister Vajpayee in his address to the Combined Commanders Conference, which was attended by members of the Cabinet Committee on Security, on November 1, 2003. See Alka Acharya, and G.P. Deshpande, 'India-China Relations: The Territorial Imperative: Past and Present', *Economic and Political Weekly,* Mumbai (November 8, 2003): 4729-4730.
76. Acharya, "Irresistible Attraction" and Implacable Reality: The President's China Visit', p. 2094.
77. Ibid.

78. 'PM's Statement in the Lok Sabha on the Visits of Chinese Premier and Pakistan President', New Delhi, April 20, 2005; 'PM's Statement at Press Interaction with Chinese President', New Delhi, November 21, 2006, both available at http://www.meaindia.nic.in/.
79. 'PM's Statement at Press Interaction with Chinese President', New Delhi, November 21, 2006, available at http://www.meaindia.nic.in/.
80. Samudra Gupta Kashyap, 'Arunachal Our Land of the Rising Sun, Says PM in Itanagar, Eye on Beijing', *The Indian Express,* February 1, 2008.
81. 'Sunshine State', *The Indian Express,* February 2, 2008; Pranab Dhal Samanta, 'India Puts China Border Roads on the Fast Track', *The Indian Express,* November 5, 2006.
82. 'Summary of the Press Briefing by the Official Spokesman of the MEA, 8 March 2000', available at http://www.meadev.nic.in/news/20000308.htm.
83. Mohan, *Crossing the Rubicon,* p.148.
84. Dixit, *India's Foreign Policy and its Neighbours,* p. 253.
85. Mohan, *Crossing the Rubicon,* pp.161-162.
86. Brahma Chellaney, 'The US-India-Japan-Australia Quadrilateral Initiative: New Great Game', *The Asian Age,* June 2, 2007.
87. K. Subrahmanyam, 'Deal Essential to Counter China's Might in Asia', *The Times of India,* August 20, 2007; K. Subrahmanyam, 'New World, If Only China Could Sea', *The Indian Express,* August 14, 2007.
88. This three-point proposal includes: increasing the exchange of personnel between the two parliaments, establishing a parliamentary friendship group, and strengthening the two parliaments' cooperation in world affairs.
89. 'Prime Minister's Statement to the Press During His Visit to China', Beijing, January 14, 2008, available at http://www.meaindia.nic.in/.
90. *Declaration on Principles for Relations and Comprehensive Cooperation between the Republic of India and the People's Republic of China,* June 23, 2003, available at http://www.meaindia.nic.in/.
91. *Joint Statement of the Republic of India and the People's Republic of China,* New Delhi, April 11, 2005, available at http://www.meaindia.nic.in/.
92. Singh, *China-India Economic Engagement,* p.97.
93. Sun Yuxi, 'India-China Relations: Report', in *Emerging Trends in India-China Relations,* ed. Mohan Guruswamy (Gurgaon: Hope India Publications, 2006), p. 202.
94. Nirupama Rao, 'The Future of India-China Relations', a speech delivered at the Asia Society, Hong Kong, May 8, 2007, available at http://www.indianembassy.org.cn/press/070518_1.htm.
95. Singh, *China-India Economic Engagement,* pp.104-105.
96. 'PM's Address at the India-China Economic, Trade and Investment Summit', Beijing, January 14, 2008, available at http://www.meaindia.nic.in/.
97. Nirupama Rao, 'The Future of India-China Relations'.
98. Singh, *China-India Economic Engagement,* pp.104-105.
99. *A Shared Vision for the 21st Century of the Republic of India and the People's Republic of China,* Beijing, January 14, 2008, available at http://www.meaindia.nic.in/.

100. Indrajit Basu, 'India, China Pin Down $573m Syria Deal', *Asia Times Online,* December 22, 2005, available at http://www.atimes.com/atimes/China_Business/GL22Cb06.html.
101. Saibal Dasgupta, 'India, China for Joint Sourcing of Crude: Aiyar', *The Times of India,* January 13, 2006.
102. The China-India Expert Group was set up in 1993. It consists of diplomatic and military experts who are respectively appointed by each side of the JWG. Its task is to assist the JWG in dealing with the boundary issues. It meets once a year.
103. *Declaration on Principles for Relations and Comprehensive Cooperation* (2003).
104. Acharya and Deshpande, 'India-China Relations: The Territorial Imperative: Past and Present', pp. 4729-4730.
105. Ranganathan and Khanna, *India and China: The Way Ahead,* p.192.
106. 'PM's Statement in the Lok Sabha on the Visits of Chinese Premier and Pakistan President' (2005).
107. 'Wen Jiaobao Address Delhi Institute of Technology', April 12, 2005, available at http://www.chinaembassy.org.il/eng/xwdt/t191998.htm.
108. Pranab Dhal Samanta, 'Delhi, Beijing Agree on Roadmap to Settle Border', *The Indian Express,* January 16, 2008.
109. Cited in Acharya and Deshpande, 'Talking of and with China', p. 2942.
110. 'PM's Statement in the Lok Sabha on the Visits of Chinese Premier and Pakistan President' (2005).
111. *Agreement Between The People's Republic of China and The Republic of India on Trade and Intercourse Between The Tibet Region of China and India,* April 29, 1954, available at http://mea.gov.in/treatiesagreement/1954/chap94.htm.
112. *Joint Statement of the Republic of India and the People's Republic of China* (2005).
113. See the annual defence report of India since 2001.

6

Conclusion

Security perception is a state actor's strategic culture or ideas about security. It basically involves three aspects, i.e. threat perception, types of security, and approaches to security. Threat perception is the appraisal and judgment of the status or condition of security. Types of security are the sectors or dimensions of security classified by the character of threats. When nations categorize their own security, they generally establish an order of priority at the same time. Approaches to security are the methods or ways taken by a state in dealing with its security issues to accomplish or preserve its national security. Based on Wendt's Constructivism, which postulates that ideas matter more than interest and power in terms of their effects on international politics, the objective of this book has been to examine the role of security perception in the evolution of China-India relations, especially in the transformation since the end of the Cold War.

According to Wendt, state actors and the international system are mutually constituted. The evolution of an international strategic culture thereby has an effect on the respective security perceptions of China and India, and vice versa. Since the end of the Cold War, the international strategic culture has been undergoing a major change, namely, from the Cold War mindset to the post-Cold War new security perspective. The first aspect of change pertains to the source of threat. The Cold War mindset postulates that capability outweighs intention in the construction of threat. Therefore, the major threat to a nation's security is derived from the military superiority of its opponent. The new security perspective assumes that intention is far more important than capability. States are not born aggressive. The second aspect lies in the categorization and prioritization of security. The Cold War mindset takes the military and political characters of security for granted. It believes that military threats are always at the core of a nation's security consideration. The threat facing a nation will be greater if its opponent enjoys a divergent ideology. The new security perspective extends the dimension of security from military and political to economic and other non-traditional aspects. In the post-Cold War era, many countries are convinced that military capability should be underpinned by economic strength. Therefore, they see economic security as important as military security. Third, nations with the Cold War mindset rely on self-help security and alliance security to preserve their national security. However, the new security perspective advocates common security, cooperative security and comprehensive security, which ensure a nation's security by growing mutual trust and common interests through cooperation.

At a time when the transformation of the international strategic culture is still underway, each country's security perception is influenced by both the Cold War mindset and the new security perspective, though to a different extent. As a result, some countries incline to the new security perspective, some continue to cling to the Cold War mindset, while others stay in between. As far as China and India are concerned, the post-Cold War era has witnessed major changes in their respective security perceptions.

On the part of China, there has been a shift from the Cold War mindset to the new security perspective. First of all, since the end of the Cold War, China has adjusted the parameter by which it defined threat. During Mao's era, China considered that the imbalance of military power and ideological confrontation among nations were major sources of threat. As a newly liberated and weak country, the China of this period had been staying in a shadow of an imminent Third World War as well as a possible military invasion by the superpowers, i.e. the United States in the 1950s, both the United States and the Soviet Union in the 1960s, and the Soviet Union in the 1970s. Although in the early 1980s Deng Xiaoping started to downplay the role of the imbalance of military power in constructing threat, he had to keep an eye on the political and ideological pressures on China by the Western countries at that time. He warned against the threat of "a third world war without gunsmoke" launched by the Western countries to promote "peaceful evolution" in the socialist countries. In the light of the fact that the post-Cold War competition among nations is characterized by comprehensive national strength rather than military power alone, China attributes its sense of insecurity mainly to its backward economy. Economic security thereby made a formal appearance in China's national security consideration after the Cold War.

Second, China in the Cold War took the military and political characters of security for granted. It was also convinced that military security preceded political security in importance all the time. After the Cold War, however, China started to seek comprehensive national security, including economic security, military security, political security and non-traditional security which involves issues like terrorism, transnational crimes, environmental degradation, drug trafficking and epidemics. In the first decade of the post-Cold War era, when China set economic development as the central task of the whole country and required all other work, including national defence, to be subordinated to and serve this strategic objective, it accorded priority to economic security. When the urgency of defending China's territorial integrity has mounted due to the rising risk of 'Taiwan Independence' since the beginning of the new century, China has upgraded military security to the same level as economic security.

Third, China has replaced alliance security with common security in defending its security interests. During Mao's era, China adopted alliance security along with self-help security as the major approaches to security. On the one hand, China gave the army the priority in access to the limited resources China had at that time in order to build a strong army including the establishment of its own nuclear arsenal. On the other hand, China forged alliances with the two superpowers at different periods, as well as exploring a moral alignment with the Third World countries. In 1982, Deng Xiaoping started to drop alliance security and tried to safeguard its national security through economic cooperation and international security dialogue. Since the end of the Cold War, in spite of China's insistence on the important role of 'active defence' in safeguarding its territorial security, Deng's strategy has been reinforced particularly by the PRC's emphasis on common security. Believing that common interests and good political relationships can play a more effective role in addressing its security problems, China has developed strategic partnerships with all major powers and good-neighbourly relations with surrounding countries.

As far as India is concerned, much like the development with regard to China since the end of the Cold War, India's security perception has also undergone a great change. First of all, India has broadened the definition of threat. During the Cold War, the successive Indian leaders looked at the threats facing India through a narrow prism of purely military and political contexts. India attributed its sense of insecurity to its inferiority in national power, especially in military strength. Though it did not see any prospect of direct military invasion by the superpowers, India had been haunted by a sense of being encircled for decades, especially since 1962. It believed that the two-front threat was enhanced by the Sino-Pak collaboration since the mid-1960s, that the Sino-US alliance in the 1970s and 1980s had a strategic bearing on the India-China disputes, and that the smaller regional states tried to counterbalance India by developing military cooperation with the major powers. After the Cold War, the economic crisis made India realize the implications of economic strength for its national security. In the mid-1990s, it also started to pay attention to other non-traditional problems like drug-trafficking, terrorism and organized crime.

Second, India has reorganized its security structure. Like China and many other countries in the world, India in the Cold War assumed that national security had only military and political dimensions. While Nehru and Rajiv Gandhi attached equal importance to military security and political security, Indira Gandhi obviously accorded greater importance to military security. After the Cold War, India gradually accepted that national security should be viewed as a comprehensive issue encompassing military, political, economic and other non-traditional elements. Unlike China, India has never downgraded the significance of military and political security, but emphasized that more attention should be paid to economic security in the contemporary world.

Third, some changes have occurred in terms of India's approaches to security. During the major part of the Cold War, India, like Mao's China, was heavily dependent on alliance security and self-help security to safeguard its national security. While attaching great importance to its own military build-up, including the explosion of a nuclear device in 1974, India viewed its quasi-military alliance with the Soviet Union since the early 1970s as a major provider of security. After the Cold War, however, India started to adopt comprehensive approaches to security. Alliance security has been replaced with new partnership, security dialogue and cooperation, and economic diplomacy, which could be attributed to common security, cooperative security or comprehensive security. By emphasizing military and technological self-reliance, India still regards self-help security as a significant approach to security for India in the post-Cold War era. This has been especially manifested by India's decision to go nuclear in defiance of the strong international opposition.

The mutual perceptions of China and India have been the consequence of their respective security perceptions. How they looked at each other has determined their respective policies toward each other, and has consequently shaped their overall relationship.

As history has witnessed, for most part of the Cold War era, China and India saw and dealt with each other through the prism of the Cold War mindset; and hence underwent a three-decade-long 'cold' relationship. The China-India 'honeymoon' around the mid-1950s emerged at a time when they attempted to keep aloof from the then prevalent international strategic culture. Obviously, it was the determination of Nehru and Mao to befriend each other that had led the bilateral relationship to such a height as 'Hindi-Chini Bhai Bhai'. As China and India got further involved into the Cold War to different extents, however, the mutual distrust inherent in their respective security perceptions gained momentum with the passage of time. Since both Nehru's India and Mao's China took each other's expansive nature for granted, they were very sensitive to any change in their power relations. China's gain in Bandung and military act in Tibet appeared to be alarms for Nehru; Nehru's sympathy for the Tibet rebellion, claim to the British legacy of the Sino-Indian border and intimacy with Khrushev were in turn a series of warnings for Mao. The mutual distrust led to mutual misperceptions, culminating in the armed conflict of 1962.

From 1962 onwards, China and India formally dubbed each other as threats or adversaries. For China, the real threats derived from India's quasi-military alliance with the Soviet Union, China's major enemy at that time, as well as the ideological difference between China and India. For India, who was haunted by the humiliation of its defeat in the 1962 war, China's proximity to Pakistan, its later alliance with the United States, and its pursuit of nuclear weapons and missile capacities, were all India-directed. In fact, the hostility between China and India appeared to be formally fixed in the structure of Cold War confrontation since the 1970s, with the US-China-Pak strategic collaboration on one side and the Soviet-Indian alliance on the other.

It was Deng Xiaoping who brought some light into the China-India relations. In 1982, when he was determined to keep aloof from the Cold War and put China's focus on its economic development, Deng Xiaoping suggested that the two countries should treat each other not as threats but close neighours and friends, and that they could normalize their relations without predicating the process on the resolution of their boundary dispute. India accepted this proposal only by late 1988 when Rajiv Gandhi made some adjustments in India's security consideration according to the changes of the international situation. Rajiv Gandhi's visit to Beijing in December 1988, broke the impasse of the process of normalization between the two countries and led China-India relations into a new stage of increasingly positive interaction.

As their respective security perceptions have transformed in general since the end of the Cold War, China and India have looked at each other more and more through the new security perspective. China, guided by the 'new security concept' which lays stress on comprehensive national power and common security, believes that a new-type partnership with India is in its fundamental interests. With the good-neighbourly policy becoming an important approach to security, even the Indian 1998 nuclear tests did not shake China's resolve to befriend India. Although China started to accord equal priority to economic security and military security in 2002, the rising threat in the east has consolidated its determination to strengthen peace and stability in other directions including the west. Therefore, in recent years, China has started to seek a strategic partnership with India.

In the early 1990s, India on its part was convinced that an 'inward looking' China did not have an intention to threaten India. A good working relationship with China would serve the interests of the similarly 'inward looking' India at that time. As it started to take a more comprehensive security perception in the mid-1990s, India perceived more opportunities than challenges in its relations with China. It visualized a constructive cooperation with China, both at the bilateral level and on the multilateral fora. Although some Indian top leaders continued to warn against the 'China threat' in 1998, it was not a manifestation of a return to the negative China perspective of the Cold War period. Rather, it was more of a tactical attempt to justify India's nuclear tests. As history has witnessed, shortly after the Pokhran II, the Vajpayee government once again reiterated India's commitment to the development of a friendly, cooperative, good-neighbourly and mutually beneficial relationship with China. Entering the 21st century, India regards China as a partner rather than an adversary. Although there are still some old security concerns regarding China, like China's military build-up and its military relations with Pakistan, India is adopting approaches beyond military confrontation to solve these outstanding differences with China.

Treating each other as new partners rather than adversaries and acknowledging the need for comprehensive approaches to national security, both China and India have accordingly adjusted their respective policies toward each other since the end of the Cold War. Irrespective of their specific expectations from this relationship, both countries converged on the understanding that a stable and cooperative relationship between them would best serve their respective national interests in the post-Cold War era. This meant that they would maximize their own interests only within the framework of friendship, and that on occasion, they would even accommodate their requirements to the concerns of the other. China's attitude toward the Indo-Pak tensions and India's stance on the Tibet issue can be cited as such examples.

Not everybody is satisfied with the pace of the development of China-India relations, but no one can deny that this relationship has experienced an impressive transformation, from normalization to partnership, since the end of the Cold War. The last decade of the 20th century witnessed the two countries emerging from their three-decade-long cold relationship and replacing it with a normal one. In spite of the brief hiatus after Pokhran II, the inability of the Indian nuclear tests to derail the China-India relations has demonstrated the degree of maturity this relationship had reached on the one hand. On the other, it also represents a strong affirmation of this research's major hypothesis that perceptions construct relations. If there were no perception changes in China or India, there would be no change in their relationship. Walking out of the shadow of India's nuclear tests, China-India relations in the new century have entered a new stage of comprehensive cooperation and the establishment of strategic partnership.

On the future of China-India relations, the debates are still hot in both countries and around the world, however, notwithstanding the consensus reached in 2006 between China and India that "there exist bright prospects for their common development," and that "there is enough space for them to grow together".[1] Since perceptions construct relations, this author believes that the direction of this relationship will basically depend on the evolution of their respective security perceptions and their mutual perceptions thereby. Lessons of the past have indicated that the Cold War mindset leads nowhere but confrontation while the new security perspective make cooperation and win-win games possible. Therefore, whether "there is enough space for them to grow together" does not depend on the size of Asia or the belief of the two governments, but on how much they can deal with each other on basis of the new security perspective.

Wendt points out that there is an interaction between state actors and the international system. Since the international system[2] is still in a transition period, the respective security perceptions of China and India will be continually affected by the evolution of international strategic culture. Meanwhile, as the two most important nations in the world of the 21st century, both China and India can play a significant role in the construction of the new international system. If the new security perspective prevails in China and India, an international system characterized by cooperation and win-win games may probably first emerge in Asia. This will be the greatest contribution by China and India to the transformation of Asia and the world.

Notes

1. *Joint Declaration by the Republic of India and the People's Republic of China,* November 21, 2006, available at http://www.meaindia.nic.in/.
2. It needs to be emphasized here that, for constructivists, the structure of the international system is a "distribution of ideas" rather than a "distribution of power".

Index

Afghanistan, 41, 50, 54, 74, 114
Africa, 36, 37, 113
Alexander Wendt, 2, 3, 4, 5, 6, 7, 8, 9, 12, 17, 18, 19, 27
Andhra Pradesh, 103
APEC, 82, 113
ARF, 20, 83, 115, 157
ASEAN, 20, 82, 113, 116, 148, 157
Asia, 36, 37, 72, 75, 177
Atal Behari Vajpayee, 60, 87, 101, 106, 108, 109, 110, 111, 113, 119, 120, 121, 122, 147, 159, 162, 163, 176
Australia, 83, 157

Babri Masjid, 104
Bangladesh, 50, 51, 52, 53, 55, 103, 113, 116, 152
Beijing, 35, 39, 54, 55, 60, 88, 89, 118, 138, 140, 147, 148, 151, 156, 175
Bhutan, 47, 113
Bihar, 103
Bill Clinton, 87, 119, 121, 147
BIMST-EC, 116
Britain (UK), 4, 43, 48. 83, 115
Burma, 49

CENTO, 34, 44, 124
Chiang Kai-Shek, 34, 35, 77
China, 1, 7, 8, 12, 17, 22, 23, 24, 25, 26, 27, 33, 34, 35, 36, 37, 38, 39, 40, 41, 42, 46, 47,
48, 49, 50, 51, 52, 53, 54, 55, 56, 57, 58, 59, 60, 61, 69-94, 102, 103, 107, 108, 109, 111, 113, 114, 116, 117, 118, 119, 120, 121, 122, 123, 124, 125, 126, 135-164, 171, 172, 173, 174, 175, 176, 177
China's Security Perception after Cold War, 69-94
- assessment of its security environment, 69-76
  - better security environment than ever before (1991-2002), 70-74
  - complex picture (2002 till present), 74-76
- India's perspective, 85-92
- national security strategy, 76-85
  - national security interests, 78-80
  - national security policy, 81-85
  - objectives of, 76-77
- nature of change in, 92-94

Cold War Mindset and China-India 'Cold' relations during Cold War, 33-61
- China's security perception, 33-42
  - Deng's era, 38-42
    - assessment of China's security environment, 38-39
    - India's perspective, 41-42
    - national security strategy of China under, 39-41
  - Mao's era, 34-38
    - assessment of China's security environment, 34-35
    - India's perspective, 37-38
    - national security strategy of China under, 35-37
- Cold War Mindset and its implications for China-India relations during Cold War, 56-61
- India's security perception, 42-56
  - Mrs. Gandhi's era, 49-54
    - assessment of India's security environment, 50-51
    - China's perspective, 52-54
    - national security strategy of India under, 52-52
  - Nehru's era, 43-49
    - assessment of India's security environment, 43-45

China's perspective, 47-49
national security of India under, 45-47
Rajiv Gandhi's era, 54-56
assessment of India's security environment, 54-55
China's perspective, 55-56
India's national security strategy under, 55
Conclusion, 171-177
CTBT, 89, 103

Dalai Lama, 137, 141
Deng Xiaoping, 33, 38-42, 55, 56, 57, 60, 70, 81, 85, 86, 91, 92, 94, 136, 150, 172, 173, 175
Deve Gowda, 101
DRDO, 112
Dr. Subramanian Swamy, 41

ECOWAS, 19
ETA, 16
Europe, 18, 19, 102, 103, 107, 108, 111

France, 83
Friedrich Kratochwil, 2

George Fernandes, 88, 119, 120, 121, 147

Hobbesian, 5, 6, 8, 17
Hong Kong, 40

IAEA, 151
I.K. Gujral, 101
IMF, 2
India, 1, 7, 8, 12, 17, 23, 24, 25, 26, 27, 33, 37, 38, 41, 42, 43, 44, 45, 46, 48, 49, 50, 51, 52, 53, 54, 55, 56, 57, 58, 59, 60, 61, 83, 85, 86, 87, 88, 89, 90, 91, 92, 94, 101-126, 135-164, 171, 174, 175, 176, 177
India's Security Perception after Cold War, 101-126
assessment of its security environment, 101-107
China's perspective, 116-123
national security strategy, 107-116
interests of, 109-111
national security policy, 111-116
objectives of, 107-109
security perception in transformation, 123-126
Indira Gandhi, 43, 49-54, 55, 58, 59, 111, 124, 141, 157, 174
IRA, 16

Jammu and Kashmir, 44, 47, 90, 102, 103, 106, 137
Japan, 20, 23, 75, 83, 102, 107, 111, 113, 114, 157
Jawaharlal Nehru, 37, 38, 42, 43-49, 50, 51, 52, 54, 57, 58, 59, 60, 107, 108, 111, 123, 174, 175
Lal Bahadur Shastri, 43

Kantian, 5, 6, 8, 17
Kenneth Waltz, 2, 4
K. R. Narayanan, 122, 150, 151, 152, 153, 155, 158
K. Subrahmanyam, 114

Lockean, 5, 6, 8, 17, 18

Maldives, 55, 113
Manmohan Singh, 101, 104, 123, 154, 155, 159, 163
Mao Zedong, 33, 34-38, 56, 57, 58, 59, 60, 70, 92, 93, 125, 172, 173, 174, 175
McMahon Line, 49
Mikhail Gorbachev, 38, 39, 56
Mongolia, 83
Morarji Desai, 43
Moscow, 39, 55
Myanmar, 103, 105, 115, 116, 117, 119, 152

NATO, 19, 105
Nepal, 47, 49, 50, 52, 55, 113, 116
New Delhi, 88, 89, 118, 123, 137, 138, 140, 147, 148, 151
New York, 16
Nicholas Onuf, 2

North Korea, 4, 21
NSG, 151

Pakistan, 43, 44, 45, 46, 47, 48, 49, 50, 51, 52, 53, 54, 55, 58, 60, 83, 89, 90, 102, 103, 106, 107, 115, 117, 119, 121, 122, 124, 126, 136, 137, 141, 153, 154, 156, 175, 176
Perception Change and Transformation of China-India Relations since 1991, 133-164
  new stage of China-India relations (July 1999-till date), 150-164
  perceptible improvements in China-India relations preceding Pokhran II (1991-April 1998), 136-145
    China's India policy, 136-138
    improvements in, 141-145
    India's China policy, 138-141
  Post-Pokhran II Hiatus and Fence-Mending Efforts (May 1998-June 1999), 146-149
Pervez Musharraf, 106
P. N. Haskar, 56
P. V. Narasimha Rao, 101, 112, 120, 121, 141, 142
Punjab, 54, 102
Rajiv Gandhi, 43, 54-56, 60, 116, 124, 126, 138, 139, 140, 142, 143, 174, 175

SAARC, 113
SAFTA, 116
Sardar Vallabhbhai Patel, 48
SEATO, 34, 44, 124
Security perception and constructivism: A new Approach to Analyze China-India Relations, 1-27
  components of, 9-23
    approaches to, 17-21
    contents of, 11-13
    security and, 9-11
    types of, 13-17
  evolution of international strategic culture, 21-23
  parameters of, 23-27
    assessment of security environment, 24-25
    mutual perception, 26-27
    national security strategy, 25-26
  Wendt's constructivism: effects of ideas on international relations, 1-9
Shankar Dayal Sharma, 118, 119
Sikkim, 47, 52, 163
Sonia Gandhi, 159
South Africa, 83, 115
Soviet Union (USSR), 18, 20, 22, 33, 34, 35, 36, 38, 39, 41, 42, 43, 44, 46, 47, 50, 51, 52, 53, 54, 55, 56, 57, 58, 59, 69, 70, 79, 85, 92, 94, 102, 103, 104, 111, 125, 172, 174, 175
Sri Lanka, 50, 55, 103, 113, 115, 115, 116

Taiwan, 34, 35, 40, 41, 73, 74, 75, 76, 77, 79, 84, 147
Tanzania, 36
Thailand, 83, 116
Tibet, 35, 37, 38, 48, 49, 57, 60, 74, 80, 89, 118, 119, 136, 137, 138, 140, 141, 143, 163, 175, 176

United Nations (UN), 2, 15, 18, 19, 41, 50, 74, 157
United States (US), 4, 6, 16, 18, 21, 23, 25, 26, 33, 34, 35, 36, 37, 39, 40, 43, 44, 46, 48, 50, 51, 52, 53, 54, 55, 56, 57, 58, 60, 70, 71, 73, 74, 75, 76, 81, 82, 83, 89, 90, 92, 102, 103, 106, 107, 111, 112, 113, 114, 119, 124, 126, 145, 151, 157, 172, 173, 175

Vietnam, 41, 82, 116
V. P. Singh, 43

Washington, 50
West Bengal, 103
World Trade Centre (WTC), 16
World War II, 19, 44

Xinjiang, 35, 74

Zambia, 36
Zhou Enlai, 49